Bollywood in the Age of New Media

D1477389

For Dr Subrata Basu and Dr Bimalendu Basu

Bollywood in the Age of New Media

The Geo-televisual Aesthetic

Anustup Basu

Edinburgh University Press

Edinburgh University Press Ltd
22 George Square, Edinburgh

www.euppublishing.com

Typeset in Monotype Ehrhardt by
Servis Filmsetting Ltd, Stockport, Cheshire, and
printed and bound in Great Britain by
CPI Antony Rowe, Chippenham and Eastbourne

A CIP record for this book is available from the British Library

ISBN 978 0 7486 4102 4 (hardback)

Contents

List of Figures

Acknowledgments

This book has been long in gestation. The idea started in my head during those heady years in the mid-1990s when I was a film critic for *The Telegraph* in the city then known as Calcutta. It was then, when one was compelled to go beyond the staple Bollywood quota and watch up to four films a day in order to fill columns, that I got a glimpse of a new cinematic idiom. Coming in the wake of mighty barbarisms and equally mighty transformations, it was a different opulence altogether. The rumbles of the new were first adjusted to, engaged with, and theorized in the company of remarkable minds in the political and intellectual scene of Calcutta. Friends and peers like Jayeeta Bagchi, Nandinee Banerjee, Pallavi Banerjee, Manabendra Bandyopadhyay, Saswata Bhattacharya, Gautam Basu-Thakur, Prasanta Chakravarty, Swapan Chakravarty, Suchetana Chattopadhyay, Supriya Chaudhuri, Anirban Das, Amlan Dasgupta, Rajarshi Dasgupta, Mallika Jalan, Bodhisattwa Kar, Udaya Kumar, Bodhisattwa Maity, Amitava Malakar, Aniruddha Mitra, Reshmi Mukherjee, Sajni Mukherjee, Urvee Mukhopadhyay, Kavita Panjabi, Ashish Rajadhyaksha, Abhijit Roy, Airindrajit Saha, Amitrajit Saha, Pratim Sengupta, and Ravi Vasudevan have played crucial roles in my development as a scholar during these years. Madhava Prasad has been an inspiring presence and an unerring but gentle guide. Moinak Biswas was the first to teach me how to think about cinema and develop an abiding scholarly love for it; Suman Mukhopadhyay did the same while making exquisite films. For the last two decades, Sibaji Bandyopadhyay has been the single most important influence in my life of the mind. It would be presumptuous to gauge how much I owe him in terms of my thinking and my being.

My doctoral years at the University of Pittsburgh were spent in a vigorous intellectual climate fostered especially by Jonathan Arac, David Bartholomae, Elizabeth Bledsoe, Amy Borden, Malkiel Choseed, Nancy Condee, Petra Dierkus-Thrun, Lucy Fischer, Brenda Glascott, Jeffrey Hole, Melissa Lenos, Ignacio Lopez-Vicuna, Adam Lowenstein, Neepa Majumdar, Amy Mueller-Hurwitz, Dana Och, Vladimir Padunov, Stanley Shoshtak, Anja Ulanowicz, Sergio Villalobos, Chris Warnick, and Stefan Wheelock. Kirsten Strayer has extended a friendship very rarely found and an invaluable intellectual camaraderie. J. Paul Narkunas, Richard Purcell, and Henry Veggian have been special partners in scholarly crime. During the initial consolidation of this project, Eric Clarke taught me how exactly one can, with rigor and innovation, bring to bear classical legacies of the Enlightenment into new horizons of thought like Queer Studies. Colin MacCabe was a sharp interlocutor, whose profound knowledge of world cinema was invaluable. Ronald A. T. Judy's admirable powers of generative thinking aided me immensely in better understanding a post-9/11 world. Paul Bové's seminars and numerous *addas* in his office opened up intellectual horizons I did not know existed, especially in relation to understanding the United States as an historical formation. He is the one who truly taught me how to think in exile. It is impossible to account for the profound influence Marcia Landy's presence and intellect has had on my life and on my mind. This project was conceived in its present form during countless hours of stimulating conversations with her, especially about Karl Marx and Gilles Deleuze. Whatever merit this book has, I owe her. The faults though are entirely mine.

I am indeed blessed to have a wonderful set of supportive colleagues at the University of Illinois at Urbana-Champaign. I am especially grateful to Rob Barrett, Dale Bauer, Sandy Camargo, Martin Camargo, José B. Capino, David Desser, Jed Esty, Peter Garrett, Behroze Ghamari, Jim Hansen, Debra Hawhee, Trish Loughran, Feisal Mohammad, Becky Moss, Hina Nazar, Cary Nelson, Susan Koshy, Tim Newcomb, Curtis Perry, Sarah Projansky, Siobhan Somerville, Zohreh Sullivan, Deb Stauffer, Renee Trilling, Ted Underwood, and Joe Valente for living, thinking, and in some cases facebooking in the twin towns such wonderful affairs. Ramona Curry, from the very outset, has been a wonderful mentor, whose wisdom and selflessness are rare commodities. Bob Parker, Bill Maxwell, and Bob Merkley, apart from being wonderful colleagues, have provided useful feedback, as has Matt Hart, despite being a supporter of the English cricket team. Michael Rothberg and Lauren Goodlad have been formidable intellectual interlocutors; as past and present directors of the Unit for Criticism, they have also organized timely reading groups and colloquia, which have vastly influenced this project and contributed to my growth as an intellectual. I thank these fantastic colleagues, along with the Department of English and the Research Board of the University of Illinois, for the logistical support they have given me. In the extended world of the North American academy, I am especially grateful to Bishnupriya Ghosh, Sangita Gopal, Nitin Govil, Priya Jaikumar, Suvir Kaul, Ania Loomba, Amit Rai, Bhaskar Sarkar, and Amy Villarejo for their immensely helpful advice and feedback. Esmé Watson and Daniel Bourner of the University of Edinburgh Press have been resourceful and patient editors. I thank them, along with the two anonymous reviewers, for providing insightful comments.

The unflinching moral and intellectual support that Ambar Basu and Mahuya Pal have provided over decades has long since transcended any common idea of friendship. I thank them, along with my other set of special friends who deserve to be called family: Ayan Gangopadhyay, Meheli Sen, and Philip Webb. Among the wonderful members of my extended family in Calcutta and elsewhere, I am especially grateful to Ananya Basu-Gupta, Biman Basu, Noel Nag, Niloy and Esha Nag, Banani Saha, Rahul Saha, Rohan Saha, Taraknath Saha, and Probir Sur Roy. My mother, Mita Basu, and mother-in-law, Kamala Basu, have been inspirational presences. Manisha Basu's contribution as partner, critic, resuscitator, and movie-watching companion (for well over 1,001 nights) cannot be spelled out in words. It comes from what we share, and for that I continue to thank her with all my heart. Lastly, I recall with gratitude the contributions to my life and being from the late Dr Subrata Basu and the late Dr Bimalendu Basu. I inherited only some of the former's razor sharp intellect and absorbed a fraction of the latter's untimely wisdom. This book is dedicated to their lasting memories.

Anustup Basu
Champaign, Illinois
Winter 2009

Part I

Introduction

CHAPTER 1

Cinematic "Assemblages": The 1990s and Earlier

Rakesh Roshan's 1995 film *Karan Arjun* (*Karan and Arjun*) offers a typical cinematic example of a Dharmic[1] intervention into human affairs. What is ushered in, in a moment of acute crisis, is a cosmic power that is able to close the gap between the fallible word of human law and a divine ontology of justice. Law, it must be remembered, is for judgment, not justice.[2] The former is an earthly discursive phenomenon, prone to error and adjustment; the latter is a divine ideal toward which historical procedures of judgment aspire but never quite reach. Yet, in the present case, as we shall see, judgment and justice coincide. This is what makes Dharma (which is at once divinely ordained duty, ethics, and religion) a cinematic picture of theodicy.[3] The incident takes place immediately after the diabolical *thakur* Durjan Singh and his men kill Karan and Arjun, the two young sons of a widow called Durga. The distraught mother runs to the temple; the surroundings grow elemental and it seems that nature itself is outraged. The sequence inside the temple begins with a Dutch-angle close-up of the goddess Kali, signifying a world that is out of kilter. Durga looks accusingly at the deity and says that her sons cannot die, since one mother—that is, Kali herself—cannot empty the bosom of another one. She then demands the impossible: that Karan and Arjun be restored to her by Kali's grace. This momentous utterance is accompanied by thunder on the soundtrack. Next, there is a close-up of Durga who begins to bang her head on the sacrificial platform in front of Kali, the divinity of power. Alternating shots of the crazed but unwaveringly faith-driven woman are interspersed with more skewed close-ups of the idol, bridging the two figures with an imaginary affiliating power that is of another time and another world. A slow use of the zoom, intimating every shot/reverse-shot exchange of looks between the acolyte and the divine and a rising crescendo of music bring the prayer and the inevitable moment of deliverance to a critical proximity. The two meet in a dimension that is alien to the editorial intelligence of a cause–effect realist cinema.

   A groundless cut-away to a distant hospital follows, where a doctor is delivering a baby. While a young woman struggles through her labor, there are inserts of lightning flashes filling the sky. The scene switches back to Durga still banging her head in front of the goddess. A close-up of Kali is followed by another cut-away to the hospital, where the baby is pulled out of his mother's womb. When the newborn cries out, a sound bridge carries the wail to the next shot of Durga in the temple, who lifts her head as if to register a distant miracle. She becomes calm now, and looks up at Kali with grateful eyes. The camera tilts up toward Kali and zooms to a close-up. It then cuts away to a second hospital, where another baby is being born. This is followed by Durga folding her hands to thank the goddess. It is after this moment, when she is touched by the knowledge of a divine retribution that will take place in a future already imminent, that the title sequence of the film begins to roll. It is also from here that Durga is clinically and socially diagnosed as insane because she believes in an inevitable return—otherworldly and mythic—that is at odds with the humdrum and disenchanting experience of daily life. Durga spends the next two decades telling friends and foes alike that Karan and Arjun will return to avenge the injustice perpetrated on her.

What is thereby launched is a chronicle of vendetta already foretold. The two babies, born to distant, unknown lineages, inevitably grow up to be the exact replicas of the murdered Karan and Arjun. Compelled by a powerful uterine call from another birth, they come to reunite with their mother of unfulfilled past lives and then wreak a terrible revenge on the evil Durjan Singh. The rest of the film is a run-of-the-mill action spectacular which uses the diverse resources of the world—the kickboxing powers of Karan and the gun-toting rodeo skills of Arjun—to bring about a dénouement that is familiar to Hindi cinema. All along, it is the piety of Durga—which is announced to be mad precisely because, in order to preserve an unflinching steadfastness of belief, she has to totally shut out the historical world of injustice and chance—that holds the ontology of the Dharmic constant. The mother simply endures and waits for the wheel of time to turn, while the cynical world lives according to the emptiness of the calendar.

Karan Arjun, like many other potboilers of its kind, is an adroit mixture of home-grown and foreign generic prototypes: the action-adventure, the mythological, the spaghetti western, and the family melodrama. Heroic powers, skills, and styles are freely borrowed to redress the abomination and restore the ethical universe. Like many of their cinematic ancestors and descendants, Karan and Arjun display a transnational *chutzpah* and art of war while scrupulously bearing an epic mantle bestowed by traditional memory and faith. As in many other popular Hindi films, the brothers are named after epic heroes and warring estranged siblings of the Pandava clan in the Mahabharata, while Durga is named after a ten-armed deity, who is herself an aspect of Kali in the Hindu pantheon. The ontology of being, therefore, remains steadfast while the instruments and spectacles of wish-fulfilling revenge are upgraded to match the increasingly globalized environment of the early 1990s. In its visual attributes and narrative presentation, *Karan Arjun* combines the old and the new, uterine memories of home and spectacles of the world. Throughout the film, a messianic temporality curves into chronometric time; perceptions keep shifting from the individual to a cosmic point of view that is not a secular world-historical one; and movements of realist narration are boosted by mythic transformations.[4] However, it is crucial to note that in this film, as in many others of its kind, such binaries are not always antagonistically poised, but eclectically combined, often in quite radical ways. I intend to theorize this process of assemblage.

Secondly, while such assemblages (like that between the memories of the epic Mahabharata and the visual allures of the spaghetti western) are not new to Hindi popular film, they acquire an entirely new dimension in the globalizing electronic media ecology inaugurated in India during the early 1990s. I shall eventually propose that the assembling impulse of Hindi film becomes increasingly "informatic" and "geo-televisual" during that decade. The "home" as an ethical and visual postulate changes as a result, as does the world that hovers around and sometimes imperils it. All the more, the dividing lines between these two abstract domains of tradition and modernity become osmotic and the energies of desire, faith, remembrance, power, intellect, and sensation commerce between them in a manner more pronounced than in the past.

The inquiry into this electrified field of exchange—the new Indian media world of the 1990s and the concomitant universe of commercial Hindi film – forms the heart of this book. It is a study of recent, top-bracket Hindi cinema, roughly between 1991 and 2004, in the light of three elemental changes in the Indian situation: the opening up of the economy to transnational capital and consumer goods, the spectacular rise of the Hindu Right, and the ushering in of a borderless, global system of electronic media exchanges. Let me propose a few early lines of inquiry. What becomes of an aspired-for "Indian" modernity amidst this kinetic, worldly traffic of goods, bodies, and images? How can core, organic postulates like national culture and national sovereignty be rethought in this fast-globalizing scenario? How does a so-called dialectical relationship between "modernity" and "tradition" change? How did this period of titanic, techno-financial modernization also witness paradoxically the rise of a "pre-modern" ideology of *Hindutva*, hitherto languishing among the urban petit bourgeois and some agrarian-feudal quarters of north India? This project is therefore not just an excursion into film and media theory, but also a political analysis of the globalization of culture and urban life in a third world situation. It is not a conventional examination of a national cinema as such, but an exposé of how planetary flows of information, the spread of cottage piracy, and various cybernetic and digital intermedia ecologies besiege static notions of the same—in other words, the idea of cinema as part of an endogamous national culture protected by classic vertical institutions of modernity, such as protected economies, state-owned television, censorship, distribution quotas, and import/export laws.

The traditional Hindi film crossed several frontiers of "homeliness" in this environment of semiotic mergers. The hard boundaries between proposed and constantly revised national selves and the world at large appeared virtual, permeable, and awry in a novel ecology of information. Films flirted with issues and themes that were once seen as "foreign" or taboo to a dominant Brahminical imagination: swinger lifestyles, polygamous fantasies, homosexuality, premarital sex, live-in relationships, and a host of other tempting metropolitan propositions. Hindi cinema became a global phenomenon increasingly known in the West and to the Indian upper classes as "Bollywood."[5] The trial of conservative ideology—which, in the Indian context, draws predominantly from a Brahminical mindset—seemed to lie in wading through a sea of pluralities and somehow affirming a core "Indian self" in the end. As I shall demonstrate in the following chapters, this was achieved not so much by rounding up a story of tradition, but by setting up, through agonistic passages as well as irreverent spectacles, a complex stratum of urban normalcy that was largely Hindu. A new nationalism thus asserted itself more by its affective strength—the establishment of a neurological stratum of habit and regulation of shock—than by the precision of its definitions or its narrative resolutions. It did so by inventing a new syntax for the times, a negative syntax that flouted older, more mordant ways of connecting the noun to the event, pictures of the world to a constitution of the self. A fresh cinematic style uprooted signs from sites of "tradition" and institutions of the modern, rendered them afloat, and set them into a complex concert. The idiom acquired the capacity to cannibalize and combine matters from disparate avenues of global life, like transnational advertising, MTV, video games, pop *Hindutva*, high fashion, international travel, consumer goods, gadgetry, computers, spiritualism, and dogmas of neoliberal development. Historical spaces merged, as did temporalities of a past self, a transformative present, and a contested future.

It is this fungible yet sensuous style—one that begins to operate at the level of the tissue and the nerve—that I shall theorize as the geo-televisual aesthetic of contemporary Hindi film. In an opened-out ecology of imported media pressures, bodies were irremediably touched by splits between desires and anathemas, or fascinations and pathologies. Their libidinal and affective capacities could not be tempered into an axiomatic and consolidated national subjectivity, either borrowed from the past or finalized in the present. After a point there was no emphatic and singular "guardianship of view" on the part of a nationalist upper-caste/class-cultural authorship that succeeded in resolving such matters through top-down hegemonic or proscriptive measures.[6] These hegemonic efforts did exist, but had limited powers of intervention. However, this overall instability need not be considered as a weakness or a non-arrival of the national self at a tryst with a destiny long desired. Rather, I shall argue that it is a cluttered but innovative dynamism in Hindi cinema in the age of global media that is indicative of the ways in which a new metropolitan Hinduness, of which militant *Hindutva* is only a small part, asserts itself. The cinema of the 1990s and after was thus largely not a case of classical or alternate modernity enunciated into an historical form, but a picture of what I shall elaborate in the next chapter as *informatic modernization*. Under the auspices of the latter, the nation increasingly did not have to be narrated with plausible realism (although such efforts persisted). It could be sublimated micropunctually as a shining specter—airy but robust—through an overall informatization of social life. Its mythography could actually be manifest, not as a closed book of the world, but as a disaggregated body of spectacles or a grandly tactile and sensuous ambience of particularized bits and bytes.

But I am getting ahead of myself here, so let us return to first principles: what is the *assembling* process in popular Hindi cinema, and what exactly happens when cinematic assembling becomes "informatic" in a global sense? I shall first examine the philosophy of the Indian cinematic assemblage, its ontic moorings and historical scopes of permissiveness. In doing so, I shall also indicate how the assembling processes have always responded to ecological shifts in politics, media, and fields of knowledge. The objective will therefore be to formulate a new theory of form for popular Hindi cinema, one that is consistent with its genealogies. Hence, for now, we shall travel freely between the decades after Independence to look for examples of assembling. Once that ground is established, in the next chapter, I will look at how assemblages in Hindi film transform in the information environment of the 1990s.

The Realism Debate

A format of classical realist narration in cinema can be abstracted, in a general way, from the terrain of Western film theory. In this, an overall valorizing of realism is based on a reckoning of the cinematic apparatus as emulating the phenomenology of the individual. This prototype accords a few dominant conventions to filmic narration: a faithful contiguity and seriality of time, space, and movement; a synthetic part–whole relationship between the frame and out-of-field; and a punctual cause–effect arraying of perception, motivation, and action.[7] The schema thus largely corresponds to an intellectual/existential/historical horizon of the human subject inaugurated by a line of Western metaphysical thinking starting with René Descartes. The machinic eye of cinema as such has to faithfully intersect with or run in parallel to the cognitive mappings of the individual, the earthly limits of his movements (in metrically calibrated space and time), and the finitudes of his general being in the world. In other words, there has to be an anthropologism of cinematic signification and an anthropomorphic cast of action. Realism as such, with its imperative of looking at the world through the lens of Cartesian "doubt," was seen to have a primary function: to reproduce a scientific and rational world picture devoid of miracles. It is already clear that the sequence in *Karan Arjun* described above violates almost all of these rules. But it is also true that, for a good part, Rakesh Roshan's film conforms to many basic principles of American continuity cinema—eyeline match, the 30 and 180 degree rules, POV shot, correct screen direction, and match-on-action cuts.

Geeta Kapur, Ashish Rajadhyaksha, Ravi Vasudevan, and Madhava Prasad, among others, have, in different ways, richly explored this critical interface between Indian popular cinematic forms and the normative, realist bent of film theory.[8] These studies provide us with lines of inquiry: the tension between a mythic impulse of storytelling and an analytical/descriptive seriality of Hollywood; a combination of codes, like the iconic stasis, tableaux, and linear narration; dualities between historical spaces and magically transformative milieus; and a messianic, "thick" temporality interspersed with the empty calendrical time of the modern. Stylistic borrowings were, of course, never restricted to American cinema. They covered a wide range, from V. Shantaram's early interest in German Expressionism and *Kammerspiel* during the late 1930s, the influence of neo-realism and socialist realism in the 1950s, sensationalist genres like the Italian peplums in the 1960s, to Hong Kong action cinema during the 1990s.

Reading such eclectic combinations between a globality of cinematic style and indigenous modules of affect, expression, and memory often gives rise to violent translations between epistemes. The critical challenge starts at the point where one tries to earmark a domain of unsullied natality for the "indigenous" and distinguish it from a plethora of worldly influences. Problems arise, for instance, when, in relation to a modern imperative of realist narration, one broaches *Rasa* as a cosmological schema of aesthetics in the Indic tradition. In *Rasa* theory[9] the human onlooker is just a locus and not an active agent in what is a global alchemy of properties and perceptions. As a result, it is after a point irreconcilable with the aesthetics of the integrated subject of the Enlightenment, conceived along the lines of Kant or Hegel. It would, for example, be unfair to read an outpouring of *Karuna Rasa* as a punctual equivalent of what is known as sentimentalism in the Western tradition.[10] The same can be said of Dharma as an inhuman theodicy that often exists over and beyond the movements of detection, discovery, reasoning, and proof in modern methods of justice. The preponderance of this horizon of belief in commercial Hindi films is what has prevented the detective genre from making substantive inroads.[11] One can also talk about the impasses between *Maya* as a metaphysical postulate of illusion that rests on a negation of any abiding truth in the created universe, and Western empirical models for discerning rational facts through logical deduction.[12]

"Traditional" postulates like *Maya*, Dharma, and *Rasa* are undeniably part of a vocabulary of pertinence in relation to popular Hindi cinema. As categories, they abound in basic dialogic situations, worldviews, references, and lyrical-aesthetic modes. However, a normative approach of "film theory" frequently does not know what to do with them, apart from bracketing them anthropologically. That is, more often than not, they are accounted for, with awkward or surreptitious evasions, as purely decorative markers or signs of an obstinate heritagism that, in a contemporary episteme, command neither authentic memory nor belief.[13] The point, however, is not to marshal Dharma, *Maya*, or *Rasa* as pure, untainted concepts in a battle between a so-called Indian essence and an alien modernity that always threatens to engulf it. Nor is it to arrange them neatly into tables of cultural difference. Rather, the trial is to critically appreciate the ways in which postulates like *Rasa*, Dharma, or *Maya* are always already cited, dialecticized, semiotically contaminated, translated, and rendered discursive by modern cinematic formats. Conversely, these forces of "tradition" too disturb, strike wonder in, and vernacularize the positivism of the modern. The putative diagrams of the latter are always entering into complex assemblages with the powers and qualities of the former. They form assemblages of perception which are refracted or aggregated ways of looking at things and can splinter into many visions of the cosmos.[14] In other words, what is not produced is a disenchanted subjective point of view, one that is unified and also dominant. But let me repeat that while this aggregational form might be diagnosed as a symptom of weak or incomplete modernity, it can generate intense affects towards statism and capitalist modernization without any obligation to liberalism. This factor becomes especially important in understanding Indian popular cinema and the Indian political situation itself from the 1990s onwards.

An important caveat is called for here. This genealogical picture comes with a host of terms which can be broadly lumped under the rubrics "traditional" and "modern," but only after acknowledging that the specter of a pan-Indian tradition comes without an unblemished claim to originary authenticity. "Tradition" was a discursive invention of the modern as its own intimate enemy. This grand Orientalist/Indological project perhaps began in earnest with the publication of Charles Wilkins' English translation of the *Bhagwad Gita* in 1785, followed by the Warren Hastings administration's adoption of the Laws of Manu as the Hindu Book of Law, and the subsequent works of a legion of Indian and European scholars headed by luminaries like William Jones and Friedrich Max Müller. These early Orientalist attempts to catalog and comprehend a quintessentially "Indian" tradition of the self were enthusiastically taken up by various nationalist cultural projects from the middle of the nineteenth century. As far as cinema is concerned, the idea of assembling becomes crucial in relation to an agonistic, incessant extraction of "tradition," not just as a native counterpoint to the Occident and the modern, but also tendentially absolved of the influences of eight centuries of Islamic culture.

Assemblages pertaining to form in Hindi cinema have to do with how indigenous theatrical and artistic traditions like the Parsee Theater, *Ramlila, Jatra, Swang, Tamasha, Lila, Theru,* or the *Nautanki* regularly contend with Western genre templates. In terms of filmic organizations of the "look," for example, features of frontality and epic depthlessness (Geeta Kapur, Anuradha Kapur, Ashish Rajadhyaksha) in theatrical and painterly traditions, or the institution of *darsana* (Prasad) in public encounters with the deity, have combined with individual points of view, depth of focus, and other Western psychologisms.[15] Exchanges between the worlds of style and selfhood in Indian film were, from the outset, both infra- and international. In early Hindi cinema manifold attributes of an imperial-cosmopolitan universe entered into highly flexible mixes with cultural-literary forms of Bengali modernism, the Marathi reform novel, or the sonorous, high-flown rhetorical structure of Urdu poetry. The outcome was a complex and highly flexible mode which encompassed variegated powers of knowledge, memory, and expressive form.

I am calling this a critical template of "assembling" precisely because it allows and actually revels in complex folds of ontology. Rajadhyaksha, for instance, has pointed out a persistent feature of "double Orientalism" in the works of the early twentieth-century pre-eminent Parsee playwright Aga Hashar Kashmiri. Kashmiri's adaptations of Shakespeare, in *Sufaid Khoon* (*White Blood*, an adaptation of *King Lear*) or *Said-E-Havas* (*Greed*, based on *King John*), display a Western look towards the East, but via Persian, Arabic, and Moorish legend, through their Orientalist variations in the European baroque.[16] Kaushik Bhaumik has suggested that Bombay cinema of the 1920s and 1930s evolved through a continual osmosis between bazaar forms and bourgeois monumental styles, including Victorian Gothic sensationalism. In such a climate, the swashbuckling exploits of Douglas Fairbanks could thus be absorbed into an indigenous Gujarati nationalist project to reclaim a Rajput identity (Bhaumik, *The Emergence of the Bombay Film Industry*, 31–6). Through an insightful analysis of a segment of Mehboob Khan's 1948 film *Andaaz*, Ravi Vasudevan has noted that in the post-Independence social melodrama, one sees a dynamic orchestration of three codes: segments of linear narrative, brief moments of iconic stasis, and the tableaux, where a static visual arrangement is invested with narrative value.[17] Lalitha Gopalan[18] has more recently shown how a phenomenology of interruptions overwrites economies of continuity cinema in popular Indian film. I am proposing to bring these considerations of genre, form, perception, habituation, and memory under a constellation of assemblage theories. In other words, I am proposing that these interactive sets are not simply entities that add up to something, or exist side by side as incommensurable contradictions. Instead, they offer dynamic, interactive relations. Rather than just conceptually freeze-frame them and see how they often harbor antagonisms or inconsistencies, it would be productive to track their *movements* in themselves as a special cinematic style. This is because, while the movements may finally yield weakly modern or stubbornly traditional precepts, en route they continually generate affective, highly energized, circuitous exchanges between myth and fact, ideology and faith, knowledge and dogma.

What is an Assemblage?

In Prakash Mehra's 1973 revenge drama *Zanjeer* (*Chains*) a young police officer recognizes his parents' murderer by chance, twenty years after the event, when he sees a silver chain dangling on the latter's right wrist. Long ago, during that fateful night, the hero, then a terrified boy in hiding, had seen that same hand firing a gun.[19] The scene had been fixed in his memory ever since by an uninterrupted series of nightmares. Similarly, the protagonist in Nasir Hussain's *Yadon Ki Baraat* (*The Procession of Friends*) (1973) discovers his parents' killer when a twist in the tale reveals to him that the latter wore different-sized shoes. As projects of remembrance, the wrist chain and shoes are images that are compacts of perceptual powers; they pertain to both a psychological understanding of trauma and a signature of epic memory, like Odysseus' scar.[20] The event of recall and delayed incrimination indeterminately combine a mythic notion of infallible fate or *kismet*, as well as "luck" in a numerical chain of possibilities.[21] The bridge of memory is therefore set up by both the individual's secular navigation of the world and the momentous events of revelation accorded by the heavens.

Such narrative compacts can be called assemblages[22] in a transformed Deleuzian sense, without following his occasional tendencies toward an acosmic vitalism. Assemblages are energetic, diffuse, but practical combinations of statements, bodies, sounds, events, matter, spaces, knowledges, beliefs, or subjective stances that come together and disperse constantly, in an opportune manner, without being organized into, or even appealing to, stable diagrams of human subjectivity and consciousness.[23] In the first place, therefore, a conception of the assemblage does not seek to distinguish a material world from an ideational one. Instead, assemblages are to be understood as instantaneous but non-dualistic compositional outcomes of the materiality of ideas and the intellectual/expressive evocations that inform matter. The stone figure of Mother Kali in *Karan Arjun* is thus at once an ethnographic totem and the metaphysical presence of a deity commanding belief; it is also, as a visible sign, a stone. To think in assemblages is thus to recognize, at every point, the contending lines of force in the object-sign and the fractured universe in which it is lodged. It is all the more pertinent because, as we have seen, the stone can instantaneously pass from a universe of realist reckoning into a cosmology of pure belief.

Not only do assemblages combine memories and phenomena of different orientations, they also often violently juxtapose and switch grand systems (history, legend) by which the substances of memory and phenomena are organized in the first place. Assemblages are *opportune* because they exist for the moment and for the purpose; in them, there are often no immediately available hard forms, hard facts, or paramount earthly authorities to separate, for instance, the trauma from the epic memory. They must not be dismissed as signs of an unhappy "national" consciousness caught between the lures of the modern and the recidivism of the "traditional." Rather, they can be accounted for as formations that emerge from continual cinematic exchanges between both tradition and modernity as historical diagrams of thought and belief. To go back to an earlier example, there might be assembled moments when invocations of *Karuna rasa* might indeed be adjacent, in the same cinematic movement, to melodramatic structures of sentimentalism. It is an adjacency inextricably linked to the historicity of the Indian postcolonial situation in itself. Assembling is the movement of the split, the fork, the folding, or the gestation within that space of critical proximity.

Assemblages of Totality

Assemblages are not positive entities that can be extracted and separated as additives that point to a fulfilled whole; rather, they become discernible with all their powers precisely at the moment when they are inscribed onto other assemblages, and when the consequent "whole" itself (the world, nation, history, tradition, modern, God, Dharma) transforms or breaks at every instant, caught between knowledge systems that affirm faith and those that call for a secular skepticism. When we "read" assemblages, we undeniably and necessarily subtract signs, statements, bodies, ideologies, and dogma from a moving, transforming plenitude. However, to affirm the assemblage is also to understand that the world or "totality" it may point to—by which attributes of the mise-en-scène relate to the shot, the shot to the sequence, the sequence to the narrative—is not a consummate universal. This is similar, but not identical to what Deleuze says in relation to the dynamic sets in the whole of the Western moving image. The sets yield a totality that is not a closure or a universal, but an opening out.[24] In the case of Hindi film and its wide liberties with cause–effect narration, the process is more pugnacious and awry. The given assemblage might have already diminished the affects of the previous one and turned away from it; it might already be in the process of being replaced by newer assembling energies. The assemblage cannot be looked at as a simple snapshot without its tempo or its breaking tenacity, by which it has already disfigured the totality that has claimed it.

    Let me elaborate the assembling sets in Yash Chopra's *Darr* (*Fear*) (1992) to demonstrate how this happens. The narrative arc of the film—with a clear beginning, middle, and end—can be easily outlined: an obsessive psychopath stalks a woman, puts her and her husband in danger, and finally gets his just deserts at the hands of the latter, who acts on behalf of the democratic state as well as the order of the feudal clan. A composite picture of authority is also provided, comprising juridical statements

1.1: The psychotic orphan "gets" the girl in *Darr*.

(it is illegal to stalk a woman or take her against her wishes), medical-psychological diagnoses (the orphan is mentally disturbed), modern ideas of individual rights (the woman is not interested), and feudal–patriarchal norms of propriety and custodianship (the woman belongs to the husband). Justice meted out at the end (the husband kills the stalker) is thus at once self-defense from the legal angle and absolute punishment from the perspective of the upper-caste North Indian feudal extended family. There are, however, matters in the middle that could be of critical interest. These interim assemblages bring the profane ardor of the anti-hero, Rahul, and the body of the heroine into spectacular proximity, especially in the lusty song sequences that are projections of illicit male fantasies. In these, the figure of the woman becomes a disengaged, lurid body, devoid of psycho-biography or moral identity. The musical segments voluptuously consolidate on screen precisely that which is foreclosed by *just* narration and by traditional patriarchy as well as secular-legal rules of consensual sex. In the "Tu Mere Samne, Main Tere Samne" ("You and Me, Face to Face") sequence, the good woman writhes in a translucent, wet sari, lying on a grand piano played by the crazed orphan. Later, he sprays a bottle of champagne over her when they are on board a luxury boat. In the magnificent valleys of Switzerland, she alternately adopts ethnic and urban attire, striking up stylized poses of sexual assertion and submission.

The sequence, of course, is a fantasy, a set of virtual projections in relation to the real grounds of narration. However, its strong affective power brings about telling ruptures in the ethical wholes of the state as well that of feudal-bourgeois patriarchy. An understanding of the latter two in terms of totalities is thus deemed possible only when they are already in the process of being opened up by the rude and irreverent winds of a new order. The dynamic ensembles of femininity, objects, and landscapes point to transforming universes: a protectionist national past that is dissipating and a global future in the process of germination. The battle between a legitimate patriarchal custodianship and a yuppie but psychotic male desire, therefore, becomes complicated. In affective terms, matters are not settled by the simple question as to who gets the girl at the end; the picture becomes complex when the query is where, in which space— virtual or real—has the girl been in the meantime?

Darr is a significant moment in relation to an altered political and informatic Indian situation, and the defining male stardom of Shahrukh Khan, because it harbors unspeakable energies of a new age urban adventurism—a baroque adventurism if you will. The spectacle generated by the cinematic assembling of the faithful wife, the psychotic villain, and a mise-en-scène of transnational consumerism, tourism, and lifestyle, remains an obstinate expression of unremitted desire. It is a perverse, but much more "enticing" picture of consuming the female in the high tide of globalization. This body of affects can neither be mitigated nor absolved by a formal coming together of the subject, unity, and law when the villain finally receives his punishment. The expressive virtual moments leave a powerful residue in death, potent enough to blast the continuums of the very protectionist totalities that terminate it. This particular form of obsession in *Darr* is the forbidden delirium that precedes the arrival of a planetary neo-liberal order. It is a stylized, hyperbolic presentation of a new credo of individualism which had already made its historical entry in an opened-up India. The orphan's psychosis is an ensemble of male desires for money, goods, women, and power which are presently retailed but yet to be named or given community recognition. He is fascinating precisely because between the stammer in Khan's acting and the dying smile of the maniacal stalker, he has already announced the irresistible arrival of a community of sons demanding a new covenant from the fathers of old: the Nehruvian welfare state, as well as the agrarian feudal class.

It is therefore the movement itself, and not the simple and static part-whole relation, that is the assemblage.[25] It is the unfettered energy of cinematic figuration and not the fixed nature of identity (the psychotic stalker, the good woman) that is of crucial concern in assembling. This is the reason why the notion of assembling can lend itself to processes of relentless contagions, but not to identitarian, anthropomorphic ideas of hybridity that abound in postcolonial and diasporic studies. The latter is largely a

Hegelian postulate, of a forbidden intercourse between master and slave, producing an historically synthetic offspring who can perhaps now claim a name from the Father. Mixing between races, cultures, languages, and different forms of life is undeniably good, but to valorize its consequences as anthropomorphic resolutions to long drawn-out and bitter battles of identity, empire, and history is to be satisfied with nominalist tics of liberal humanism. It is, among other things, to address the global struggles against colonialism and the cultural and political wars of the 1960s by a happy sleight of hand and foreclose foundational questions of class or, for that matter, gender, caste, or race. It is to play into the hands of a largely American, now increasingly global multiculturalism that is able to preserve structures of class power and privilege and practice a post-racial racism that is increasingly not predicated on organic or biological notions of race.[26] But here I digress. This partial qualification, in terms of identities and assemblages, will be highly pertinent in subsequent discussions about femininity, caste, and Islamic figures in Hindi cinema.

It is the assembling principle—of wonders, edicts, attractions, or dogmas—that has been paramount in the classic Hindi film. The narrative itself has been a grand assemblage, often a series of what the director Manmohan Desai calls "highlights."[27] It is this aggravated power of assembling that lends a supple and versatile character to its genres. That is, such cinematic formations can cut across a world of variables with a greater tempo than the entrenched, "classic" style of Hollywood. This is not because the latter does not work in cinematic assemblages; rather, we can say that Hindi cinema is capable of an assembling impulse that overrides the centralizing economies of the modern—namely, authorial/subjective narration—and a metalinguistic grammar of plausibility, broadly called realism. I accord the cinematic assemblage a status of autonomy without championing it as a form of third world "alternate" becoming; it goes without saying that, as a cinematic tendency, it can produce powerful utopias by demanding the impossible from both capital and the state, as well as give impetus to some of the most dominant and violent myths of our times.

Assemblages of Temporality

In Yash Chopra's 1965 film *Waqt* it is the father's hubristic-secular utterance ("Man makes his own fate," he smugly declares) and the consequent earthquake that breaks up the family of five, separating the parents from each other and their three sons for decades. After that, two processes—one of this material world, the other, more transcendent—reunite them: a

secular murder investigation and subsequent trial, and the father's repent-
ance and prayers in the *longue durée*. More than twenty years later, Lala
Kedarnath, by then humbled by the judging powers of an otherworldly
time, chances upon a courtroom where the prosecuting counsel, the chief
witness, and the prime suspect are his three long-lost sons. Time in *Waqt*
is a cinematic calibration of events in a linear temporality (the crimino-
logical detection that leads to the lost son) as well as a curve of mythic
recall that holds constant: there is no temporal gap between hubris and
atonement; both are enactments of an eternal exemplum. The momentous
utterances in the film are both dialogic speech-acts between interacting
individuals in an historical process, and words that are emblazoned in an
epic sky of meaning.[28] The sky, usually rent by thunder, is a stock dramatic
close-up in popular Hindi cinema. Exactly as in the case of *Karan Arjun*,
it signals disorder in a lawful patriarchal order, but at the same time it can
assure, without any Cartesian suspicion or doubt, that a restorative power
is already imminent. Both the past and the present inhere in the elements,
as in a palimpsest. This is precisely why the epic cast of the narrative in
Waqt, as is the case in all "lost and found" themes that abound in popular
Hindi cinema, is a tale already told through thunder and lightning. It is an
already present dictation of the Dharmic order, which says what is lost will
be found. It is only in between that the wayward procedures and violent
landscapes of history have to be endured.

It is also the unerring governance of deep time which manages the
world of chance and prevents accidental incest between long-separated
siblings in lost-and-found films. The sons who fall in love with their
sisters in Raj Khosla's *Bambai Ka Babu* (*Babu from Bombay*) (1960) and
Ravi Chopra's *Zameer* (*Conscience*) (1975) turn out to be imposters, the
first a repentant murderer on the run and the second a conman.[29] The
movements of lost orphans, as they wade through an historical landscape
of privation, unemployment, sleaze, and crime, are thus never external
to a greater assemblage of the temporal, one that binds the here and now
with the omniscient and profound guidance of a greater order. Often the
course of justice in deep time extends to the next birth when vengeance
is wreaked (*Ab Ke Baras* [*This Season*], Raj Kanwar, 2002) or the lovers
united (*Hamesha* [*Forever*], Sanjay Gupta, 1997).

Postulated Resolutions

It is because Hindi cinema rarely presents a completely disenchanted
world that the event of resolution—an arrival at a *telos* through a mapping
of meaning and action—is often "postulated" in such tales. Postulation,

in this sense, lies between a hypothesis of "real" knowledge and a "postulate" in the specific etymological sense of "prayer." Escaping danger or bringing peace and stability are frequently achieved through a compact of secular and celestial forces. Postulation is located in the middle ground, intersecting a degraded modern world of history and chance, as well as a different but contiguous universe of mythic belief and otherworldly hope. This form of "prayer" demands a form of deliverance for which there are yet no political grounds, for the state is seen to be a weak entity that has not secured its monopoly of violence in the troubled milieu. The mother's prayer in *Karan Arjun* was thus a "postulation." In terms of the milieu of the story and the visible resources of the mise-en-scène (the state was distant and Durjan Singh's feudal sway was absolute), it was a utopian demand for the impossible.

But resolutions in Hindi film are not necessarily postulatory. This tradition of filmmaking has always had a potent realistic dimension which has especially come to the fore in some genres since the mid- to late 1990s. Meanwhile, it can be said that postulated resolutions have been central to Hindi film in its classic incarnation of the feudal family romance[30] and in the action melodramas that dominated the angry 1970s. Postulation can be cast as a theoretical fiction in contrast to another limit case, that of "real" resolution as a dominant Western paradigm.[31] As opposed to the latter, prayer as postulation is directed at once to the Almighty, the state, and the composite figure of the hero as citizen and demigod. However, this also means that it is a secular heresy; it does not affirm a realistic and resolute faith in the modern legal apparatus and its panoptic workings of governance—that is, a modern killing of God and a scrupulous submission to the state. The tension between celestial and earthly authorities is especially acute when the will of the gods exceeds lawful parameters or calls for the temporary suspension of statist affiliations. In a divided world of patriotism and mythic belief, there is a volume of *agon* in between that renders the *Bildung* of the protagonist incomplete. The science of the citizen cannot be clearly distinguished from and privileged over the faith of the acolyte.

In many cases, such assemblages include the agency of the anthropomorphic or divinely motivated animal, which, in mythic terms, can be called the *vahana* or vehicle for gods and their ministrations. A tiger saves the hero's mother in Manmohan Desai's *Mard* (1985) and salutes her. The hero of the same film is aided in his battle against the British colonial powers by a dog and a horse endowed with supernatural intelligence and agency. The blind protagonist of Asit Sen's *Bairaag* (*Asceticism*) (1976) regains his sight when he is bitten by a snake. In Desai's other film, *Amar*

Akbar Anthony (1977), a snake protects the figure of the mother from the clutches of unsavory characters.[32] In Sooraj R. Barjatiya's *Hum Aapke Hain Kaun* (*What Am I to You?*) (1994), it is the dog, Tuffy, that saves the day and gets the lovers united.

Postulations extend beyond the archives of the state and the skeptical knowledge systems of the modern without necessarily abjuring them wholesale. In David Dhawan's *Aankhen* (*Eyes*) (1993), it is a compact of state power and the irresistible flow of cosmic justice that mobilizes humans as well as a car-driving "humanoid" monkey to combat high conspiracy against the nation and the government. In Vijay Reddy's *Teri Meherbaniyan* (*By Your Grace*) (1985), video footage of the killing (a recording performed by destiny itself, since no one was "manning" the camera) and the memory of the faithful dog come together to create an avenging agency. Sometimes postulation can be an ensemble of body, matter, space, and the Word (prayer that ascends to the heavens) that can affect decisive transformation; in Desai's *Coolie* (1983), the blessed air of Haji Ali's *dargah* the holy shroud that magically envelops the hero's body and the recited Qur'anic verses render him immune to the three bullets that hit him. In the climax of Abbas-Mastaan's *Soldier* (1998), it is an assemblage of human, divine, and naturalistic forces—the praying mother, the deity in a deserted temple, and an elemental sandstorm in the desert – that scatter the army of evildoers. The groundless return of the Dharmic thereby saves the besieged hero, beats the odds, punishes the guilty, and restores order.

Assemblages, as I have said, are *opportune* compacts of evocative powers drawn, often haphazardly, from reason, prejudice, or faith. I call them opportune because they provide contingent solutions without leaving enduring bridges between opposites in their wake. Hindi films very often organize narrative matters into binary modules—religious/secular, country/city, traditional/modern, poor/rich, masculine/feminine—without resolving them in a progressive, dialectical way. This is precisely why assembling can be intensely mobile assertions of the status quo, involving a politically passive dynamic. The retribution assemblage, for instance, is frequently divided between two figurations, one linked to the legal order, and the other to criminal, lower-class forces. These sets, often cast in the form of estranged brothers or friends working on opposite sides of the law, share a zone of filial affection where the administration of Dharma takes place. This is seen in numerous films, from *Ganga Jumna* (*Ganga and Yamuna*) (Nitin Bose, 1961) to *Aatish* (*The Mirror*) (Sanjay Gupta, 1994) and beyond. Sometimes the body of the star itself has to be divided into twin assemblages—good/bad, dutiful/roguish, pacifist/

militant—which are then reincorporated into a superset of justice. This is seen in the emblematic "double role" films which are common in Hindi cinema. Dilip Kumar plays the twin siblings in *Ram Aur Shyam* (*Ram and Shyam*) (Tapi Chanakya, 1967), Hema Malini in *Seeta Aur Geeta* (*Seeta and Geeta*) (Ramesh Sippy, 1972), Sridevi in *Chalbaaz* (*The Player*) (Pankuj Parashar, 1990), or Salman Khan in *Judwa* (*Twins*) (David Dhawan, 1997). This narrative function allows a bucolic, often "Gandhian" spirit of the nation to affectively share the face of the male star as the face of the Dharmic, with sad but necessary illegal/industrial agencies in an overall age of degeneration.[33]

The Thing-in-the-Assemblage

Let us now consider the "thing-in-the-assemblage"; that is, entities we understand as "objects" that can be surveyed and ratiocinated by a singular subjective consciousness. It is also important to probe further the complicated relationship between multi-directional assembling of signs and an expected linear tempo of subjective narration; that is, the manner in which objects can be grafted onto and rendered communicable in an event of cinematic thought. I shall discuss a host of objects familiar as well as alien throughout this book, but especially when discussing lyricism in Chapter 4. Let me approach this present task with an early, provisional suggestion: that the relationship between assembling and linear narration is an "eccentric" one. That is, the kinetic mobilization of objects often overrides stable subjective frames of reckoning. I shall take up two unusual entities for our inquiry—blood and alcohol—and, *ergo*, talk about the two not as matter *qua* matter, but blood-in-the-assemblage and alcohol-in-the-assemblage.

In *Amar Akbar Anthony* (Manmohan Desai, 1977) three brothers, who were separated from each other and their parents decades ago, come together in a hospital by chance as well as by destiny. In one among many such moments of dramatic irony, they donate blood to a blind woman who is actually their long-lost mother. The cinematic blood transfusion becomes an epic merger of a feudal theme and modern instruments of medical science. Three tubes carrying blood from the bodies of the heroes mingle in one bottle; the collected reservoir is simultaneously transfused into the mother's body. In this poignant moment of non-recognition, the attributes of a medical impossibility (even if the blood groups match, blood from three different donors cannot be simultaneously administered) are appended to emotives from a feudal imaginary (blood [*khoon*] as a marker of lineage; the mother as a font of being and meaning in the world), and an ironic dictation of destiny. In another of Desai's films, *Dharam Veer*

(*Dharam and Veer*) (1977), the hero puts his blood mark on the forehead of a haughty and "shrewish" princess, declaring that the imprint will take a long time to be effaced. The princess discovers this to be true, especially when she compares the virile viscosity of the mark with the watery blood of her "effeminate" and cowardly fiancé. Here a patriarchal fantasy of mythic virility is released through an image of biological absurdity; "blood" ceases to be scientific matter with organic qualities but is abstracted as a direct inscription of pedigree. From a different epistemological framework, one can argue that blood, as the thing-in-the-assemblage, is rendered miraculous by a cosmic intelligence not beholden to realism. That is, in an overall evoking of *karuna rasa* or *veer rasa* through an alchemy of elements earthly and divine, the sign of blood lodges itself inseparably between two worlds.

Assemblages often "make do" by collecting objects and exaggerating their qualities to mythic dimensions. That is, sometimes they bring about acute, morally "impossible" passages in the melodramatic dispensation of the narrative, when the narrative itself staggers between the sacred and the profane. They often give rise to a temporary separation between desire and ethics, allowing the protagonist to perform functions without culpability. In films like *Himmat Aur Mehnat* (*Courage and Sweat*) (K. Bapaiah, 1987) and *Vardi* (*The Uniform*) (Umesh Mehra, 1988), the stigma of pre-marital sex/rape is mediated by alcohol as the object in the assemblage. The heroes in both films undergo total inebriation, a temporary dispersal of their ethical-civic selves. They get drunk and have "non-consensual" sex (rape) with their respective heroines. The issue of force, however, does not have much to do with the woman's individualism, freedom, or juridical identity, but pertains to the permissive limits of patriarchy. Alcohol here serves as a force of linguistic and phenomenological "dissolve," which not only suspends the juridical perception of things (which is why rape is not an issue) but also for the moment waylays the usual Dharmic parameter of storytelling.[34] Rather, to put it differently, it can be said that such events take the memories of Dharma to the extreme, by invoking the most grotesque and lowly ones of the eight types of marriages mentioned in the *Dharmasastras* or *The Laws of Manu*: the *rakshasha* (ogre) marriage and the *pisacha* (ghoul) marriage. The first takes place when "a man forcibly carries off a girl out of her house, screaming and weeping, after he has killed, wounded, and broken," and the second when a man has sex with a girl "who is asleep, drunk, or out of her mind" (*The Laws of Manu*, 46).

Alcohol as object thus enters into an assemblage with the figure of the hero, reinventing him as a beastly automaton—a grossly naturalistic body of masculine robustness completely devoid of ethical consciousness and therefore capable of a primal patriarchal appropriation of the woman. The body of the woman is captured as a territory for the transit of unleashed libidinal drives in a state of subjective "black-out." Later, after a sobering total return of moral focus, the contrite hero prevents the heroine from committing suicide by offering to marry her and reinstate her social standing.[35]

The inebriation of the self is precisely that which forecloses "modern" charges of subjective hypocrisy or attribution of culpability in terms of law. The subject, in the alcoholic assemblage, is not proposed as a modern one with individuated responsibilities and blameworthiness. This is why the figure under the influence can be subsequently recuperated in a feudal melodramatic schema of forgiveness and restoration. It can thus be said that it was not the traditional Indian self that acted, but the body as instrument, under the spell of alcohol as the sole, demonic agent of perception as well as desire. In the feudal world, the unfortunate interregnum cannot alter the "surface" aspect of goodness and virtue because surface is all that there is. One cannot say that alcohol merely allowed hidden or deep, underlying demons to surface because there is no subjective "depth" in the first place.[36] Booze, as an object in the cinematic assemblage, is thus an absolute sign of bestiality that draws powers of signification from a totalized Gandhian prejudice.[37] When alcohol as such is allowed to enter the body, it switches off the human in a total manner.

The alcoholic assemblage thus effects an infantile regression to a stage where it is no longer possible, on a plane of cognition, to separate the self from the environment.[38] This is precisely why it is often used in comic scenes. In S. U. Sunny's 1960 swashbuckler *Kohinoor*, the hero, played by Dilip Kumar, enters the villain's den and finds himself in front of his arch-enemy, who is drunk. He pretends to be the drunken man's image in a mirror, imitating the latter's hand and body gestures in the way of stereoscopic reversals. The villain, of course, cannot gauge the authenticity of his own reflection, and the hero makes good his escape.[39] In perhaps the most famous scene of this type, the character Anthony (Amitabh Bachchan) in Manmohan Desai's *Amar Akbar Anthony* (1977) gets drunk at a party and is then beaten up by the heroine's bodyguard. On returning home, he applies bandages to the injured parts of his image in a mirror instead of his actual body.

The Body-in-the-Assemblage: The *Dalit*

It is clear at this point that the notion of assemblage does not accommodate a strict subject–object arrangement presiding over the lineage of visuals and sounds. Nor does it conform to a Descartian dualism and a hierarchical ordering of the mind over the body. When I speak of *affects* in relation to the assemblage, I imply a parallelism of the mind and the body, which I shall clarify in the next chapter. The guidance of a humanistic phenomenology is not wholesome in assembling because the mind is not imperial here; the body is often an automaton, intelligence is frequently cosmic, and matter miraculous. The hero's taxi in *Khuddar* (*The Autonomous*) (Ravi Tandon, 1982) beeps a warning whenever dubious merchandise is loaded into it. The holy tuft of hair on the Brahmin hero's head in *Hum Se Badkar Kaun* (*None Bigger than Us*) (Deepak Bahry, 1981) stands up of its own volition, like an antenna, whenever there is mischief afoot. Assemblages are immanent clusters of realistic and uncanny factors that produce effects of power, authority, and intelligibility outside the ambit of the modern, although modern perceptions, like any other, can be easily included in them. Through somber reckonings as well as carnivalesque laughter, they discursively create situations and the partitioned subjectivities that fulfill, mediate, and war over those very situations. This understanding will be of utmost importance in the larger discussion of Hindi cinema in the age of globalization and information because it is from the 1990s onwards that assembling bodies and objects proliferate with ferocious intensity.

What is being questioned in these elaborations is an imperialism of the signifier over the sign and the privilege of the integrated individual subject at ground level. In that case, what happens to a body, encoded as a pure visual sign, or proposed as a proper name, when it is *in* assemblage? That is, what occurs when the body, in being anterior to an assembling process, cannot be immediately secured by a dominant syntax and grammar of meaning? After Jacques Derrida and Paul de Man, it is quite insufficient to state the obvious: that the relationship between the figure and the identity, just like word and meaning, is that of a temporal disjunction (in which the historical act of reading is to be lodged), or that the relationship between the signifier and the signified is that of a perpetual *difference*. I shall pose the question in a manner that touches the nerve center of an ongoing debate about the language of cinema itself, and whether, and to what extent, cinematic language can be systematized into a narrational but punctual grammar of plausibility.

It is pertinent here to invoke Tejaswini Niranjana and Vivek Dhareswar's insightful discussion of a musical setpiece in Shankar's 1994 film *Kaadalan*.[40] The sequence in question features the dazzling dancing talents of the southern star Prabhudeva. Staged in a setting that approximates the spaghetti western, the "Muqabla Muqabla" song is quite detached from the narrative, which is of a staple modern love story threatened by a tyrannical father. The beginning of the scene rewrites the figure of the hero: he is now dressed in the dusty attire of the Wild West, astride a horse, and about to be hanged. Two white "villains" are seen to be presiding over his execution. At this juncture, the heroine rides into the scene and shoots the noose from the gallows. The condemned escapes with the heroine and is instantly transported to a utopian/dystopian setting that combines scenic attributes of the western with those of the MTV musical. The song-and-dance sequence that follows is a transnational pastiche of movements and rhythms. Later, the white villains shoot at Prabhu's (Prabhudeva's character in the film) dancing figure, eliminating his head, hands, and feet. After a dramatic pause, it is the cinematic grapheme of the body, outlined by the clothes, that continues the dance. The bodily verve tenaciously remains intact even after the body *qua* body is exiled from the assemblage. Dhareshwar and Niranjana point out that the persistence of the ghostly caricature that survives the bullets can be linked, in terms of memory and affect, to a sequence preceding the "Mukabla Mukabla" one, in which Prabhu is tortured by the goons of the dictatorial governor. He is punished by a rich, powerful, evidently upper-caste patriarchy because of a transgression that cannot be legally named in a democratic dispensation. The temerity of the lower-class, dark-skinned hero can only be acknowledged as that which must be extinguished through a form of violence that precedes the formal law of the republic.

The fact that Prabhu has fallen in love with a woman from the upper echelons of society is only part of the problem. The very cinematic figuration of the dark and decidedly non-Aryan Prabhu, animated by the irreverent energy of the street and in assemblage with the plenitudes of globalization, is something that has wider political resonances. According to Dhareshwar and Niranjana, this is thematically established in the film. From the very outset Prabhu and his sidekick are seen to declare "freedom" from the order of Brahminical papas. They gleefully cannibalize the opened-up spaces, commodities, bodies, and styles (from peta-rap to Bharat Natyam) of a liberalized order, violating an older patriarchal system of distributing goods and women as privilege or tribute. At the same time, Prabhu is presented as a survivor who can subsist on insects in straitened circumstances. As far as a naturalized feudal mindset is concerned, Prabhu and company present a disconcerting, post-Mandal[41] picture of a world turned upside down: that of the *dalit* inheriting the earth.

Prabhu is a *dalit* figure, but not as a matter of positive identity. His is a *dalit* body in assemblage, only within "a signifying space for a new politics." The image of dark-skinned untouchability, against an historical backdrop of an endogamous class/caste social arrangement, becomes immanent precisely in those moments of interface between a terminal statist violence and tenacious irreverence. It comes into being when an undying expressivity meets with and survives the bullets of erasure, when the dance continues even after Prabhu is dispatched. This is because the gunshots do not actually interrupt the rhythm of the piece; rather they bring to the fore the power of the assemblage itself; that is, how, in combining dark skin with zoot suits and bleach-blond hair, it has already violated a habit of grouping signs. The actual body in the assemblage—the *dalit*—comes into being at the very moment the dark-skinned human figure is violently sent to spectral disembodiment. The body-in-the-assemblage is at once the figure of Prabhudeva, the gunshot, the rhythm of movement, and the dance of the digital. The filmic picture of the obstinate *dalit* is consolidated between life and death, between music and firepower, in the assembling *graphe-motion* of cinema itself, and not in what cinema is supposed to represent or reflect—that is, exactly when a dynamic of hybridization goes to a celebratory space beyond stable, anthropomorphic 'hybrid' identities.

The assemblage, however, is only a moment in the film. It congeals some disparate lines of energy (feudalism, new urbanity, caste politics, globalization, violence, and planetary desires) and in a moment of cata-chrestic maturation, foregrounds the tensions between conflicting sign systems. However, what if, as in the case of *Kaadalan*, the narrative of the film is nothing special? That is, the story is inconsequential as a socially symbolic act, and at times quite regressive in its sexist ideological bearings? Why should more importance be accorded to the part than the whole, the assembling process rather than the narratological one? That is because, as mentioned earlier, Indian cinema is as much a perpetually assembling field of phenomena as is the Indian modernizing process itself. In either of these cases, there is no single story of being or becoming that dominates the horizon and transcodes the rest. Rather, multiple stories—national, regional, mythic, developmentalist, traditional, or modern—contest and intertwine with each other. Here propositions are never isolatable in states of splendid transcendence; they are continually proposed, simultaneously contaminated, and incessantly purified. The assemblage is thus sympto-matic in its elemental implosion of sign systems, rather than in the light of Shankar's intentions as author, or the manner in which he "rounds up" an act of conscious or unconscious narration.

The task is thus not to ignore storytelling procedures altogether, but to devalue the status of the narrative as the supreme ideological and aesthetic instantiation; that is, to concentrate analysis more on *how*, in an historical field of problems and semiotic engagement, the stories of the nation are told. This argument can, of course, be connected to an abiding question of cinematic language and grammar. In the course of their exegesis on *Kaadhalan*, Dhareshwar and Niranjana usefully point out why there is a need to move beyond the structural impasses of semiology/narratology:

> As Christian Metz . . . argues: "Enunciation is the semiological act by which some part of the text talks to us about this text as an act." . . . Metz rightly claims that the cinematic enunciation is reflexive rather than deictic . . . . And yet Metz seems confused about how to clarify the nature of cinematic enunciation without inheriting the anthropomorphism of a linguistics of deictics. He inherits this confusion, or so it seems to us, from the linguistic monism of semiology. Gilles Deleuze, who opts for Peircean semiotics precisely to avoid this confusion, offers a diagnosis of the confusion inherited by a semiology of cinema: "We . . . have to define, not semiology, but 'semiotics', as the system of images and signs independent of language in general. When we recall that linguistics is only part of semiotics, we no longer mean, as for semiology, that there are languages without a language system, but that the language system only exists in its reaction to the *non-language material* that it transforms. *That is why utterances and narrations are not a given of visible images, but a consequence which flows from this reaction.*" (Dhareshwar and Niranjana, 212; emphasis added)

Narrative closure as a global gesture and the ideological statement as a local one are thus abstract diagrams in the Deleuzian sense. As afterthoughts, they can be considered *end-statements* that have curved around and claimed for the moment a critical volume of wanton signs. Moral, ideological, or legal strictures do attempt to domesticate the body as a repository of hoary appetites and energies, but never quite succeed. Trajectories of storytelling are undeniably useful to chart regularities and compelling pressures of dominant power. However, the story as such cannot propose a destinying horizon of meaning, even as meaning is being generated, particularized, and proliferated. I will examine this aspect in greater detail later in this book when talking about difference and repetition in Hindi cinema.

The Body-in-the-Assemblage: The Woman

I shall conclude this chapter with a slightly extended discussion on assemblages of femininity. This is because a large part of the nationalist discourse on Indian modernity has been centered on the idealized figure of the Hindu woman as the prime cultural civilizational product, that is, as an artwork of spiritual interiorities unsullied by colonialism.[42] Her figure is perpetually an odd gravitational site, in which the specter of the modern both emerges from, and is in turn engulfed by, the vortex of tradition. In popular Hindi cinema, the cinematic coming into being of the feminine body is usually a complex process of "distilling" visibilities, by which a form is abstracted gradually by a calibration of *eros* and *jouissance*, between the world and the home, into a postulate of "traditional" patriarchy or of its intimate enemy, the modern. The movement of the woman both diurnal and exceptional, her body and its paraphernalia both exotic and mundane, her proximities and affinities with other bodies and objects, the spaces she occupies, the judicious and moral segmentations of those very spaces, her attire, her speech, her language, her vocabulary and terms of reference, her profession, her proclivities toward habits and poesis, her needs and desires, the basis of determining what is need and what can be articulated as desire, her nature and the naturalization of that very nature—all form a formidable assembling field. It is in this combustive sphere that statements of tradition are abstracted, necessities of political economy and imperatives of culture formulated, and the historicity and essence of womanhood both lamented and celebrated. The female body is always in a stage of esoteric re-drawings, being reified into both the spirit of the nation and its torrid others—the putrid vices that prevent the nation from coming into being. Which is why "narrating" the woman is an anxious as well as furious undertaking, perpetually geared toward foreclosing that moment when the female form, as a *bodily* cluster of errant appetites, becomes apparent in passing *between* abstract diagrams of virtue and vice that mutually contend over, intersect, and occupy it. Cinematic women[43] are therefore kinetic assemblages *par excellence*. Rather, one can say that there are no women *qua* women in film, only assemblages of femininities, figures, spaces, principles, and situations of political economy.

In his insightful reading of Mehboob Khan's landmark film, Moinak Biswas has pointed out that at a crucial moment in *Mother India* (1956), the figure of the title character becomes an expression of crisis in "national narration."[44] I take up this illuminating instance especially because, in Chapter 6, I shall discuss the cinematic transformation of the iconic mother figure in Khan's film, from the naissance of the new republic to the globalized environment of the 1990s, through several remakes of the classic. *Mother India* depicts the life of an ordinary village woman who suffers great hardship to bring up her two sons after the death of her infant daughter and abandonment by her husband. The epic sweep of Khan's narration elevates the story of Radha (the mother) to exemplary status, as that which sublimates an essential, abiding spirit of the nation in a changing landscape of history. The body of the woman is perpetually assembled with evocative environments pertaining to a pastoral romantic conception of the land and its people, as well as with internationalist idioms like socialist realism. The figuration of the mother as national artwork is a relentless tussle between historical pictures of agrarian poverty, the "natural" body, a syncretic iconology, and stipulates of Dharmic motherhood. The moment I am focusing on is one in which this building process, oscillating between diurnal movements and iconic arrests, comes precariously close to unraveling.

The incident takes place after Ramu, Radha's disabled husband, has left home in shame. A flash-flood devastates the village; their daughter dies and Radha is left destitute. With no help in sight, she turns to Sukhilala, an unscrupulous moneylender. It is clear from the beginning that the lecherous old man will give her money only in lieu of sexual favors. Radha thus has to compromise her honor (*izzat*). But what is interesting here is that the indecent proposal is posed in an intersection between illicit male desire and the ethics of motherhood. Sukhilala tells Radha that she has to submit to his wishes because it is her Dharma *as mother* to save her sons from starvation. In his reading, Biswas points out that since Radha's body is already claimed by another Dharmic statement of marital fidelity (which can, of course, subsist without the physical presence of the husband), there is a crisis in ethical narration whereby the body of the woman cannot be made to pass "naturally" from womanhood to motherhood. She is asked to choose between the two. This is thus an event of severe catachresis. The mother-nation is supposed to be wholesomely occupied by a unified and organic code of Dharma, but historical circumstances seem to have fractured Dharma itself. It is in this chasm that the body of the woman, now deserted by legitimate patriarchal authority, threatens to expose itself as an abject repository of appetites and needs. Radha's arms slip to her side in a gesture of almost somnambulist surrender; she stands transfixed as the leering Sukhilala keeps circling her, breaking the decorum of the veil (*ghunghat*)—of only frontal and carefully nuanced sightings of another's wife—and making her a consummate object of his gaze.

The moment of crisis, however, is not limited to a realist reckoning of the situation. A dejected Radha begins to address the idol of Lakshmi, Sukhilala's ancestral goddess. The moneylender's movements around the frame are interspersed by tight close-ups of the accusing mother who complains to the Devi about the inertia of the heavens. Sukhilala and historical time are rendered out of focus as there is a frontal broadcast of the Dharmic question; Radha raises her eyes to the heavens and asks the goddess about the veracity of a covenant written since eternity. After this moment of supine maturation, the woman's body is once again assembled with the Dharmic. A scuffle ensues when Sukhilala attempts to oust the distracting deity from the premises. In the mêlée, Radha finds out that the *mangalsutra* she had angrily thrown at Lakshmi has been tellingly returned to her. This incident reaffirms the horizon of faith; Radha pushes the villain aside and runs out to join her sons.

Radha's exit does not, of course, solve the problem of hunger and despondency that besets her and her sons. She boils a tuber to feed her family, but meanwhile the villagers prepare to leave the doomed village en masse. For Radha, there is thus the imminent danger of losing the village community to compound the loss of her husband. She herself cannot leave because that would mean ending the possibility of being there for her husband if and when he returns. Given the diegetic context, the overall material crisis in this case cannot be solved through an historical coming into being of a developmentalist state (the law, flood relief, the apparatus of political economy in the form of government-run rural banks, etc.). The country is still under the colonial yoke; the welfare state is a distant one, not yet figurable in the landscape. It is at this crucial moment that the body of the woman is transformed in an epic manner, absolving her of the bad side of history. Radha begins work in her field, singing a passion-ate song and urging the villagers not to abandon the land that is like their mother. The toiling body of the mother is reinscribed through an iconic stylization of socialist realism. A series of low-angle mid-shots of Radha and her sons carrying the plowshare elevate them to an affective sphere that transcends the devastated mise-en-scène. The body of the woman is now a part of an overall lyrical-divine assemblage that quickly acquires cosmic dimensions. Radha is touched and delivered of her predicament by a mythic power of time. She falls down while tilling the field and is helped to her feet by her two sons, Ramu and Birju. A lap dissolve takes place and the woman who is lifted up is now old; her starving children who help her do so as robust young men.

As Biswas points out, this momentous shift in time achieves two things at a single stroke: it bypasses all historical roadblocks to bring the body of the woman home to patriarchal shelter in the form of a community of sons; and it frees her from that very sexuality that had come in between and blocked her diurnal passage from being a woman of flesh to the abstract icon of the mother/wife. Radha is the exemplary maternal figure now; her close-fitting, weather-ravaged sari replaced by hermit-like attire, quite outlandish for tropical climes and reminiscent of Maxim Gorky's Mother. The postulated assemblage here combines the historical promise of a socialist internationalism—an architectonic of science, industry, and revolution—with a mythic idea of justice. The stance of cinematic melo-drama here is about incubating affections and memories of Dharma and

1.2: Signatures of socialist-realism in *Mother India*.

then unleashing them, in a single stroke, toward a sovereign occupation of the ravaged land and the imperiled woman.

Radha's test was to hold fast to the eternal while enduring a painful historical rite of passage. The lines of tension in assembling the feminine can, however, appear at a much more basic level, with problems of identifying and naming the woman, and attendant questions of proprietorship and legitimacy. In L.V. Prasad's *Sharda* (1957), for instance, the hero undergoes a baroque disintegration when his father enters into an arranged marriage with his beloved. The narrative is elaborated at that severe interface between the preordained, epic dictation of fate and a modern tragedy of "chance." The hero's emotions and duties are painfully dispersed between the woman as object of private desires and the woman as a public incarnation of the mother, as announced by patriarchy's absolute name-giving rights. The melodrama of subject formation in the new republic[45] is consequently torn between the inflexible commitments of the feudal scion and the creeping guilt of Oedipus.

Assembling anxieties continue with the problem of grasping the woman as national being incarnate and squaring that act of apprehending with historical horizons of progress, capital, and desire. It therefore pertains to locating the woman in some ground of reckoning before monumentalizing her, for the horizons are already split between the country and the city. The hero in *Talaash* (*Search*) (O. P. Ralhan, 1969) is caught between the country girl, Gauri, and her lookalike, the modern, foreign-educated Madhu (with Sharmila Tagore playing both roles). For him, the ethical choice is between staying true to a natality of being (with his widowed mother as the usual powerful influence) and compromising it for the new order. Madhu is his boss's daughter and comes with the promise of class advancement. Ralhan's film is, of course, only one among many. We could recall other situations in which the divergence between interest and desire, between an alienating mode of capitalist industrialization and an agrarian spirit of the nation, is resolved within the aegis of the feudal extended family: the twin brothers in *Ram Aur Shyam* (*Ram and Shyam*) (Tapi Chanakya, 1967) or *Kishen Kanhaiya* (Rakesh Roshan, 1990) complete a symmetrical yet assembled picture of national conjugality with one marrying the city/modern girl, and the other the rural/traditional one.

The woman thus assembles historically with theorems of modernity and tenets of tradition in the ceremonial interiors of the home and the shock and the traffic of money and bodies in the urban space. The classic postwar melodramas of the 1950s predominantly presented the bipolar extremes of the whore and wife. In films like *Baazi* (*The Deal*) (Guru Dutt, 1951), *CID* (Raj Khosla, 1956), and *Howrah Bridge* (Shakti Samanta, 1958), feminine bodies are charted along testing paths of fire and shade, between the humble abode and the smoke-filled bars that form the criminal underbelly of the city. These polarities, as we know, have become less acute in later decades, when women, more than ever, start getting caught up in the swirl and bustle of the industrial order. However, what is of critical importance is to understand the scope and complexity of these secret or scandalous mergers; that is, the manner in which the woman is configured as abominable or enticing in a zone of barters between principles and prejudice. In Raj Kapoor's *Bobby* (1973) the Indian "teenager" can be made figurable only by assembling the swimsuit or the miniskirt with an ethnographic infantilism of a Goan fishing community. In Kapoor's *Satyam Shivam Sunderam* (*Love, Truth, and Beauty*) (1978), the "fashion model" body of Zeenat Aman is combined with the ethnographic profile of the tribal woman. The former imparts an urban tonality and architecture to the abstract postulates of the latter, while the coveted body of Aman is in turn claimed by an earthy ontology of fantasized "tradition." It is precisely because of this assembling stratum that devotional energies can be brought into secret concert with expressions of appetite. In the title song sequence, Roopa (Aman), while bathing the Shiva lingam and preparing it for worship, embraces and kisses the phallic emblem.

Roughly from the 1970s, a more kinetic assembling arena of femininity entailed an unavoidable publicness of the woman in the nucleated existence of the city, amidst the skewed movements of the commercial order and in the elemental political environment leading up to Indira Gandhi's notorious declaration of Emergency. The urban space suddenly became full of temporarily or permanently "orphaned" women, exposed to education and paid employment, both necessary for the sustenance of the emerging social model of the nuclear middle-class family. It was not just the circulation of female bodies in different public avenues that was worrying for a patriarchal custodianship of culture, but also the inevitable traffic of temporalities, violence, and memories. These could pertain to disconcerting partitions between desire and ethics caused by profane psychological emotives of the times: *ennui* (Rajinder Singh Bedi's 1971 *Dastak* [*Knock*]) or memories of lost loves (Basu Bhattacharya's 1971 *Anubhav* [*Experience*]). The assembling of the woman as artwork, in line with a feudal idea of principled stewardship, was complicated when the cinematic city assumed an aura of the real, when it offered itself as a potential harbinger of secrets or schizophrenic violence. In *Achanak* (*Suddenly*) (Gulzar, 1973) the soldier husband kills the wife he dearly loves because of her infidelity. In *Shaque* (*Suspicion*) (Aruna Raje and Vikas Desai, 1976), the wife thinks that her devoted husband is a murderer; in *Sheesha* (*The Mirror*) (Basu Chatterjee, 1986) there is a nagging suspicion that the husband is a rapist.

The problem of safeguarding the woman, of assembling her very being as a set of punctual affections and commitments, crops up not simply due to the collapse of feudal paternalism; indeed, numerous instances can be cited where women are kidnapped and carried off to the *haveli* of the overlord. However, the bordered spaces that were seen in the feudal family romances of the 1950s and 1960s ensured that the ethical assemblage of the woman could be habituated diurnally, even in a horizon of fatality, between the fixed spaces of the *ghar* and the *kotha*—in what is a general course of money as tribute or woman as tribute. The crisis, as far as the location of the woman in an open map of urban modernity is concerned, pertains to the difficulties in customizing womanhood in relation to gathering storms of democratic rights, feminism, production, class warfare, and the circulation of bodies and money. In a haphazard flow of visibilities, the ceremonial postures of worship, confinement, and devotion demanded from the ideal woman became increasingly difficult to be held in the static.

A profane publicness of the woman in the atomizing city in the twilight of the Nehruvian order produced a generation of rape victims: B.

R. Chopra's fashion model heroine in *Insaaf Ka Tarazu* (*The Scales of Justice*) (1980) or the raped housewives and sisters in *Ghar* (*Home*) (Manik Chatterjee, 1978), *Pratighaat* (*The Retaliation*) (N. Chandra, 1987), and *Aaj Ki Awaaz* (*The Cry of the Times*) (Ravi Chopra, 1984). In a film like *Benam Badsha* (*The Unnamed Emperor*) (K. Ravi Shankar, 1991), the melodramatic juxtaposition of pathological violence and principled femininity is taken to a ludicrous extreme when the woman hounds her rapist until he reforms and marries her. One of the most scandalous assemblages of femininity in the turbulent city can be seen in *Zakhmi Aurat* (*The Wounded Woman*) (Avtar Bhogal, 1988). Here a band of violated women pool their various professional, intellectual, and physical resources (police officer, surgeon, temptress) to entice and trap rapists at large. The men are anesthetized and taken to a secret operating theater to be neutered. The city in this film thus becomes the assembled site of a frontal encounter between warring postulates: fear of rape and fear of castration.

Conclusion

These diagrams of past femininities serve as counterpoints to a neo-traditional womanhood that comes to the fore from the early 1990s. In the next chapter I will elaborate on how a resuscitated version of the essential Indian/Hindu woman as an emblem of ceremonial interiorities can be announced only by cutting the chords with the Nehruvian middle-class home. The new Hindu-metropolitan woman is cinematically fielded in such cases in conjunction with the heady richness of the times, in the splendid isolation of super-rich north Indian upper-caste mansions. The women in these films can be reinstated in a newly built neo-traditional platform only by removing them, almost in a total sense, from the money markets and public grounds of the historical city. The anachronistic extended families that we see in this genre of "marriage melodramas" stake a claim to be ideal Hindu ones not because they have wealth, but because they have the wherewithal and the commitment to remove their women from the prostituting and cannibalizing spaces of the globalizing city. In the process, such families effect an exemplary housing of the woman as national deity and transform their diurnal into a pure spectacle of interiorities, a perfect homesteading of virtue away from political economy, and the steadfast *geist* of a national heritage exhibit.

For now, however, having elaborated, to some extent, the assembling tendencies of classic Hindi film, and having highlighted its tensile and elastic features, let me propose a few qualifying characteristics of the period I shall next focus on. While acknowledging fully the national and worldly scope that has always been true of the Indian cinematic assemblage, I shall, at this point, suggest three provisional theorems that mark, in an increasingly cumulative fashion, the films of the 1990s and after:

1. Assemblages in top-line, mainstream Hindi films (and in many south Indian films as well) achieved a pronounced geo-televisual aesthetic from the 1990s onwards.
2. Assemblages have become geo-televisual in a special way: they have become *informatic* in a global sense.
3. In our times, a picture of metropolitan Hinduness has come into being that is not an alloy of a constitutionalist idea of modernity, but is a *modernization* that is informatic and not necessarily or automatically beholden to liberalism.

It is important to acknowledge that assembling, especially in forms of postulation, often conforms to a politics of the passive revolution in the Gramscian sense. In a rather banal manner, it can be said that the modalities of wish-fulfillment in commercial Hindi cinema often offer only cosmetic or simplistic solutions to entrenched social problems of class, caste, region, and gender. They particularize these issues or, in some cases, evade them altogether. As a broad cultural phenomenon, Hindi film has been rightly interpreted by Prasad and others as bearing reformist ideological baggage characteristic of a feudal-bourgeois national elite. Partha Chatterjee has theorized this heterogeneous Indian ruling bloc as an unstable coalition marked by a protracted "war of positions" between different contending forces.[46] Another Gramsci-inspired reading by Ranajit Guha describes this rag-tag ruling group as one that exercises a catastrophically balanced domination, without the properly formed palliative hegemonic apparatus of state and civil institutions.[47]

It is my contention that, since the 1990s, another situation of power has gradually manifested itself in the Indian context. The older structures of dominance are still very much present, but figures of thought need to be adjusted in line with a new scenario. The metaphor of territorial/trench warfare in Chatterjee's Gramscian formulation, for instance, presumes a tendentially modern order of spaces, enclosures, and movement. This cartography of political maneuvers has been *informationized* to a large extent in the past decade and a half. In other words, what I am gesturing toward is a new planetary regime of power/information that has supplemented or in some cases replaced the power/knowledge paradigm of bourgeois discipline brilliantly studied by Michel Foucault. As far as the Indian political battleground is concerned, many of its solid features have been rendered ethereal and airy, similar to how, in the history of warfare, the technology of carpet-bombing transformed the strategic status of the old survey map. The Andersonian components of the "census, the map, and the museum" have thus been electrified. Indian popular cinema was part of that virtual topography which unfolded beyond the classic enclosures of the modern paradigm. The city still retained vertical institutions of pedagogy, representation, and governance, but a good part of it also became the screen. The age-old regimes of power did not disappear, but they had to withstand the inundation of what we shall theorize in the next chapter as geo-televisual information. They thus had to morph and acquire new capacities. The rest of this book is the story of this adjustment.

Notes

1. Bimal Krishna Matilal has illuminatingly suggested that a proper discussion of Dharma as a moral philosophy can begin in a better fashion with a consideration of the epics (*itihasas*) Ramayana and Mahabharata (*Ethics and Epics*, 2002, 22–3). That is, much more than the *Dharmasastra* texts—which are lists of duties, ethics, virtues, and vices—the moral element in the Sanskritic-Brahmanical tradition can be derived from its exemplary instantiations in the *itihasas*. This is because, as Matilal notes, the ancient Indian *Sastras* are not primers in morality. Neither in the Vedic Brahmana tradition nor among the recalcitrant *Sramana* sects, such as the Buddhist, Jaina, or *Ajivika* groups, does one find God referred to as the ultimate authority on Dharma (51). In the *Isa* Upanishad, it is said that the face of truth remains hidden by a circle of gold (*The Upanishads*, 50). The *Kena* Upanishad too posits Brahman as that which is beyond the known and the unknown. In the *Chandogya* three sets of Dharma are mentioned: rituals (*yajna*), the study of the scriptures (*adyayana*), and austerities (*tapas*). Manu himself outlines an eclectic, potentially conflict-ridden process of deriving the Dharmic from five sources in his laws: the Vedas, Dharmasastras, virtues cultivated by the Vedic scholars, the good conduct of the honest, and mental satisfaction. The ways to purify Dharma are ethics, *pramanas* or perception, inference, verbal testimony, and debate as *tarka* or *hetusastra*. He describes Dharma as that which is honored by the learned, followed by those who are above greed, and approved in the hearts of people (*The Laws of Manu*, 17–18). It is with a special modernist textualization of the *Bhagwad Gita* during the nineteenth century that the notion of Dharma is assigned to a single, oracular source that can potentially be affiliated to a general monotheism of the nation-state as well as to a consolidated "Hindu" identity. It is only then that Dharma emerges as a mytho-poesis devoutly desired by political dispensations, as precisely that divine entity that can bridge the gap between the horizontal proliferation of daily life and the vertical immanence of the state. See also *Atho Ma Faleshu*

Kadachon (2003), the groundbreaking work on the *Bhagwad Gita* by Sibaji Bandyopadhyay.

2. See, for example, Georgio Agamben, *Remnants of Auschwitz* (2000): 18.

3. Two such laws, both frequently repeated in popular Hindi films, are *Satyameva Jayate* (Truth always Triumphs) and *Bhagwan ke ghar der hai, andher nehi* (Justice may be Delayed in the House of God, but it is Inevitable).

4. Perhaps the best critical elaboration of a temper of the "world historical" in Kantian-Hegelian modernity and its intimate connection to realist narration can be found in Georg Lukács, *Theory of the Novel: A Historico-philosophical Essay on the Great Forms of Western Literature* (1971) and in "Reification," in his *History and Class Consciousness* (1971).

5. Ashish Rajadhyaksha, in "The Bollywoodization of Indian Cinema" (2003), has argued that big-budget Hindi cinema as such is only a part of an overall transnational culture industry called "Bollywood." The latter ranges from star-studded entertainment shows held abroad, pastiche-like indices in Western fashion, music, tourism, installation art, to cell phone ring tones. In an equally insightful article, Madhava Prasad ("This Thing called Bollywood," 2003) has argued that the proper name should be used to designate a body of films that privilege a back-to-the-grassroots NRI (non-resident Indian) nostalgia, with the newly emerging urban middle class in India absorbing that as a part of its own self-projection in the world. Prasad notes that these films are being made in the UK and Canada among other places (excluding Bombay) and are marked by the replacement of Urdu by English as the dominant aesthetic and ideological metalanguage of Hindi film.

6. The most famous example is the cultural ban on the screen kiss in Hindi cinema, explored by Madhava Prasad in *Ideology of the Hindi Film* (1998): 88–113.

7. The classic study is David Bordwell et al., *The Classical Hollywood Cinema: Film Style & Mode of Production to 1960* (1985).

8. See Geeta Kapur, "Mythic Material in Indian Cinema" (1987), and "Revelation & Doubt: Sant Tukaram and Devi," in *When Was Modernism?: Essays on Contemporary Cultural Practice in India* (2000); Ashish Rajadhyaksha, "Neo-Traditionalism: Film as Popular Art in India" (1986), and "The Phalke Era, Conflict of Traditional Form and Modern Technology" (1987); Ravi S. Vasudevan, "The Politics of Cultural Address in a 'Transitional' Cinema: A Case Study of Popular Indian Cinema" (2000), and "Shifting Codes, Dissolving Identities: The Hindi Social Film of the 1950s as Popular Culture" (1999); and M. Madhava Prasad, *Ideology of the Hindi Film: A Historical Construction* (1998).

9. See chapter 6 of Bharatmuni, *Natyasastra* (Vol. 1, 1961); Priyadarshi Patnaik, *Rasa in Aesthetics* (1999); G. N. Devy's Introductory Note to Avinavagupta's "On *Santarasa*: Aesthetic Equipoise" (2002): 61; Edwin Gerow, "*Rasa* as a Category of Literary Criticism" (1981); Susan Schwarz, *Rasa: Performing the Divine in India* (2004); and Eliot Deutsch, "Reflections on Some Aspects of the Theory of Rasa," in *Sanskrit Drama in Performance* (1981). The

Natyasastra lists and elaborates eight fundamental *rasas: śringāra* (love), *hāsya* (comic), *karuna* (pathos), *raudra* (anger), *vīra* (heroic), *bhayānaka* (fear), *bībhatsa* (disgust), and *adbhuta* (surprise). Each *rasa* corresponds to eight fundamental *sthāyi-bhāvas: rati, hāsa, śoka, krodha, ursāha, bhāya, jugusā,* and *vimaya*. In later years, possibly during the fifth century, *śānti rasa* (peace) was added to the list of *rasas*.

10. See Moinak Biswas, *Historical Realism: Modes of Modernity in Indian Cinema* (1996): 171–87.

11. Ravi Vasudevan has commented on the absence of a detective function in *Awara* (*Vagabond*) (Raj Kapoor, 1951) and *Baazi* (*A Game of Chance*) (Guru Dutt, 1951), despite the latter adopting many of the chiaroscuro lighting effects of the American *film noir*. See "The Melodramatic Mode and the Commercial Hindi Cinema" (1989): 39. Guilt is deduced through intuitive functions and broad indices, such as dress, facial typologies, and habits. These narratives harbor no enigma in the Barthian sense. This, however, does not mean that there were no films constituting a "mystery" genre. Films involving mysteries or different, uncanny incidents were plentiful, but the dénouements usually involved a series of chance coincidences rather than logical deductions by an individual protagonist. Often, as in Raj Khosla's *Woh Kaun Thi (Who Was She?)* (1964), the apparent ghostly apparition is revealed to be a fake at the end of the film, without completely tying up all uncanny ends within a framework of reason. It is thus not clear why this human entity, if she was not a ghost after all, could make the windshield wipers of a car stop in a key scene early on in the film merely by her presence.

12. *Maya* or illusion sometimes becomes a veil to go beyond, sometimes a darkness to be penetrated, and sometimes "etymologically that which is not there tomorrow" (Sharma, *The Hindu Gita* [1986]: xiii).

13. Exceptions include the works of Sumita S. Chakravarty (1993) and Vijay Mishra (2002). Noting that cinema has only been "partially integrated into notions of an Indian visual aesthetic" (*National Identity in Popular Indian Cinema*, 29), Chakravarty outlines a complex realist tendency that not only oscillates between an Aristotelian mimesis and a Lukácsian elevation of consciousness, but is also pregnant with what she (following Ananda Coomaraswamy) calls a "Hindu worldview." In this metaphysical dispensation, the phenomenal universe becomes "the reflection of reality in the mirror of illusion" (82). It is because of this myriad assembling of expressive powers and ontologies that a turn of the republic realist *auteur* like Bimal Roy can append a global apparatus of realist representation (including its socialist and classical principles) to the Vedic metaphysical postulate of *atmanam bidhdhi* and to *Rasa* aesthetics. Vijay Mishra has situated *Rasa* as a spectrum of affects between the dual afflictions of Goethe's Werther: *Weltschmerz* (unease with the world) and *Ichschmerz* (unease with the self). In his understanding, *Rasa* emerges as that body of expressive powers that is commanded by neither a home-in-the-world nor a self (*Bollywood Cinema*, 25).

14. The colonial assault on indigenous visual perspectives started early. Christopher Pinney (2003) points out that during the 1850s art schools in Madras, Calcutta, and Bombay were brought under the direct control of the Department of Public Instruction. The governing idea was to wed public taste to scientific attitudes. From the administration's point of view, fostering an ability to "draw objects correctly" meant an analytic reorientation that would finally collapse the "Hindu dream-world." Naturalism was thus a powerful aesthetic call to "deny the magical origin of images." See Christopher Pinney, "A Secret of Their Own Country" (2003): 115.

15. See also Kajri Jain, "Figures of Locality and Tradition: Commercial Cinema and the Networks of Visual Print Capitalism in Maharashtra" (2005); and Gayatri Chatterjee "Icons and Events: Reinventing Visual Construction in Cinema in India" (2005) for a more extensive discussion on the various visual impulses that combined in popular cinema.

16. Ashish Rajadhyaksha, "Epic Melodrama: Themes of Nationality in Indian Cinema" (1994): 64, and the entry on Aga Hashar Kashmiri in *Encyclopedia of Indian Cinema*, 123.

17. Ravi Vasudevan, "Shifting Codes, Dissolving Identities: The Hindi Social Film of the 1950s as Popular Culture" (1999).

18. Lalitha Gopalan, *Cinema of Interruptions* (2002).

19. Valentina Vitali (*Hindi Action Cinema* [2008]: 216–17), in an insightful close reading of the scene in which the young Vijay witnesses his parents being murdered, has commented on the inconsistent points of view. From his vantage point in the overall spatial organization of the setting, Vijay could not have seen the culprit or his hand.

20. See Erich Auerbach, *Mimesis* (1957): chapter 1. When Odysseus returns in disguise from his adventures in Homer's epic, his old nurse, while bathing him, recognizes the scar the hero had acquired in childhood during a boar hunting expedition. In his magnificent reading of this moment of recall, Auerbach points out that Homer's epic enunciation does not harbor any suspense in terms of revealing a "background." Narration in *The Odyssey* is peripatetic; the moment of recall, the "flashback" as it were, is an immanent present in the architecture of time. There is no "background" or hidden past to be subjectively discovered after an interval of suspense.

21. These are not unique to popular Hindi narratives; they occur frequently in spaghetti westerns and Hong Kong martial arts films of the 1960s and 1970s.

22. See Gilles Deleuze and Felix Guattari, *A Thousand Plateaus: Capitalism and Schizophrenia* (1987). Also Gilles Deleuze, *Foucault* (1997).

23. In appending the Deleuzian assemblage to his sociological method in *Bollywood: Sociology Goes to the Movies* (2006), Rajinder Dudrah points out that in a theory of assemblages, "desire is considered as part of the formation of an effect, a sensation that is part of and articulated between actual and metaphoric bodies" (43).

24. See Gilles Deleuze, *Cinema 1* (1986): 12–28.

25. It is, however, important to partially distinguish the Hindi cinematic assemblage in movement from the typologies (movement image, time image) that Deleuze proposed in his seminal study of largely the classical narrative cinema of the West and the European avant-garde. This is because the formal attributes of Hindi film were never as hardened as those of realistic continuity film, and departures from cause–effect narration—a flowing "sensory-motor schemata" of phenomenological representation—do not automatically produce the time image as an avant-garde interruption of a dominant tempo of sign arrangement. It would be a gross formalist reduction of Deleuze's philosophy of cinema if one were to use it as a tool box to say, for instance, that the song sequences in *Darr* are exemplary forms of the time image, or the discontinuities in the cinema of Manmohan Desai, in their collisions with high modernist sensibilities, achieve the same aesthetic result as that of Jean-Luc Godard. It must be remembered that there is an important historical dimension implicit in Deleuze's work: he discerns a break in the Western sensory-motor schema (that which rests in the faith in the integrated human subject) after World War II, with the advent of the street-fighting 1960s, the Cold War, decolonization, and the crisis of the official Left.

26. Although I have severe problems with the book as a whole, I agree with the drift of Hardt and Negri's argument about a post-civil society racism. See *Empire* (2001): 3–21; and Michael Hardt, "The Global Society of Control" (1998). Etienne Balibar's observations in "Is There a New Racism?" *Race, Nation, and Class: Ambiguous Identities* (1991): 17–28 are also telling. For a more nuanced perspective on a global expansion of governmental violence directed toward "disposable" populations beyond the representational pieties of liberal civil society, see Ronald Judy, "Provisionary Note on Formations of Planetary Violence" (2006).

27. See Willemen and Rajadhyaksha's discussion of Desai's *Amar Akbar Anthony* (1977) in *Encyclopedia of Indian Cinema*, 430.

28. The category epic is used here to designate a modernist ideogram which, in the case of Indic cultures, involved, to a certain extent, the ordering of the multiple literary and oral traditions of the Ramayana (a *kavya*) or Mahabharata (an *itihasa*) into an unstable, but tendentially monolithic body of "epic" referents for a national culture.

29. The realist art-house director Shyam Benegal parodied this trope in *Mandi* (*Market*) (1983). In this film, the brother and sister (a prostitute) elope, but she suddenly loses interest in consummating the relationship.

30. See Madhava Prasad, *Ideology of the Hindi Film* (1998): 30–1.

31. We do see postulated resolutions in other popular cinemas of the world, for instance in the climax of Steven Spielberg's *Indiana Jones and the Last Crusade* (1989).

32. In this context one can mention the numerous films on the snake-man transmogrification myth. See, for instance, Manjunath Pendakur, *Indian Popular Cinema* (2003).

33. Apart from a horizontal dispersal of energies of war and peace in the form of identical twins, the star double role assemblage can also be deployed in a vertical axiomatic of the generational conflict (as a particular instance of the so-called traditional-modern dialectic). Perfect examples of this feature would be the father and son duos played by Amitabh Bachchan in *Adalat* (*Court*) (Dilip Deka, 1976), *Mahaan* (*Great*) (S. Ramanathan, 1983) and *Aakhri Raasta* (*The Last Road*) (K. Bhagyaraj, 1985).

34. Alcohol is once again an affective function in Abrar Alvi's *Sahib Bibi Aur Ghulam* (*The King, Queen, and the Knave*) (1962). In this film the youngest daughter-in-law of the aristocratic Chaudhury family drinks to emerge as a memorable cinematic instance of tragic melodrama. It is alcohol that allows the ideal wife to keep her philandering husband at home when she allows herself to be recast through intoxication—as a physical automaton that approximates the seductive figure of the courtesan.

35. Similar passages can be achieved in myriad ways. In Manmohan Desai's *Aa Gale Lag Jaa* (*Come Embrace Me*) (1973), it is an assemblage between ice-water, the body of the woman, the voluntarism of the hero, and medical science that creates an "emergency" ground for premarital sex. The hero is forced to bring his body into intimate contact with the woman's in order to transmit heat and save her life after she falls into a freezing lake.

36. The feudal order of representation is confined to surfaces. Here one can recall the beautiful Kantian metaphor which Lukács echoes in the beginning of *The Theory of the Novel* to depict this: "Happy are those ages when the starry sky is the map of all possible paths" (29). We can think of another object in the assemblage to illustrate this. Ravi Vasudevan, in a brilliant reading of a moment in Mehboob Khan's *Andaaz* (*Style*), talks about the function of a mirror. In the film, a "friendship" develops between a rich modern girl (Nina) and her estate manager (Dilip). At one point, Nina sees Dilip's image instead of her own on a mirror. He declares his love for her. Dilip at this point does not know that Nina is already engaged to Raj, who lives abroad. The first part of the film, hitherto, had been confined to Dilip's point of view, thus effectively allowing the woman to harbor what, from a modern perspective, would be repressed desire for another man. The mirror in the assemblage here thus disallows a subjective culpability of having indulged in the forbidden by bringing matters to the surface and displacing Nina's own voice or intuition. See Ravi Vasudevan, "The Melodramatic Mode and the Commercial Hindi Cinema" (1989): 42.

37. Indeed, alcohol in cinema has consistently been policed by the Gandhian elite as vice in an overall realm of vice that is cinema itself. Aruna Vasudev (1978) points out that the Bombay Censor Board decided to implement prohibition in films on April 1, 1947 (*Liberty and Licence*, 78–9). In 1976, during the Emergency, drink was again the issue: "no scenes of drinking or drunkenness or of display of bottles containing alcoholic drinks are to be permitted in films" (160).

38. In Anil Devgun's *Raju Chacha* (*Uncle Raju*) (2000), it is Viagra that performs the function of alcohol.
39. This scene is inspired by the famous Groucho and Harpo Marx mirror scene in *Duck Soup*.
40. See Vivek Dhareshwar and Tejaswini Niranjana, "*Kaadalan* and the Politics of Resignification" (1999).
41. In 1990, following the suggestions of a Commission instituted in 1979 and headed by the parliamentarian B. P. Mandal, the Indian government decided to increase the quota of jobs for "backward castes" in the public sector. The urban upper caste and middle classes reacted violently; protests were held throughout the country, especially in the north. Several students publicly immolated themselves.
42. See chapter 7 ("Women and the Nation") of Partha Chatterjee's *The Nation and its Fragments*; the essays in Kumkum Sangari and Sudesh Vaid, eds., *Recasting Women: Essays in Colonial History* (1989); Indira Chowdhury-Sengupta, "Mother India and Mother Victoria: Motherland and Nationalism in Nineteenth Century Bengal" (1992); and Jyotika Virdi, *The Cinematic ImagiNation: Indian Popular Films as Social History* (2003): chapter 2. For an account of how the nationalist icon of the mother accumulated cultural power after the publication of Bankim Chandra Chattopadhyay's novel *Anandamath* (1882), see Jasodhara Bagchi, "Representing Nationalism: Ideology of Motherhood in Colonial Bengal" (1990); and Tanika Sarkar, *Hindu Wife, Hindu Nation* (2001). In her insightful essay "Visualizing India's Geo-body: Globes, Maps, Bodyscapes" (2003), Sumathi Ramaswamy demonstrates how an assembled perspective—one that combines a voluptuous mythic projection of the nation as mother with the empty cartographic frame of the map—marked a popular visualization of India-in-the-world in early twentieth-century calendar art.
43. See, for example, Asha Kasbekar, "Hidden Pleasures: Negotiating the Myth of the Female Ideal in Popular Indian Cinema" (2000).
44. See Moinak Biswas, *Mother India O' Roja: Jatir Dui Akhyan* (1996).
45. Prasad's film was screened after the Hindu Marriage Act (the Sharda Act) banning Hindu polygamy was adopted in 1955, as part of the Hindu Code Bill (which included denominations such Buddhism, Jainism, and Sikhism within the legal parameters of "Hindu"). It was followed by the Hindu Adoption and Maintenance Act of 1956. The Hindu Succession Act of 1956 accorded women greater property rights. Feminist scholars have rightly pointed out that it is gratuitous to claim that Hindu personal law was "reformed" during the 1990s; it was merely codified.
46. See Partha Chatterjee, *Nationalist Thought and the Colonial World: A Derivative Discourse* (1986): 48–50.
47. See Ranajit Guha, "Dominance without Hegemony and Its Historiography" (1989).

CHAPTER 2

The Geo-televisual and Hindi Film in the Age of Information

Introduction

Assemblages in A-grade popular Indian films became irresistibly geo-televisual from the beginning of the 1990s. The nation's overall media space gradually began to open up to a global dispensation of electronic satellite exchanges after the beginning of liberalization in 1991. Life-worlds of a relatively protected, apparently endogamous domain of national culture were inundated with new vistas, spaces, goods, bodies, forms of pleasure, and style. Filmic templates in the Bombay and regional industries had to morph and adjust to this new ecology. They had to withstand, through complex measures of absorption and recoil, a plethora of sensuous pressures from a worldly outside. As briefly stated in the previous chapter, the geo-televisual, in a simple, even idealist initial sense, means the projection and reception of words and images over great distances. It has nothing *essentially* to do with television, although television, like many other technologies and practices, is a part of it.[1] In its pure idealist incarnation, the geo-televisual might intersect with or gravitate toward avenues of thinking devoted to cosmopolitanism, multiculturalism, and other universally aspiring pieties of a now rather tormented, but not quite buried humanism. It is, however, not my aim to keep this conceptual postulate in its pristine form. Rather, I shall try to elaborate on why geo-televisual exchanges come with uneven kinetic distributions and why these processes coincide with a planetary regime of power and governance. It will also be my objective to find out why this dispensation, in an epoch marked by an overall production of social life, becomes indistinguishable from (and not a reflection of) the flows of capital. The geo-televisual thus becomes informatic, where the latter is to be understood not as a simple, quantitative state of bolstering *qua* technology and speed, but as a direct expression of a global regime of value.

It is often noted that compared to an earlier epoch of the "all-India film" (a portmanteau genre to "narrate the nation"),[2] big-budget "Bollywood" of the 1990s and later "virtualized" India. That is, it increasingly catered to the escapist tendencies of metropolitan audiences at home and abroad, presenting a sanitized, "unreal" milieu devoid of dirt, poverty, hunger, and other unwashed and unhappy aspects of history. A-grade productions became unashamedly urban, often in an absolute sense. The image of the countryside was reassembled through modes of tourism (the idyllic Punjabi mustard fields of Aditya Chopra's *Dilwale Dulhaniya Le Jayenge* [*The Brave Heart Will Take the Bride*], 1995) or by recastings of quotidian ethnic figures by way of city fashion (the dancing rural fruit-sellers on the roof of a moving train in Mani Ratnam's *Dil Se* [*From the Heart*], 1998). Sometimes this cinematic rewriting of what used to be the agrarian heart of India took over the entire visual space. In Rajeev Kapoor's *Prem Granth* (*The Book of Love*) (1995) the milieu is an assemblage of bewitching vistas of the lush South African landscape, studio space, designer attires, and designer lifeware. Predominantly, however, the village itself vanished from the high-end screen, as did migrant, deracinated figures from a national backwater at large. Ranjini Mazumdar has provided us with a penetrating analysis of this stylization in relation to the popular filmic figure of the *tapori* in Hindi cinema.[3] What is remarkable, however, is the fact that while the *tapori* prospered, his abode in the city began to disappear, except in the largely minoritarian gangster film. It was during the 1990s that the *bustee* (shanty-town) film gradually lapsed into obsolescence or was relegated to B- or C-grade industries. The screen was overwhelmingly taken over by a decorative milieu that assembled, often without obligation, varied aspects of a new urban consumerism, lifestyle choices, novelties, boundless imaginations of space and time. It is this fungible cinematic style of the geo-televisual that I intend to theorize as *informatic*.

We have earmarked a period between 1991 and 2004 for our inquiries into a theme of the geo-televisual as informatic in Hindi cinema. But what is unique about this period? How was it different from earlier phases, and what exactly changed after that? This early proposition, that the 1990s inaugurated a transformative scenario, however, does not seek to posit an origin. By marking this period as a point of reckoning, I am only identifying a moment in which a relational concept of the geo-televisual dazzles itself into existence as Benjamin would say, when it enters, with undeniable corrosive power, an historical field of ideas. However, in doing so, it instantly claims an anterior past for itself, even as it points to a new *agon* of the gestating future. That is, one can say that while matters were always televisual, from the 1990s onwards it becomes so in a breathlessly informatic manner. Compared to earlier epochs, the powers and qualities of the geo-televisual assumed an airy, boundless, and robust form that uprooted them from a previously moderated system of movements between the home and the world at large. The zippy geo-televisual mores of the 1990s assumed an autonomous mode of functioning, increasingly independent of stories of an arrested Indian modernity, or a former Nehruvian arc of national destinying. It therefore blasted the given continuums of narrating and becoming and made signs available in an anchorless, mobile form. These particularized clusters of signs, wonders, and affect became available to a different ontology. I am suggesting that this new ontology draws its randomly associative powers from an overall environment I will theorize towards the end of this chapter as one of an "informatic" or "advertised" modernization. That is a form of pure techno-financial modernization (ecology of affect, regime of spectacle) that owes no allegiance to the multi-pronged, dialectical stories of an Indian modernity devoutly desired. In the visible realm of political publicity, this ecology sublimated into many expressive forms: the valorization of a new technologically embellished, consumerist urbanism; spectacular achievements in avenues of nuclear militarization, space technology, or software; and the paramount image of an "India shining" spectacularly conjured up by the Bharatiya Janata Party (BJP) as the central motif of its unsuccessful 2004 general election campaign. In this and the next chapters I intend to theorize a stratum of the cinematic/informatic—a baseline of spectacle and affect, rhythm, and resonance—that is an essential part of this ecology. The purpose, however, will be not be to investigate cases of crude *Hindutva*[4] ideology negotiating with capital and media, but to understand a form of urbanization—both in its consolidated forms and desirous, often breathtakingly utopian projections—that sets up Hinduness as a normative state of life itself, that is, a picture of life that draws its powers more from horizontal flows than axiomatic narratives and sublimates a form that is deemed worth living.

I propose 2004 as a cut-off date because that is roughly when the Multiplex revolution in India came into its own. The scenario that it inaugurated after that has undergone many complex transformations that remain outside the ambit of this project. I shall propose some caveats in this direction in the short Conclusion to this book. Here I am earmarking the period between 1991 and 2004 as a relational and not a positive measure of time. It was then that the cinematic publicity of informatic modernization took a delirious shape. A new technologically equipped and globally aspiring metropolitan Indian elite sought to present its life and ceremonies themselves as artwork, complete with principled decorative interiorities of neo-traditionalism and brave overtures toward manifold desires and goods available in the world at large. What was seen during this period was a new form of hegemonic power that did not necessarily work in a top-down manner. Instead, it set up novel ways to pass off technology as myth and create fresh informatic circuits of transfer between what can be provisionally called a Hindu folklore and an urban "globalizing" common sense.[5] That is, unlike a previous unease between techno-financial worlds and what was considered to be an abiding agrarian spirit of "India" there came into being a new dispensation in which many attributes of technology, "removed from their content and more or less distorted, constantly fall within the popular domain and are 'inserted' into the mosaic of tradition."[6] I shall elaborate this field of inquiry in this chapter, first by providing a brief historical account of transformations in the media and film industries. After that I will trace a critical genealogy of the geo-televisual in relation to Hindi film, selecting two transformative periods for detailed examination: first, a nationalist monitoring of the geo-televisual in relation to an "Indian culture" (1947–88), and second, the age of globalization and new media (1991–2004), which is, of course, our primary object of study.

The Indian Situation after 1991

Although the Indian government took its first significant IMF loan in 1981 and liberalization of the economy was well under way during the premiership of Rajiv Gandhi (1984–9), 1991 is usually flagged as the watershed year in which India entered the globalizing process. This was when Manmohan Singh, then Finance Minister of the Congress government, passed his legendary annual budget, beginning to curb the powers of what is often called a protectionist Nehruvian "license permit" bureaucracy, removing obstacles for foreign direct investment (FDI), and initiating a culture of privatizing public sector undertakings.[7] The same year the Indian government took its second significant IMF loan to meet the demands of an escalating foreign debt and a threatening national deficit. The reform process inaugurated an era of steadily increasing financial and political exchanges between the Indian state and the World Bank, along with other Bretton Woods organizations. This new dispensation effectively dismantled the Janata Party government's 1978 Foreign Exchange Regulation Act and the prescriptions of the Monopolies and Restrictive Trade Practices Commission which had effectively led to the termination of trade licenses for Coca Cola, IBM, and other multinationals. These corporations returned and others, like Pepsi, started operating in the Indian market for the first time. Throughout the 1990s and after, there was a series of measures ostensibly adopted to reduce the fiscal deficit: disinvestment of state-owned enterprises, encouragement of FDI by the state, and permitting the entry of private players into core infrastructural sectors (power, telecommunications, mining, roads). The consumer goods sector in Indian markets started to grow exponentially. The rupee began its long journey toward becoming fully convertible on the international money markets.[8]

It was in this environment that cable television emerged from its obscure, illegal beginnings during the late 1980s to define India's media ecology from the mid-1990s onwards. The medium stopped being a monopolized instrument for a developmentalist pedagogy of the state, which is how it was largely envisioned in the Indian context for three decades, since its experimental beginnings in 1959. The paradigm shifted to what Rajadhyaksha and Willemen call a postmodern code of "info-tainment," involving big corporate media, international advertising, the fashion and travel industries, consumer products, and brand culture.[9] Multinational operatives like CNN, MTV, and Star, and Indian firms like Eenadu, Sun TV, and Zee, began to challenge the dominance of the state-owned Doordarshan[10] with the latter's market share steadily falling from an absolute monopoly in the late 1980s to 19.58 percent by the end of 2005. Television ownership in India grew from 34.9 million in 1992 to 108 million in 2005, while the number of cabled homes shot up from 1.2 million to 60.82 million in the same timespan, making India one of the largest cable-connected nations in the world, along with the US (about 70 million) and China (110 million).[11] Meanwhile, in 1997, India signed the Information Technology Agreement (ITA) of the World Trade Organization, paving the way for a phased reduction in import tariffs on IT products. By the end of 2005, India's media business was worth about US$9 billion, still a small fraction of the global outlay of approximately US$1,375 billion, but well placed to grow at a breathtaking rate, with the major areas of expansion being digital theaters, multiplexes, broad-band, satellites for DTH (direct-to-home), and set-top boxes for pay TV. The animation industry alone was estimated at $550 million by Arthur Anderson in 2002, and forecast to grow to $15 billion by 2008.[12]

The globalization of the media space was not a seamless process marked by carnivalesque and libertine appropriations of alien wonders. Nor was it simply a belated settling of the long-standing recommendations of the B. G. Verghese Report of 1977 which, in the aftermath of the notorious suspension of rights and freedoms during the Emergency, had advo-cated a decrease of governmental control over broadcasting media. The protectionist impulses of the state, as well as conservative culturalist backlashes of different kinds, continued to assert themselves periodically. The government tried to retain control through occasional legislation like a Bill to regulate cable TV in 1993, and an ordinance passed to the same effect in 1994. In 1999, Pramod Mahajan, then Minister of Information and Broadcasting, proposed a comprehensive Broadcasting Bill to regulate the activities of private TV channels. Sushma Swaraj, Information and Broadcasting Minister in the short-lived Vajpayee administration of 1998, expressed dislike for sleeveless blouses and alcohol advertising and imposed a blanket ban on condom advertising for the thirteen days that the government was in office.[13] The erosion of state control over electronic media took place in fits and starts, following an overall gradualist scheme, prompted by a landmark Supreme Court judgment in relation to the telecast rights to the Hero Cup International Cricket Tournament in 1995, by which the Indian airwaves were declared public property.[14]

Even outside the works of the state, in the era that witnessed the grotesquely spectacular rise of militant urban *Hindutva,* there were strong expressions of hostility and anxiety against the new dispensation of often irreverent energies, commodities, ideas, and images. On July 6, 1998 a New Delhi magistrate issued an arrest warrant against Rupert Murdoch (whose News Corporation, by July 1995, had acquired the Hong Kong-based company) for failing to appear as a defendant in a public interest litigation against Star TV for showing obscene movies.[15] The Hindu right-wing groups protested vehemently against the lesbian love story in Deepa Mehta's 1997 film *Fire.*[16] In 1998 there was much hullaballoo when the Spice Girls were due to perform at the temples of Khajuraho which are adorned with erotic sculptures. The Karnataka Farmers' Association (Karnataka Rajya Raita Sangha) attacked a Kentucky Fried Chicken outlet in Bangalore in September 1995. The Mahila Jagaran Samity threatened acts of self-immolation to protest the Miss World Pageant held in Bangalore in 1996; several other women's groups, across a wide ideological spectrum encompassing the Right and Left, also actively canvassed against the commercial exploitation of women, as did the right-wing students' association Akhil Bharatiya Vidyarthi Parishad (ABVP).

The Question of the Subject

It is not my objective to give a detailed historical picture of this many armed and complex process which spanned over a decade and a half. The overall transformative field included dynamics of not just culturalist absorption of incoming global pressures, but also instant reinventions and reifications of national and regional selves in relation to the world at large. The distributions of these energies, both in line with and antagonistic to an overall financialization of the economic and cultural spheres (to the point where it becomes redundant to discriminate between the two), can be mapped in conventional ideological grids only to a limited extent. That is, it is my contention that movements for and against globalization in relation to the nation cannot be sufficiently analyzed in terms of enunciating selves (entities that simply tell a story of the self and contest head on other stories) that have marked the grand ideological battles of modernity. Such aspirations for self–other metanarratives undeniably exist. But they often follow a typically "modern" discursive format diagnosed by Bruno Latour.[17] In these instances the *agon* of shoring up "tradition" as a picture of the national/eternal lies in an absolute modernist separation between what Latour identifies as zones of naturalization, socialization, and deconstruction. All three can have their epistemological privileges provided they remain sealed off from each other (*We Have Never Been Modern* [1993]: 5). The incessant unrest with modernity would thus pertain to the fact that such total divisions are never quite possible. Tradition is incessantly naturalized through sovereign pronouncements, emphatically socialized through projects of memory, but also always behind one's back as it were, irresistibly contaminated and deconstructed by the circulation of images and bodies as capital. One can never quite become modern or, for that matter, traditional, precisely because of the osmosis between contending spaces, structures (East/West, private/public, state/religion, national/global), and their sign systems. The discursive test in claiming the erotic figures of Khajuraho within a singular imaginary horizon of tradition (from which the Spice Girls were naturally to be excluded), therefore, involved a separation of spirit from flesh and stone, the extraction of a pure allegory of form-as-transcendence from the otherwise profane voluptuousness of the gendered female body. The problem, however, is that in the ecology of irreverent media contagions, such vertical acts of monitoring become increasingly anachronistic.

Secondly, what is of crucial importance here is that the cinematic-informatic interface brings infectious energies over and beyond the parameters of any marked national subjectivity or state-of-the-public. I am, therefore, suggesting a study method beyond a conventional ethnography that surveys and extracts subjective confessions as "truths" and then enumerates them in tabular, either/or reckonings. The latter, while providing us with useful pointers, also tends to abridge a world of variable affects and desires—conscious or otherwise, stated or unstated—that occupy a volatile space in between subjective standpoints and anthropological profiles. The individual can indeed have a principled stance against Cola culture; that, however, does not mean that s/he is not affected, in myriad ways, by an overall capitalist dispensation of value and production of social life itself that privileges such a culture. The point, therefore, will be to investigate precisely those crucial assembling points where a moral Brahminical-Victorian abomination of alien pleasures can no longer be separated from secret fascinations towards them. In this sense, subjectivities capable of moral or ethical assertions are ephemeral "positionalities" that do not emerge from the depths of a transhistorical human/Indian psyche, but are formations of power in an historical field of problems. I am, therefore, for the moment, tying the question of the subject in the kinetic information ecology with a formulation by Michel Foucault, one that he draws from Maurice Blanchot, in which the different positions of the speaking subject are located within a "deep anonymous murmur" that characterizes an epoch.[18] And yet the theory cannot travel as easily. The disenchanting "anonymity" of the murmur perhaps presumes, to a great degree, that the epoch is already marked by a modern killing of God. Murmur is possible only when there is no monotheistic donation of meaning and the singular Almighty has been replaced by an infinity of subjections. There is thus a crucial question of ontology here that needs to be attended to, not to dispel Foucault's idea of power, but to contextualize it properly and prevent its ironical transformation into a negative theology. Apropos the Indian situation, the question of God in itself is further complicated by a question of a possible Hindu monotheism, as a necessary ground for the historical emergence of a proper axiomatic Hindu nationalism.[19] We shall investigate this further in the following chapters. For the moment, let us locate the clamor of subjection in the ecology of information, between the neutral, globally expansive hum of technology and the receding whispers of inclement gods.

The Hindi Film Industry after 1991

As briefly noted at the beginning, the Indian film industry underwent significant changes in the new order. The demise of the all-India film was prompted by the gradual rise of a newly empowered urban technocratic middle class at home and the significant extension of Hindi film markets overseas. The industry thus segmented its output into elite productions addressing domestic and overseas metropolitan audiences, the latter group including not just the forty million or so Indian diasporic populations in more than sixty countries, but also multicultural viewers fascinated by "Bollywood." Indian films, for quite some time, have had foreign markets in parts of Africa, Mauritius, Malaysia, Fiji, Trinidad, Singapore, parts of the Middle East, and South East Asia. However, the scale and rate of growth of overseas markets roughly from the mid-1990s was formidable. In 1982, the Indian film industry as a whole earned about 14.6 million rupees from overseas. By 1998 this figure had risen to 4 billion rupees; and by 2003 was expected to be approaching 7 billion.[20] The crucial difference was the entry of "Bollywood" into first world sectors like the US, Canada, UK, Germany, and Australia.[21]

The segmentation of the industry took place on several fronts. In terms of scales of production, big-budget films gradually acquired a metropolitan idiom affiliated to consumer culture, international travel, the fashion industry, and upscale advertising. Erstwhile major genres of the all-India film, like the dacoit saga and the rural melodrama, were relegated to B- and C-grade productions or regional cinemas. Some previously minoritarian genres, like the sci-fi film, the superhero fantasy, the *film noir*, and the sex comedy, were either upgraded or imported, while the historical, languishing in a state of obsolescence for decades, was revived. The new millennium, toward the middle of the first decade, also witnessed the gradual rise of a mid-budget "multiplex cinema," often totally or largely in English.[22] This division of cinematic worlds was thus much in alignment with a non-synchronous political-cultural space caught between indigenous silicon valleys and farmer suicides; between a third world past and the future of a techno-financial global power. However, the entire spectrum of the cinematic world had to contend with the inundations of the geo-televisual by devising different appropriative and cannibalizing styles and moral economies.

The general atmosphere of liberalization also accorded, for the first time since Independence, a legitimate industry status to commercial filmmaking. The initial declaration to that effect came in 1998, but it was only in 2000 that the business of cinema was notified under the Industrial Development Bank of India (IDBI) Act of 1964. Around the same time there was a Federation of Indian Chambers of Commerce and Industry (FICCI) conference on the entertainment business. By 2000 several media companies (Pritish Nandy Communications, Mukta Arts, and Adlabs) were raising money on the stock market. In the same year Shringar Cinemas became one of the first enterprises to garner private equity when it sold a significant portion of its shares to GW Capital.[23] The government also allowed total FDI in films, encouraging firms like Columbia Tristar and Paramount to make forays into Indian production. These efforts toward the corporatization of what used to be the largest unorganized industrial sector in the Indian economy have strengthened in recent years. The transformations in production were accompanied by major shifts in the distribution-exhibition sectors, instigated by the Multiplex revolution (aided by the government's tax relief policy) and the spread of digital screens. By 2004 multiplexes accounted for only 0.6 percent of

Indian screens, but brought in 30 percent of the domestic take of the year's premium releases.[24]

In the ecology of globalization and new media, the "Bollywood" phenomenon in itself was consolidated as an assemblage of dispersing and circulating commoditized affects. That is, cinema in its classically integrated form contributed about 35 percent of the total revenues generated by an average top-line production in the form of domestic box office.[25] The film otherwise immersed itself, as a whole or in disaggregated parts, into a plethora of media–capital circuits: music and satellite industries, software for film-based television channels like Channel V, MTV, or Zee Music, online portals, mobile phone ring tones, product placements, brand tie-ins, and FM radio. Multi-pronged publicity blitzes and saturated releases in tune with the blockbuster format, or the filmic phenomenon itself as a media event, are of course not unique to Indian cinema. However, I shall later argue that the contrapuntal assemblages between cinematic narration and awry flows of information at large assume special features in the Indian situation of the 1990s and after. For now, let me begin with a proper theorization of what I have been calling the geo-televisual.

The Concept of the Geo-televisual

One can begin this elaboration by recalling the anxious overture with which Hannah Arendt begins her monumental book *The Human Condition* (1958). For Arendt, the 1957 launch of the Russian space satellite Sputnik was a momentous event in the history of mankind, for it was said to have marked the first step in eventually freeing man from his earthbound state. What was important, however, apart from the futural promises of excursions into other worlds, was the coming into being of a cosmic perspective that humans could henceforth command; that is, the very ability to see and enframe the earth in all its planetary roundness, from a panoptic vantage point. For Arendt this was the culmination of a modern secularizing process that began with a turn away from God the Father and ended with "an even more fateful repudiation of an Earth who was the Mother of all living creatures under the sky" (*Human Condition*, 2). What she discerned was a final, wistful split between the horizon of human expectations and the ground for natality of being. Human artifice had transcended the very earth that used to be "the quintessence of the human condition." For Arendt, the cosmic vision of the world from outer space was an event that created for man a new existentialist bond with the skies. It was no longer a vertical one of aspired transcendence—neither of waiting for the gods nor of killing them. It was at this point that what I am calling the geo-televisual had attained a special dimension of reckoning.

The geo-televisual, as stated above, has nothing essentially to do with television, although TV technology, like many similar ones, is a part of its phenomenal procedures. In a primary sense, it pertains to the exchange of sights and sounds[26] across global distances that human cultures have always undertaken, through nomadism, commerce, kinship, friendship, and warfare. That is, it involves the perpetual incursions of "alien" pictures and hearings that always challenge and transform resident notions of the self, along with dialectical reckonings of the home in relation to the world. The geo-televisual, therefore, precipitates transformed imaginings of space and time. The first (along with the second) alters the map itself when the world shrinks and the home expands. The second (along with the first) renders any internal time of the home as diseased by planetary flows of multiple tenses—the here, the now, the "has been," and the already. That is, the home/nation/locale finds itself in a relational position in the uneven landscape of historical time, according to contested indices of backwardness or progress. These "tenses of adjacency" disturb entrenched customs, flout dynastic orderings, explode or wear out given frameworks of culture, and compel multiplicities into being. The invention of the telescope, for instance, was one of the signal events that created the human as a postulate of a global modernity; indeed, the European *anthropos* was a sublime creation which emerged from a Pascalian horror at seeing an interstellar space without the face of the Holy Ghost hovering over the margins. The telescope thus was not just an optical instrument that made distant objects appear near at hand; it also began to kill God and surreptitiously lay the foundations of an anthropocentric universe. The disenchanted birth of the modern European self was coincident with the genesis of a novel and secular cosmology, one that could be understood through cognitive functions of a transcendental human subject rather than a patient wait for revelatory occurrences. The geo-televisual, in a *secular* sense, has therefore to do with the primary epistemological tasks of the modern human subject—that of reading his degraded universe as a world-historical whole. In terms of the modern nation-state, it involved a graduated cultural process of monitoring alien visions and distilling one's own images to be projected to the world. From trade seals, to the Codex, the miniature, the coin, or the wondrous sights beheld, reported, and mythologized by the likes of Marco Polo or Ibn Batuta, the imprints of the geo-televisual can come in many shapes and forms. In terms of media archeology, it extended from "the genealogies of telematics (from antiquity's metal speaking-tube to the telephone; from Aeneas's water telegraph to the Integrated Service Data Network [ISDN]), or cinema archeology (from the cave paintings of Lascaux to the immersive IMAX), or the history of computers (from Wilhelm Schickard's mechanical calculating apparatus to the Universal Turing machine.)"[27] The history of the geo-televisual has to be understood in deep time and not in terms of any linear, inexorable progress. In the realm of modern culture under the nation-state, the consideration of the geo-televisual becomes crucial in defining a people-in-the-world by exercising sovereign control over a sea of potentially anarchic cross-border flows. For India, a typically Arendtian moment came when its first astronaut, Wing Commander Rakesh Sharma, cited a memorable line from the famous Urdu poet Mohammad Iqbal from the Soviet space ship *Soyuz T11* on April 2, 1984. He replied "Sare Jahan Se Achcha" ("The best in the world") when asked by the Prime Minister how India looked from those cosmic heights. This particular repetition of the famous line, eighty years after it was written, was special because it was no longer merely an everyday patriotic hyperbole or a mythic self-image of the nation. In being uttered from an otherworldly Archimedean vantage point, it had assembled with other mythic orbits of technologism and development to point to an overall picture of a rising India-in-the-world.

The concept of the geo-televisual assumes a different dimension when we locate its aggravated procedures in our informational world, that is, when such exchanges cross a critical threshold of speed and density and also become micropunctual, increasingly reliant on private capital and endeavors, and on miniaturized instruments, that is, in an increasingly globalized dispensation of what Bernard Stiegler has called the industrial temporalization of consciousness[28] and Miriam Hansen has described as the mass production of the senses.[29] The field of the geo-televisual was always immediately a field of power. However, in the age of information, we have to find different modes of thinking to understand the political dimensions of an altered scenario, in which the geo-televisual has become informatic. In order to do that, one has to cultivate a stance of thought that does not always refer back to the nation-state and the trinity of the subject, unity, and law. This is because the geo-televisual has been rendered boundless to an appreciable degree, beyond direct priestly ministrations of the state. But how did this opening out introduce qualitative rather than merely quantitative changes in Indian cinema? How was this process of cultural liberalization inseparable from a radical shift in the sphere of power and politics? I will approach these questions and the greater theoretical one of information itself gradually. Let us begin by tracing a genealogy of the geo-televisual in post-Independence Bombay cinema.

The Geo-televisual in the Age of the All-India Film
(1947–88)

Introduction: The Past

The Indian cinematic space has been always animated by geo-televisual attractions. By beginning this workable genealogy in 1947, we are leaving out many interesting moments, especially the period from the mid-1920s to the mid-1930s, when the film industry in Bombay was establishing itself. In his particularly illuminating doctoral research on early Indian cinema, Kaushik Bhaumik has shown that during these years, before the establishment of big studios like Filmstan and Bombay Talkies, there was free and sensational commerce between the largely cottage products of Bombay and the cosmopolitan-imperial bazaar at large.[30] The geo-televisual scope of this realm of the spectacular, in which the Bombay film was trying to find a place in the sun, was formidable. From around World War I the market was already featuring silent films from a number of Western countries (the US, UK, France, Italy, Germany, and Russia). It also had a thriving black market for films largely imported from China and Japan through Bombay, including pornographic films exhibited in baby Pathé projectors.[31] The manifold imprints of a world of attractions and lures could perhaps be seen most clearly in the stunt and the city-thriller genres which dominated this period and mediated the passage from the mythological to the social.[32] These genres combined a variegated bazaar aesthetics with bourgeois monumental styles. Many of them were influenced by serials like *Fantomas* and *Judex*, featuring female and male adventurers played by Pearl White, Ruth Roland, Elmo Lincoln, and Eddie Polo.[33] The films were often marked by a borrowed perspective of Victorian Gothic and sensationalism that was perhaps a circuitous way of "seeing the self in cinema," especially in relation to feminine figures that had to be at once embraced as iconic symbols of national being and distanced as lurid attractions.[34] In an era in which cinematic technology in itself was an instance of the geo-televisual, the filmic Bombay was therefore a locus where the home met the world. It was a monstrous, all-consuming repository of bodies, vistas, styles, temptations, markets, and magical gadgets.[35] The kiss was a common feature in Indian cinema until the mid- to late 1930s. There were also the freely associative Islamicate impulses of *Masnani* poetry, the *qissa-dastaan* tradition, and bazaar romances (Bhaumik, "The Emergence of the Bombay Film Industry" [2001], 136), which came from an overall Urdu modernism of *Afsana* literature. It was a vast, eclectic assembling field of memories and associations in which the geo-televisual attractions of Maciste and Tarzan could similarly blend with homely wrestling styles and the myth of *Bajrangbali*. According to Bhaumik, this kinetic field was curbed with the rise of film journalism, especially in Gujarati, Marathi, English, and Bengali, and an overall increase in the nationalist feudal-bourgeois interest in the pedagogic possibilities of the film medium.[36] From the mid-1930s, there would be strident cries by cultural high priests like K. M. Munshi for an overall Sanskritic reform of national culture, backed by activist enterprises, like the one by Rukmini Arundale, to extract a classical Indian dance tradition free of Islamic courtly or courtesanal institutions, and that of V. N. Bhatkande and V. D. Paluskar to invent a classical Indian music by purging *Tawaif* traditions like *Thumri* and *Kajri*. These ministrations, along with the installation of a panoptic monitoring gaze of "Indian culture," which curbed, among other things, public femininity and sexuality, gradually paved the way for an overall consolidation of what Bhaumik calls the cinematic construction of a Hindu ethnoscape.[37] It was thus through a stringent tempering of bazaar energies that the cultural template of the all-India film assumed its proper shape.

Aruna Vasudev (1978) has pointed out that cinema censorship in India became much stricter after Independence. In 1949 the Indian Motion Picture Producers Association (IMPPA) was summoned to meet with the Bombay Board of Censors to discuss a worrying hybridization of film songs. The same year the Madras High Court seriously considered a proposal to ban the portrayal of gods and goddesses on screen as it was felt that it reduced public veneration for them. The issue of film songs corrupting the haloed Indian classical traditions of music was famously taken up by Dr Balakrishna Keskar, Minister for Information and Broadcasting. His assiduous guardianship of national culture resulted in a drastic reduction of Hindi film songs in *Akashvani*, the national public radio in 1952. By then, censorship had been centralized under a national board in 1951, and the Indian Cinematograph Act of 1952 had re-emphasized the necessity to ban films that were not just against national interest, but also against amorphous considerations of public discipline, taste, or morality. This overall atmosphere of acute culturalist monitoring and suspicion was strongly abetted by powerful activists like Lilavati Munshi and by journals like *Film India*.[38] According to Vasudev (1978), the classics of the 1930s probably could not have been made in this particular dispensation: *Devdas* would be deemed controversial for alcoholism and prostitution, *Duniya Na Mane* for depicting suicide, or *Mukti* for adultery. Both *Chandidas* and *Achhut Kanya* dealt with love between a Brahmin and an untouchable and could have been seen as fomenting social unrest.[39] It is not within the scope of this project to historically evaluate the accuracy of Vasudev's assertion. The interface between the proscriptive stances of the state and myriad cinematic formations were undeniably much more complex. However, what we can earmark is a continuing sense of unease about cinema as a massified assemblage of capital, modernity, vice, and desire. It was a medium that was seen as something that could both bolster and strongly derail a grand culturalist project of defining the nation in its true, autonomous form. The errant and proliferating powers of film thus had to be relentlessly circumscribed, checked, and pulled back into a non-aligned, Nehruvian middle ground between the irreverent commerce of the world and a retiring Gandhian asceticism. The powers of the geo-televisual had to merge with this caution-filled, calibrated project of defining India in the world.

The Nation and it Moral Anthropology

Pramod Chakravorty's 1966 film *Love in Tokyo* is perhaps unique in the history of world cinema for having listed a nation – Japan – as a cast member. The film's hero, Ashok, is the scion of a rich north Indian family with obvious feudal trappings. It is with great reluctance that his mother allows him to "cross the dark waters" and go to distant Japan in order to bring back his deceased elder brother's only son. The family had cut all ties with the elder brother because many years earlier he had gone to the Land of the Rising Sun and done the unthinkable: married a Japanese woman. It is the same fear—that her younger son too might be ensnared by a foreigner—that distresses the mother before she eventually gives her permission. Ashok lands in Tokyo and meets his nephew, Chiku, but the youngster shows little interest in going to India. Ashok then tempts him with what he thinks is the lure of the ultimate spectacle: viewing the Taj Mahal. The two are inside a toy and electronics store at this point. Chiku dismisses this offer disdainfully: he has seen the Taj on television. "What is television?" Ashok asks incredulously. Chiku points toward this technological wonder, which can indeed collapse the distance between Tokyo and the Taj, displayed in one corner. Ashok's first encounter with the marvelous device assumes an immediate libidinal register when a beautiful dancing woman appears on screen. Much in line with stock situations in this melodramatic format, Ashok falls in love at first sight. However, a fortuitous incident prevents the realization of his mother's fear. It is an Indian woman, Asha, who is seen dancing and singing. Later in the film, it is Asha, largely disguised as a kimono-wearing Japanese woman, who mediates the exhilarating encounter between Ashok, the new age Indian, and the manifold allures of Japan as an internationalist picture of urbanity and postwar techno-financial progress. The love affair in and with Tokyo is conducted without the risk of miscegenation.

Chakravorty's film, like many others of its type, enframes Japan in a particular grid of spiritual and cognitive reckoning. The naturalized ethnophobia that features here is only a part of a larger stance. It rests on a Hindu nationalist sense of being that is defined by a moral economy of public and domestic femininity. This pristine sense of the self, however, secretly draws from an Orientalist-Indological perspective borrowed from the colonial discourse of the last two centuries. When this point of view is transposed to foreign shores, the imaginary institution of India automatically becomes racially privileged because it is deemed to be the cradle of Aryan civilization. It is this core, originary spirit that is seen to be preserved in Brahminical ascetic pieties and a principled Indian femininity. All the insidious lures and enabling riches of the world, therefore, have to be scrupulously measured, especially in relation to the woman as a talismanic civilizational creation. The fear of miscegenation is thus at once a palpable fear of biological contamination and a metaphysical one. It centers on the possibility of an alien intrusion despoiling an idealized interiority of the feudal upper-caste Hindu family home, one that draws its status of authenticity from a larger arc of homesteading the nation at large. The alien Other (the woman as foreign, racially different, Muslim, or *dalit*) can only be differentially included within the sphere of the ideological and biological reproduction of "India." It can be done only rarely, within the auspices of carefully modulated extensions of patriarchal benevolence.

But why exactly must India, spiritually enriched yet materially impoverished, be automatically privileged over a burgeoning, technologically advanced Japan? What is the commonsensical view of a unique historical legacy that distinguishes the genius of India from all others? One can turn to a moment in Sibaji Bandyopadhyay's brilliant body of work on Indian nationalism to understand this apparently paradoxical attitude. Bandyopadhyay, perhaps more than anyone else, has provided a critical genealogy of Hindu revivalism which marks the phenomenon as always globally aspiring. Indeed, from its earliest articulations in the late nineteenth century, especially in Bengal, this nationalist discourse bore an awesomely messianic character. The historical resuscitation of the nation as Hindu in the *longue durée* was imagined as a process that would not only make the colonized land a free and equal participant in the *durbar* of the world, but also first among equals. In his essay "Punar Bishoye Punarbibechona" ("Rethinking the Prefix 'Re'"), first written in 1994 and

subsequently expanded in 2009, Bandyopadhyay elaborates the genealogy
of this line of thinking. He demonstrates that it guides Hindu discursive,
congregational, and institutional efforts toward defining a peopleness,
from the late nineteenth-century Hindu Mela gatherings in Calcutta, to
contemporary, global formations like Swaminarayan's *Sanskritic Utsav*,
the Maharshi Mahesh Yogi's Disney-style amusement park, Veda Land, in
Orlando, Florida, or the Global Museum of the Brahmakumaris in Kenya.[40]
Through his reading of the works of public intellectuals like Bankim
Chandra Chattopadhyay (1838–94) and Swami Vivekananda (1863–1902),
Bandyopadhyay elucidates what can be understood as a tacit historical contract with the West. According to this understanding, the positive role of the
colonial enterprise was to be limited to two principal matters: first, bringing
India out of a medieval portal of time inaugurated by a millennial Buddhist
dominance followed by eight centuries of Islamic rule; and second, providing Hindus with the external knowledge and instrumentation to revive their
unique spiritual genius.[41] Once that catalysis is complete, the tide, as it
were, would turn in the Hegelian teleology. The spirit of history would not
reach its culmination in Prussia or anywhere else in the West, but return to
its origins: a reinvigorated Hindu nation in the world. This is because, as
Vivekananda puts it, the *Mokhshamarg* (path to salvation) exists in India
and nowhere else. For Bankimchandra, too, the Hindu *Anushilan* (practice),
once strengthened with material advantages from the West, can only yield
a far superior form of humanity than Arnoldian culture.[42] All measures of
science and *technē* borrowed from the world must therefore converge in a
singular project of memory and cognition: a lost, amnesiac self must see
and remember the true self. It is from this infallible spiritual bedrock that
India is to embark on a destinying narrative of progress. The appropriation
of modern instruments is to be undertaken in a deeper invagination of time
and not according to the dictates of an empty, metrical logic of development. This is precisely why India can claim spiritual superiority over technologically advanced nations like Japan or, as is clear in other films, even
over Europe and the United States.

In his earlier work *Gopal-Rakhal Dwandhwosamas*,[43] Bandyopadhyay
cites an illuminating passage from Rabindranath Tagore's 1887 essay
"Hindu Bibaho" ("Hindu Marriage"), which parodies this attitude with
devastating effect:

> We are an enslaved nation. We have been insulted by others, hence we crave respect
> at home. This is why we want to say to the British: Englishmen! The *shoshtro*
> (weapon) is paramount for you, but for us the *shastra* (scriptures) are paramount; you
> are kings, but we are Aryans. We thus seek to pretend that we still have what we had
> in the past in order to forget the pain of our present dishonor. (1991; my translation)

In the Hindu nationalist attitude Tagore mocks, the *shostro* of the West is deemed merely an instrumental, spiritually vacuous and ultimately misguided icon of progress, while India is uniquely blessed with the now revived guidance of the *shastra* and the true Dharma derived from that. The *shastric* appropriation of technology is but a profound maturation in a different temporal order; but once it happens, it is only India that can lead mankind's journey towards historical fulfillment. Consider, for instance, the thought expressed toward the beginning of Manoj Kumar's 1970 film *Purab Aur Paschim* (*East and West*). When the hero, Bharat, is preparing to go to England to be educated, his spiritual master (*guruji*) ruefully meditates on the fact that there was once a time when people from all over the world came to India to acquire *gyan* (knowledge). Now it seems that Indians go abroad to acquire *gyan*. Bharat gently corrects him, saying that what he is pursuing is *vigyan* (science): the study of dross matter that is necessary nowadays. It is not *gyan*, which he already has from his *guruji*'s teachings.[44]

It is this nationalist reckoning of the self in relation to the world that yields a strange anthropological perspective which can be seen in many popular Hindi films. It takes many forms: a moral abnegation of decadence, patronizing criticisms of other cultures, and the temporary inhabiting of "quaint" practices, objects, and forms of life through parody or decorative assimilations. In *Love in Tokyo* there is speculation on whether inmates of Japanese jails are fed frogs or cockroaches. Mahesh, the stock comic character in the film, describes a sauna as a "tandoori bathroom." He flies across Tokyo in a remarkable sequence inspired by similar ones in Disney's *The Absent-minded Professor* (Robert Stevenson, 1961) where the invention of a strangely buoyant compound "flubber" facilitated the process. It is through the hero, Ashok, that a touristic as well as moralistic reconnaissance of Japan is conducted. This includes, apart from urban spectacles, a visitation of Geisha culture and a playful approximation of local mores, especially in the "Sayonara! Sayonara!" song sequence, in which Asha, dressed as a Japanese woman, flirts with Ashok.

What is remarkable about this anthropological/ethnophobic look is that it has proved to be remarkably durable, and can be frequently seen in recent, apparently more cosmopolitan Hindi films like *Kal Ho Na Ho* (*Tomorrow May Never Come*) (Nikhil Advani, 2003). This perspective was deployed in the past across a remarkable range of geographical and cultural milieus, from England (*Purab Aur Paschim*, Manoj Kumar, 1970; *Des Pardes*, Dev Anand, 1978), France (*An Evening in Paris*, Shakti Samanta, 1967), Italy (*The Great Gambler*, Shakti Samanta, 1979), Canada (*Door-Desh* [*Faraway Country*], Ambrish Sangal, 1983), Europe in general

(*Sangam* [*Confluence*], Raj Kapoor, 1964; *Prem Pujari* [*Worshipper of Love*], Dev Anand, 1970), Africa in general (*Charas* [*Opium*], Ramanand Sagar, 1976; *Do Shikari* [*Two Hunters*], Kuljit Pal, 1979), the Arab world (*International Crook*, Pachchi, 1974), South East Asia (*Singapore*, Shakti Samanta, 1960), and indeed sometimes the planet itself (*Around the World*, Pachchi, 1967). In all these films the Hindu/Indian self is seen to traverse a circuit of visibilities and affects, experience a range of exhilarating or abominable sentiments; and yet it must emerge pristine at the end and report back only to a lonely language of natality. The latter can indeed be strengthened by such navigations, but ultimately there can be no knowledge that will not finally affirm a singular being and becoming in the world.

Helen: The Figure of Vice in the World

The consequences of this grand enframing of geo-televisual energies can be grouped under numerous headings. It is not my purpose here to offer an exhaustive catalogue, but to present a theoretical arc that can curve around, without any expected final closure, an adequate critical mass of these volatile and buoyant cinematic formations. Let me begin with a powerful and enticing picture of vice, usually expressed through song-and-dance sequences remarkable in their eclectic worldliness. Here, keeping in mind our explorations of the assemblages of femininity, one can invoke the star figure of Helen, perhaps the most celebrated vamp in popular Hindi film. Being of British-Burmese origin, Helen's exotic-alien looks were slotted into a set of typologies by the film industry: the *femme fatale*, the gangster's moll, the prostitute, the nightclub singer, the cabaret dancer. The gallery of characters she played, and the exotic spaces, memories, and affects assembled around her, are emblematic in relation to a purported, perpetually constituting national self's ambiguous relationship with capital and modernity. When the self encounters Helen, usually in fragmented spaces of the city that come between a pristine interiority of the home and the agrarian repose of the national community, this relationship assumes a libidinal dimension, a tortured dialectics between the undeniable lure of the flesh plus the attractions of urbanity and capital that inform it, and a moral economy of fear and loathing. The Helen assemblage is constituted by a host of named and nameless figures, attired and augmented by a plethora of foreign qualities, exotic memories, sound-images, and totemic values. It is under a horizon of a worldly "outside" that affirms the stringent limits of "home" that the figure of Helen can flit between an assembling range that is book-ended by a spectral West and

2.1: Helen in the hotel: a shot from Shakti Samanta's *Chinatown*.

a primordial Orient. She can thus be a Chinese dancer in *Howrah Bridge* (Shakti Samanta, 1958), a Malaysian village girl in *Singapore* (Shakti Samanta, 1960), a north Indian *tawaif* in *Gunga Jumna* (Nitin Bose, 1961), a mythical demon princess in *Sampoorna Ramayana* (*The Ramayana*) (Babubhai Mistri, 1961), a Mughal court dancer in *Taj Mahal* (M. Sadiq, 1964), a Flamingo artist in *Inspector* (1970), or a gypsy in *Sholay* (*Flames*) (Ramesh Sippy, 1975). She has played nightclub singers, gangster's molls, smuggling operators, spies, aristocrats, beauty queens, and assassins of myriad, if spurious national-cultural origins, spanning Spain to Arabia to the Far East. Such outsider figures more often than not come with orphaned Christian/Western "single" names: Miss Kitty, Suzie, Sophia, Sylvia, Cham Cham, Rita, Rebecca, Shelly, Rita, Carmen, Roma, and perhaps the most famous of them all, Monica. Helen's song and dance is indeed the rhythmic verve of the geo-televisual as haptic power. These individual routines can freely combine musical and choreographic mores across an immense range, from salsa to the twist to ballet to Flamenco and beyond, and can suspend the vertical governance of the narrative as the ultimate instantiation of ethics. The Helen dance is the manifest wonder of the geo-televisual compressed into a trajectory of movement and style that is a plastic sublime. It is a dance to death because it has to be used up in its spectacular usefulness. Helen is precisely that torrid incarnation of a worldly public femininity that cannot enter the imagined national space of interiority. She is thus the assembled entity of lurid vice in the world which has to be expunged in order to complete a melodramatic arc of returning home (for if it is true that encounters with the profane as modern is an historical inevitability, it is also true that the self can experience this only as prodigal or exiled).

A Missed Modernism / Cultural Cannibalism?

The overall geo-televisual realm of the post-Independence Hindi film also harbored an uneven, minoritarian impulse toward modernism: a weak modernism promoted primarily by artists associated with the Indian People's Theater Movement (IPTA). It did not yield an avant-garde, but set up an internationalist field of literary and filmic resonances which combined with indigenous traditions of expression. The adaptations of Shakespeare in Hindi cinema—from Kishore Sahu's *Hamlet* (1954) to Vishal Bharadwaj's recent work—are too numerous to list; we could instead take a quick survey of the range of engagement: Gogol (*Afsar* [*Officer*], Chetan Anand, 1950; *Garam Coat* [*The Clerk and the Coat*], Amar Kumar, 1955), Tolstoy (*Duniya Kya Hai* [*Resurrection*], G. P. Pawar, 1937), Flaubert (*Anuradha* [*Love of Anuradha*], Hrishikesh Mukherjee, 1960), Dickens (*Chanda Aur Bijli* [*Chanda and Bijli*], Atma Ram, 1969), Hardy (*Dulhan Ek Raat Ki*, D. D. Kashyap, 1967; *Daag* [*The Stain*], Yash Chopra, 1973), Dostoevsky (*Phir Subah Hogi*, Ramesh Saigal, 1958), or even Brecht (*Imaan* [*Honor*], Padmanabh, 1974). This weak strain of literary modernism— if it can indeed be called that—was greatly exceeded by a more potent vein of cannibalizing narratives, genres, and spectacular set pieces from Hollywood, Europe, and Hong Kong especially from the 1970s onward. Cinematic and popular-culture figures like Tarzan (*Zimbo*, Homi Wadia, 1958; *Tarzan Aur Jaduyi Chirag* [*Tarzan and the Magic Lamp*], B. Bhanji, 1966; *Tarzan*, B. Subhash, 1985) and Zorro (*Zorro*, Shibu Mitra, 1975) were incorporated into the Brahminical-feudal moral diagram of the Hindi film. James Bond prompted a legion of imitators in films like *Farz* (*Duty*) (Ravikant Nagaich, 1967), *CID 909* (M. Hussain, 1967), *Spy in Rome* (B. K. Adarsh, 1968), *Inspector* (Chand, 1970), *Wardat* (*Accident*) (Ravi Nagaich, 1981), and *Bond 303* (Ravi Tandon, 1986). The Bombay industry also continued to import an impressive array of spectacular generic conventions from across the world. Along with ones like the romantic comedy or the crime thriller that have been noted and commented upon, it also experimented with unlikely templates like the pirate film (*Baaz* [*Hawk*], Guru Dutt, 1953), the *King Solomon's Mines*-style African safari adventure (*Do Shikari* [*Two Hunters*], Kuljit Pal, 1979), the martial arts film (*Karate*, Deb Mukherjee, 1983), the caped crusader film (*Azad*, S. M. Naidu, 1955; *Jugnu* [*The Glow Worm*], Pramod Chackravorty, 1973; *Shiva Ka Insaaf* [*Shiva's Justice*], Raj N. Sippy, 1985), and even the science fantasy, with aliens from outer space (*Wahan Ke Log* [*People From Out There*], Nisar Ansari, 1967; *Chand Par Chadayi* [*Ascent to the Moon*], T. R. Sunderam, 1967). Even the western, in 'curried' guise, generated major and minor productions in *Khotay Sikke* (*Countefeit Coins*) (Narendra Bedi, 1974), *Sholay* (*Flames*) (Ramesh Sippy, 1975), *Jagir* (*Estate*) (Pramod Chackravorty, 1984), *Wanted* (Ambrish Sangal, 1983), and *Joshilaay* (*The Passionate*) (Sibte Hassan Rizvi, 1989). Valentina Vitali has insightfully theorized the series of Roman gladiatorial films (peplums) made during the 1960s with the wrestler Dara Singh playing the lead.[45]

These infusions of visual and aural energy were monitored, econo-mized, segmented into spaces, and strategically distributed in order to fit them into an overall melodramatic diagram of the feudal family romance. The Indian James Bonds almost always emerged, at the end, to be scrupulously committed to monogamy and largely unstirred by vodka martinis. Adaptations from Western sources were "Indianized," not just by absorbing their spectacular elements into the affective universe of the north Indian extended family, but also by placing them in a different temporal order of mythic restoration.[46] The interests of the state could therefore be authenticated only by assembling them with the familial and the communitarian; heroism would have to bear an ascetic dimension even as it departed from a Gandhian code of non-violence. It could not, in other words, follow a track of possessive individualism or a simple con-tractual commitment to the state. This is precisely why Subhash Ghai's *Krodhi* (*The Angry*) (1981), despite largely being an adaptation of the spaghetti western *La bataille de San Sebastian* (*Guns for San Sebastian*) (Henri Verneuil, 1968), begins with the hero's childhood, in which being orphaned and utterly destitute, he is forced into a life of crime. B. Subhash's *Commando* (1989) approximates the spectacular set pieces of *Where Eagles Dare* (Brian Hutton, 1968) in its second half. Here too the task of eliminating the enemies of the nation coincides with that of extract-ing vengeance for a father murdered a long time ago. Professional activity in the metrical, emergency time of the state is perpetually informed by a greater weight of meaning in a maturing Dharmic temporality. The state could thus only borrow a self already instrumentalized by a mythic arc of reconstitution.

The Country and the City

Between 1947 and 1989, geo-televisual attributes are cautiously pack-
aged in visible spaces of national cultural life. They are often enclosed in
urban spaces of vice like hotels, or enframed by Orientalist/ethnophobic
perceptions of tribal life in the forests. In his remarkably insightful book
on Helen, Jerry Pinto (2006) rightly points out that in popular Hindi
cinema of the classical period hotels have always featured as venues of
decadence, animated by alcohol, foreign bodies, bestial sexuality, prostitution, and illicit commerce.[47] The four hotels as houses of intrigue in
the espionage thriller *Inspector* (1970) are tellingly named: Sun 'n' Sand,
Ajanta Palace, the Ritz, and the Blue Nile. Populated by rich, lascivious
Arab sheikhs, conspiring neo-imperialists, scantily dressed white women,
or inscrutable Orientals, the hotel is also the space that can throw up perverse assemblages of consumerism and primitive cornucopia, as evidenced
in literally hundreds of unabashedly racist cabaret sequences featuring
actors in blackface, in films like *Inteqaam* (*Revenge*) (R. K. Nayyar, 1969),
Dharmatma (*The Godfather*) (Feroz Khan, 1975), and *Vidhaata* (*Destiny*)
(Subhash Ghai, 1982).

The exact locus of being-as-nation is thus never clear; it lies between
a vernacular perspective of the city that is uneasy with modes of capitalist mercantilism and industrialization and an Aryan civilizational/
anthropological one that is terrified of an absolute, "non-Aryan" state
of nature. The map of urbanity is thus dotted with dispersed bodies of
secrecy, while the jungle is the harbinger of primitivism and terror. The
first pole of this amorphous assemblage of the self has to do with a moral
reckoning of capitalism and modernity, the second with how figures of
subalternity (the *dalit*, the Dravidian, the tribal, the Negro, or the *ban-
jaran* [gypsy]) can only be differentially included within the national fold.
The subaltern does not belong to the city, and she is also not quite a part
of that pristine agrarian natality that is the heart of India. Indian jungle
folk on screen thus often bear remarkable similarities to savages encountered in late nineteenth-/early twentieth-century imperialist fictions by
Rider Haggard, Lewis Wallace, or Edgar Rice Burroughs. The pressures
of the geo-televisual—as expressive qualities of memory, affect, and cognition—are thus multivalent and multi-directional. They are distributed
and locked in striated spaces between the jungle and the agrarian village,
between the village and the city, between the home-in-the-city and the
hotel-in-the-city, or between the homeland and foreign shores. The geo-
televisual acts from opposing directions, forming combustive or tense
clusters of signification and threatening to open up portals of anti-matter

in which cosmic artworks of national selfhood themselves can recede to a vanishing point. The geo-televisual has the betrayal of the self as its limit.

Many urban entities, both solid and metaphysical, are geo-televisual because, no matter how quotidian, no matter how integral to the city itself as an historical formation, they cannot be named in a communitarian vernacular: *Marine Drive* (G. P. Sippy, 1955), *Coffee House* (Hari Valia, 1957), *Opera House* (P. L. Santoshi, 1961), *Passport* (Pramod Chakravorty, 1961), *Love Marriage* (Subodh Mukherjee, 1959), *Boyfriend* (Naresh Saigal, 1961), *College Girl* (Shantilal Soni, 1978), or, indeed, *Divorce* (N. D. Kothari, 1984). It is by getting caught up in such a web of intrigue and perverse desire that the educated younger brother, Puran, turns to debauchery and crime in Manoj Kumar's *Upkaar* (*The Good Deed*) (1967). Like the mother in *Love in Tokyo*, the mother in Shakti Samanta's *Chinatown* is unwilling to let her son go to the big city of Calcutta because it houses, in its sordid Oriental quarters, the lures of gambling and opium dens. This panoptic-moral 'tele-localizing' of the nation involves many complicated and beleaguered measures. For example, an ethnophobic distancing is frequently seen to work even when an evaluation of domestic social vice takes place. The scrutiny of evil like alcoholic decadence or unbridled greed (*Dus Lakh* [*Ten Lakhs*], Devendra Goel, 1966), and teenage pregnancy (*Julie*, K. S. Sethumadhavan, 1975) often take place in Christian Indo-European communities. In Basu Chatterjee's *Khatta Meetha* (*Sweet and Sour*), the reformist issue of marriage between elderly widowed people with children is worlded in the Parsi community, away from a core imaginary picture of Hindu national interiority.

It is because the powers of the geo-televisual work infra-nationally too that the country and the city are not absolute cinematic spaces in and of themselves; both are constantly redrawn with signatures of the fascinating and the abhorrent. The lures of the cosmopolitan city can sometimes be particularized spectacles, a pure exhilarating semiosis of the outside: the brand-new Mercedes that is spectacularly smashed up in *Qurbani* (*Sacrifice*) (Feroz Khan, 1980), or the six major characters in Manmohan Desai's *Naseeb* (*Fate*) dressing up as a matador, a Cossack, Chaplin's tramp, a Flamenco dancer, a Heidi, and an Arabian dancer for the climactic song sequence. A group of marauders in S. U. Sunny's *Kohinoor* (1960) are dressed in the robes of the Ku Klux Klan. Often the alien entity is grasped comically: the heroine, Reshma, in Sunil Dutt's desert romance *Reshma Aur Shera* (*Reshma and Shera*) (1971) spots a transistor and demands to know more about "Radowa ka bachcha" (radio's baby) which is the latest wonder to arrive from the world at the country fair.

On the other hand, the essence of the nation—the agrarian repose of an enduring Indian form of life—is a cinematic picture that is also always touched by the geo-televisual. The memorials of natality are thus often a "setting up against" the tempestuous sea of alien images. Ajanta Sircar has pointed out that it was in New Theater's 1936 landmark production *Achhut Kanya* (*The Untouchable Girl*) (Franz Osten, 1936) that the cinematic assemblage of the archetypal Hindi film rural belle was put in place.[48] This exotic assemblage of iconic femininity included star actress Devika Rani's plucked eyebrows and dark lipstick. Sircar points out that the organization of visual and aural signs in the village girl—including tonality of voice and body, speech, intonation, body language, and attire—endowed such rural figures with features that effected a discursive erasure of caste. It was only after this that they were allowed to enter emblematic pictures of national conjugality. This demure, *ghagra-choli*-clad archetype can be seen in hundreds of films, from Bimal Roy's *Madhumati* (1958) to Mansoor Khan's *Qayamat Se Qayamat Tak* (*Catastrophe to Catastrophe*) (1988) and beyond. Sirkar proceeds to make the enlightening observation that the figure of the country belle disappears with the onset of globalization. After that, as happens in Khan's film, the jeans-clad urban woman can exhibit her essential ethnicity on demand.

The Nation and the World

Let me now turn to consolidated "foreign" spaces as cinematic loci of the geo-televisual proper. It was with S. K. Ojha's *Naaz* (*Pride*) (1956), which was shot in London and Cairo, that post-Independence popular Hindi cinema began to venture into overseas locations from time to time. Such forays, while bound by a larger cultural imperative of narrating a nation-in-the-world in the spirit of a Nehruvian non-aligned internationalism, were motivated by many desires. In Raj Kapoor's *Sangam* (*Confluence*) it was Technicolor tourism in the honeymoon segment. In Feroz Khan's *Apradh* (*Crime*) (1972), it is primarily the spectacle of crime and Grand Prix racing. In Mohan Kumar's *Aman* (*Peace*) (1967), a film in which none other than the philosopher Bertrand Russell makes an appearance, it is humanitarian concern and an exemplary Indian internationalism: the doctor hero, Gautamdas, relocates to Japan after being educated in England to serve the devastated people of Hiroshima and Nagasaki. In Manoj Kumar's *Purab Aur Paschim* (*East and West*) (1970), the voyage to England is a patriotic one. The hero goes there with the aim of returning with an Oxford education in order to serve his country better.

However, in the aftermath of the Indo-China war of 1962 and the Indo-Pakistan wars of 1965 and 1971, the question of "foreign" space became increasingly tied to concerns about national sovereignty and security. The geo-televisual as amorphous, secretive images of an overall world of peril that percolates into or besieges the nation became a dominant feature in what was also a period of tremendous domestic unrest, beginning with the Maoist Naxalbari uprisings in north-eastern and central-south India, the unraveling of the consensual base of the Indian ruling class called "The Congress System" by Rajani Kothari,[49] and the general socio-economic climate of bank failures, widespread political corruption, large-scale labor unrest, rise of urban crime, smuggling, hoarding and black-marketeering that led to the declaration of Emergency in 1975. Such images of evil in the world insinuating itself into the national space assumed forms of paranoia as well as parody, covering a range of emotions from sublimity, to terror, and laughter. In *Night in London* (Brij, 1967) the object of dread is a set of diamonds that also contains in it a formula that can spell the end of the world. In *Inspector* (1970) it is a poisonous gas, "Agent Orange"; the film also has a flying car sequence. The contentious matter in *Shareef Budmash* (*The Gentleman Cheat*) (Raj Khosla, 1973) is a set of plans for a special military aircraft. In *Yakeen* (*Trust*) (Brij, 1969) it is nuclear secrets. Jerry Pinto draws attention to more objects of espionage intrigue, ones that border on the absurd: in *Elaan* (*Declaration*) (K. Ramanlal, 1971) foreign spies plot to acquire an atomic ring of invisibility developed by Indian scientists, and in the 1967 film *CID 909* it is a technological formula for world peace.[50] Such nefarious schemes were often masterminded by cartoon-like psychotic villains of unspecified exotic origins: Supremo (*Parvarish* [*Upbringing*], Manmohan Desai, 1977), Shakaal (*Shaan* [*Style*], Ramesh Sippy, 1980), Mogambo (*Mr. India*, Shekhar Kapur, 1987), or Dr Dang (*Karma*, Subhash Ghai, 1986). These encounters were marked by affects of unrest, drawing from an almost endemic duality of the imagination: technology had to find a home in a developing India and yet a spiritual essence of the nation could not be at ease with the profane possibilities of technology. In many of these films images of modern instrumentation are associated with wonder as well as dread, alienation, and despair. The hideouts of super-villains are marked by automatic doors, scanners, computers, hidden microphones, close-circuit televisions, push-button trap doors, weapons of mass destruction, submarines, helicopters, private planes, exotic pets (leopards, crocodiles, piranhas), and a spectrum of bodies and costumes from across the world. In Ramanand Sagar's *Aankhen* (*Eyes*) (1968) the scene of profane intrusion becomes complete when spies set up a secret transmitter behind an idol of the god Krishna. Unlike Bond films, for instance, this overall specter of satanic automation comes with powers of an expressive naturalism

2.2: Smuggling and vice in *International Crook*.

rather than realism. The picture of technology harbors a demonic/mythic dimension. It is then combated not so much with professional-scientific administrations of the state or with competing gadgetry and capital as in Bond, but with a home-grown agrarian physicality that has its own mythic registers. In Manmohan Desai's *Parvarish* the two heroes stop a moving submarine by tying the propeller with an iron chain. In his *Mard* (*Man*) (1985) a plane about to take off is lassoed by a man on horseback.

The foreign land, as absolute space of the geo-televisual, is often a total, undifferentiated haunt of spectacle and peril which on many occasions does not conform to the international cartography of the Cold War. In *International Crook* tracking the flow of smuggled diamonds in the world at large takes the protagonists to an undifferentiated Central Europe, Iran, and the American state of Alaska. In *Yakeen* the African republic of Mozambique is hurriedly established through a couple of grainy night shots obviously procured from stock footage. The film then moves to a den of evil where the chief villain, who looks strikingly similar to Mussolini, hatches the ultimate plot of subversion. His chief henchman, a blue-eyed man with blond hair, is a look-alike of the imprisoned hero Rajesh. The imposter's voice is modified by strange technology and his hair and eye color is also altered. He is then sent not just to infiltrate a secure space of national sovereignty, but also an ethical one of principled conjugality centered on Rajesh's fiancée, Rita. The space of the "outside" thus often requires no cinematic calibration in terms of nationality or geography. Shakti Samanta's 1969 film *An Evening in Paris* promises a touristic romance set in the European city (the "evening," as spelled out in the title song, refers to the time we spend in the theater watching the film, and not the duration of the narrative). The film, however, moves freely between the geo-specific location of the French capital to Switzerland and Germany, and stages its climax at the Niagara Falls in North America. In Manmohan Desai's 1977 costume epic *Dharam Veer* (*Dharam and Veer*), the loose, eclectically composed fantasy milieu combines elements drawn from the Japanese Samurai films, the warfare of medieval English knights, the cinematic high seas swashbucklers of Hollywood, and Roman gladiatorial contests.

The incursions of the geo-televisual are thus marked by a priestly monitoring of movement in classic postwar Indian cinematic narratives of the 1950s and 1960s, generically characterized by Prasad as "feudal family romance."[51] Journeys across the nation in such films often encompass the length of the geographical territory, from the valleys and lakes of Kashmir to the temples, gardens, rivers, and beaches of the south. The lyrical transportation of bodies in romantic song sequences creates impossible spaces for what is otherwise forbidden: *nucleated* urban desire. As a result, these utopian grounds exist between the feudal household and a pastoral state of nature. In such segments, tourist attractions like the Taj Mahal and the Vrindavan Gardens become spectacular, yet virtual zones of conjugal privacy (imbued with an aura of legend and romance, and also the modern association of the honeymoon). They are virtual spaces because they are magically emptied of paying visitors, state employees that protect its "public" status, as well as an otherwise omniscient, monitoring gaze of the national-feudal community. Having the impossible Taj to oneself is a virtuality that reinforces the essentially symbolic nature of the line of flight. It is a stance of cinema that announces that bourgeois, individual love and privacy have to be decorative entities precisely because they cannot otherwise exist in an "Indian" familial dispensation. Travel within the nation in such films is largely interiorized into a grand domestic conversation of the nation with itself, by which the *landness* of the land passes from a geographical aesthetic into a political concept. In such sequences, nascent middle-class desire for mobility and diversion from feudal dictates assemble with a cinematic depiction of national space and national heritage.

Similarly, forays into foreign shores are usually possible only after traditional rites of passage, when professional compulsions or touristic and libidinal desires are properly blessed and sanctified by the universal interests of the feudal extended family. The couple in Raj Kapoor's *Sangam* (*The Confluence*) (1964) can go to Europe and its playground of urban desires only after marriage, with their bodies all the time being encurved by stipulations of tradition: the honeymooning couple never kiss in public, but white people in the background do. Unlike their latter-day globalized compatriots who indulge in conspicuous consumption, the army officer hero and his wife have to choose between buying a vanity bag and bagpipes. In Manoj Kumar's *Purab Aur Paschim* (*East and West*) (1970), the journey is in the opposite direction, toward a melodramatic re-familiarization of the woman's body through a shedding of alien accessorial markers. In England, the hero meets and courts the heroine, Preeti, who is the daughter of a non-resident Indian. It is, however, largely due to the upbringing provided by her English-Indian mother that Preeti lacks discipline and culture. She wears revealing clothes and indulges in tobacco and alcohol. It is through the principled ardor of Bharat, the model citizen of a new India, that Preeti's self is claimed and reinvented as an ethical instantiation of a core Indianness. She comes to India and is assimilated into the culture after her vices are expunged and symmetrically replaced by emotive, topological, and lifestyle attributes of the Indian woman as a national spiritual artwork. In *Pyar Ka Sapna* (*Dream of Love*) (Hrishikesh Mukherjee, 1969), it is the illiterate village girl, Sudha, who, after undergoing a Pygmalion-like transformation in terms of etiquette and English poise and couture, goes abroad to bring back her husband from the enticements of Europe.

Human figures too become sites of contention between disparate energies of signification and memory and the arc of the statement of propriety that tries to enclose them. Raj Kapoor's Chaplinesque urban tramp, "Raju," becomes cinematically manifest in *Sri 420* (*The Gentleman Cheat*) (1954) when traits of a postwar socialist internationalism (Mera Joota Hai Japani / Patloon Englishthani/ Sar pe Lal topi Rusi / Phir Bhi Dil Hai Hindustani [My shoes are Japanese / My trousers from England / On my head is a Russian cap / But my heart remains Indian]) combine with the tempo of an optimistic Nehruvian socialist dream for the young republic. It is indeed essential that the heart remains Indian, while the body and its prosthetics change with the times. The geo-televisual in classical Hindi cinema is therefore a cautious, graduated aesthetics of "exposure." It is a closely monitored construction of an India-in-India, in tandem with an India-in-the-world, a setting forth of the picture of the nation against a world of temptations and danger, both within it and abroad. Contending

2.3: Preeti in *Purab Aur Paschim.*

with and absorbing the geo-televisual involves the calibrated extraction of
an enduring essence that can withstand the profane temporality of capital,
industrial development, and alienation. The self inevitably has to navigate
the wide, clamorous circuit of matters and desires in the world, but in
the end the self must report to the self alone. This is the impelling that
governs patriotic love in Pramod Chakraborty's *Love in Tokyo* (1966) or
Manoj Kumar's *Purab Aur Paschim* (*East and West*) (1970), patriotic espionage in Ramanand Sagar's *Aankhen* (*Eyes*) (1968), or Dev Anand's *Prem
Pujari* (*Worshipper of Love*) (1970). It is this picture that begins to become
informatic from the 1990s onwards.

The Geo-televisual as Informatic (1991–2004)

In an early sequence in David Dhawan's *Yaarana* (*Friendship*) (1995),
Raj, the hero, is completely drunk. He picks up what he thinks is a beautiful blonde mannequin from a clothing store in Mumbai, loads it into his
expensive Mercedes, and starts driving. When the car stops, it is in a lush,
beautiful landscape in Gstaad, Switzerland, and the "dummy" has come

to life in the form of the lovely heroine, Lalita. What follows is a song-and-dance sequence ("Jadu Jadu" ["Magic"]), a symptomatic assemblage of fantasy that combines attributes of high living, tourism, and unstated libidinal overtures centering especially on the Indian woman with a blonde wig. Let us, however, consider the assembled milieu here, one that is traversed in a single cinematic movement of scripting desire. It begins with quotidian life in the bustling third world metropolis of Mumbai and ends in a secluded pastoral enclave in Europe. The two spheres are not categorically separated from each other by designated proper names (India and Switzerland); nor is this method of splicing together footage shot in different continents new to cinema. In contrast to the examples we have seen in the previous section, this is a different form of engagement with the geo-televisual. I call this the geo-televisual in an "informatic" form precisely because it does not allow for any naturalistic anchoring of signs, or a persistent and unified cinematic invention of the localized milieu. If that were the case, the Swiss landscape—or any other for that matter—could cinematically participate in the determined milieu of Mumbai only through a semiological process of selecting, enframing, ordering, and familiarizing under the axiomatic control of the realist narrative. This is how, to take a stray example, London's Pinewood Studios and other English locations cinematically *become* tropical Vietnam in Kubrick's *Full Metal Jacket*. In Dhawan's film what we see instead is a metropolitan image machinery that creates disjunctive global assemblages of desiring bodies, vectorized time–space modules and lifestyle ideas in such a way that these sets can "zap" instantaneously from dust to snow, from the tropical maritime shores to the Alps, from signatures of third world poverty to a profusion of Western consumerism, and from a host of brown bodies in the background to a host of white bodies in the background.[52]

On occasion such non-obligatory departures are presented as direct expressions of impossible desires which collide with what reality and its sedentary narratives have to offer. Cinema is thus seen to be a demand for the impossible, perhaps even a questioning of whether there can be a pure realist framework of cognition in an Indian scene in which desire has been globalized and democratized, even though the means to them are not. Can there be a perfectly disenchanted reckoning (anthropological/social) of the state-of-the-slum when the "slum-eyed view" of the world is already incurably infected by geo-televisual pulsations from the city itself as screen?[53] The "informational" democratization of desire is seen in its raw form—by way of grotesque humor, cannibalizing appropriations, and spectral violence—in the crime genre of Hindi cinema which assumed an interesting form from the late 1990s. The Dubai-based uncouth, unlettered Mumbai don in Shimit Amin's *Ab Tak Chhappan* (*56 So Far*) takes his blonde mistress lingerie shopping. The mafia king in *Calcutta Mail* (Sudhir Mishra, 2003) develops an obsession for ballroom dancing. Cinema in these cases is not a reflection of the actual, but an immanent movement of desire which impinges on and transforms ideas of reality. It reveals reality to be already indistinguishable from the virtual, and the vision of the city itself to be a compound of the desire industry and the phenomenology of the everyday. In other words, there can be no picture of a new India, in terms of temporalities, spaces, artworks, labor, and production, without the immanent expressions of longing, vicariousness, and pleasure that inform them. Two significant "musicals" authored by Ram Gopal Verma can be cited as symptomatic. Verma's *Rangeela* (*Colorful*) (1995) is about an ambitious and talented lower-middle-class girl entering the film industry; his *Mast* (*Happy*) (1999) is about a youngster's obsession with a film actress. Both films begin purportedly in a downmarket milieu distinguished from the fantasy world of cinema and then the two worlds gradually merge until they are barely distinguishable. What is thereby complicated is the commerce between existence as it is and the will to a cinematic existence: life lived and the form of life that is deemed worth living. In *Mast*, for the young hero, Kittu, being in love with screen goddess Mallika is inseparable from inhabiting the exotic space of film. As it happens later, he actually meets and falls in love with the actress, rendering his life "cinematic." The narrative of *Mast* is set in India; the film was shot in foreign locations, spanning Austria and Italy to Namibia and South Africa. Of special significance are the song sequences, with many presenting self-contained, pageant-like narrative worlds suffused with cinephilic memories. The "Ruki Ruki Thi Zindagi" ("My Life Was Stagnant") sequence is an abbreviated backpack romance set in the valleys of Central Europe. The "Mere Hero" ("My Hero") segment features Kittu as an action hero, sometimes a Bogart-like trench-coated figure, a secret agent in black leather, a biker, or a cowboy on horseback, with Mallika admiring him with a supporting cast of white cheerleaders. The alien, often exotic spaces in the film set up a signifying process of cinematic coloration. The azure, non-tropical skies, the texture of Alpine grass, or the accentuated red desert are inducted into an overall cinematic stylization of landscapes, bodies, and objects into installation art within whose auspices signs of libidinal desire cannot be separated from the need to partake in a global movement of value as aesthetics as well as erotics.

Such cinematic movements of the geo-televisual can be seen in hundreds of films in the period we are examining. The song sequences in particular, often shot with independent arrangements of production value

and spectacle, were filmed as autonomous music videos which continued
to have an independent life in a variety of media (television, the internet,
the music industry, cell phone ring tones, etc.) beyond the film itself
in theaters. The set pieces of the traditional Hindi film—described by
Madhava Prasad as outcomes of a "heterogeneous mode of manufacture"[54]—assumed different life-forms through disaggregated channels
of distribution. They became, more than ever, fired up by non-linear
energies of product placement, and infomercial logic derived from transnational fashion or tourism. This, in short, was what came to be known
abroad as "Bollywood style." Without trying to provide an exhaustive
taxonomy of these myriad and voluptuous geo-televisual movements, let
me list a few working themes. In the process, I will try to answer a few
questions: how are these cinematic procedures different from ones in previous epochs, and why exactly can they be gauged as signs of an impulse
toward an informatic or advertised *modernization* rather than those of a
long-gestating Indian modernity finally coming into being?

Space and Time

In Kuku Kohli's 1995 mafia thriller *Haqeeqat* (*Reality*), the main
characters happen to be a mob hitman-turned-garage mechanic and
a young, impoverished music teacher who is a widow. The entire
action takes place in Mumbai, particularly in the slum where they live.
However, the "dream"-based song sequences transport the couple to
Alpine Switzerland, with both of them dressed in designer Western suits.
Guddu Dhanoa's 1997 film *Ziddi* (*The Stubborn*) is another crime saga
set in the dark and violent alleys of Mumbai; here too a couple of song
sequences take place in a snow-capped European location, as touristic,
disjunctive prostheses of televisual value embedded in the narrative. The
upper torso of the macho, street criminal hero is left bare in a few shots in
what is visibly a sub-zero environment. In *Jamai Raja* (*The Son-in-Law*)
(A. Kondandarami Reddy, 1990), the feudal melodrama involving the
overbearing mother-in-law and the newly-wed couple is interspersed by
unconditional move-outs, by which a sphere of private, nuclear desires
becomes immanent in a setting of Sergio Leone-style spaghetti westerns,
much like the *Kaadalan* sequence analyzed in Chapter 1. In Shankar's
Jeans (1998) the young couple, imperiled by traditional prohibitions, are
temporarily rendered afloat and free in a space of international travel featuring the Seven Wonders of the World in the sumptuously shot "Ajooba
Ajooba" ("Wonder, Wonder") song sequence.[55]

The advent of the geo-televisual in "informatic" form, therefore, opens up the frame to the world by relativizing the milieu's temporal and spatial grids or by destroying them altogether. Let me here make a brief foray outside Hindi commercial cinema, but one nevertheless fully within the ambit of "Bollywood," for a particularly illustrative example. Rajiv Menon's *Kandukondain Kandukondein* (*I Have Found It!*) (2000) is a Tamil adaptation of Jane Austen's *Sense and Sensibility*. The film depicts the travails of a high-caste agrarian landlord family when their fortunes dip. The journey toward resettlement takes the destitute mother and her three daughters to a commercially motivated, anonymous, and ruthlessly disenchanting life in the city of Chennai. There the previously protected daughters are obliged to take up undistinguished middle-class professions to support the family. Soumya, the eldest, starts as a telephone operator and then moves into software design; Meenu, the younger one, struggles with a singing career. Two of the musical interludes in the film depart decisively from the milieu of the story; not only do they open up other spaces, but also other portals of time. The title track depicts a poignant moment in the budding romance between city-slicker Srikanth and the hopelessly romantic and impressionable Meenu. The "Kandukondein Kandukondein" number begins by cutting away from the interior of a car to the lake overlooking the thirteenth-century Eilean Donan castle in the Scottish Highlands, with Srikanth dressed as a caped swordsman. Meenu features as an ethereal beauty locked in a tower, imprisoned and threatened by high walls, formidable moats, and axe-wielding medieval executioners. The depiction of utopian, third world, middle-class desire for romantic bliss which can be found only in "another time, another place," therefore, assumes the form of an ironic transposition. It involves the creation of a dream assemblage in which the native figures inhabit not just the spaces of the European aristocracy, but also temporal imaginations and memories drawn from their history and legend. The "Enna Solla Pokirai" ("What Will Your Answer Be?") number features the other couple in the film: the elder sister, Sowmya, and her struggling filmmaker suitor, Manohar. The sequence begins with a match cut that moves from a railroad crossing near the village to train tracks that traverse a desert landscape in Egypt. The feelings of the couple, beset by family obligations and uncertain futures, find a strange cinematic consolidation here, in the form of a tragic romance in the desert, with the lead pair assuming imaginary identities of Indian ethnic tribal figures somehow inhabiting a different realm of time in a transnational touristic desert featuring the pyramids and the Sphinx.

It is my contention that the "boundless" nature of these departures differs—in terms of qualities, scale of operation, and affective powers—from similar ones from the past, when the romantic couple were transported to imaginary space–times that constituted an "outside" to the monitoring gaze of the feudal extended family. I have commented on the spectacular-ceremonial exteriors like the Taj Mahal in the previous section. Here we could set up a contrast with a couple of sequences from the past that depict assemblages between desire for conjugal bliss and class mobility. The title song sequence in *Ek Mahal Ho Sapnon Ka* (*Let There be a Mansion of Dreams*) (Devendra Goel, 1975) and the "Hum Aap Ki Akhon Mein" ("If I Set My Heart") sequence in *Pyaasa* (*The Thirsty One*) (Guru Dutt, 1957) both depict the fantasies of middle-class couples beleaguered by unemployment and poverty. In the first the lovers imagine themselves to be king and queen in a secluded but sumptuously decorated palace. In the second, the lovers are in a fantasy studio space (with a staircase coming down from the heavens), dressed in smart European clothing and waltzing to the song. Yet in both cases even the imaginary spaces of interiority cannot assume the dimensions of the "private" because, along with other cinematic devices, it is the deployment of studio fog/cloud that primarily enframes the sequences and brackets them as purely symbolic or purely decorative. Ever since its groundbreaking use in the "Ghar Aya Mera Pardesi" ("My Stranger Has Come Home") sequence in Raj Kapoor's *Awara* (*Vagabond*) (1951), the artificial cloud has been a stock, almost clichéd device in literally hundreds of Hindi film dream assemblages over the decades. The cloud swirls around the scattered signs in the mise-en-scène, inducting them into a grand cinematic movement of the ceremonial that will extinguish all wayward energies with the ceremony itself. Under its auspices, the imprints of earthly desire (for the woman, for money) cannot be separated and distinguished from the ethereal, purely symbolic, originary plenitude of the sky itself.

There is no such enframing device in the "Kandukondein Kandukondein" episodes or any of the ones mentioned earlier. The expressions of yearning are not decoratively bracketed (often through primordial/primitive Freudian imagery or masochism and guilt as in Kapoor's *Awara*), but are bolstered with geo-televisual energy and *advertised*—that is, they are emphatically expressed, without formal measures of enunciation, and without fidelity to categorical separations between the home and the world. As a result, the metaphysical aspect of "being Indian" becomes instantly portable, capable of assembling with randomly visited coordinates of time and space from across the world. This felicity of movement, of presenting new, globally aspiring urban desires as artwork, comes at a price: that of a necessary disengagement from history, especially its bad sides. Sudhanva Deshpande, in his essay "The Consumable Hero of Globalized India" (2005), makes an enlightening point when he calls the new hero an entity without a past or memory.[56] Ranjini Mazumdar has theorized this ubiquity of movement and power of instant virtualization in relation to information and electronic cataloguing, drawing on Anne Friedberg's observations on "window shopping" and the postmodern condition.[57] And yet Muzumdar astutely observes that such moves are always marked by double movements of elation and anxiety, especially in relation to the task of sexualizing the female in novel arenas of consumption (*Bombay Cinema* [2007], 107).

The Out-of-Frame and Discontinuous Plenitudes

In a romantic sequence in Vimal Kumar's *Tarazu* (*Scales*) (1997) some African and Caribbean bodies arrive from an ontic source beyond the milieu of the story and sing and dance with the lead pair on a beach in Mumbai. In the "Dil Mein Hain Tu" ("You Are in My Heart") sequence in *Daava* (*The Challenge*) (Sunil Agnihotri, 1997), the off-screen space randomly invests the frame with exotic signatures like Rastafarian dreadlocks, paragliding, and rock climbing. The "Sheher ki Ladki" ("City Girl") number of *Rakshak* (*The Protector*) (Ashok Honda, 1996) features leering Arabs, black cat commandos in motorcycle gear, and hovercrafts. The formidable range and evocative powers of these arbitrary geo-televisual imports introduce splits not just in the special integrity of the milieu, but also, as we have seen, fork lineages of time and memory. The police officer hero in *Garv: Pride and Honor* (Puneet Issar, 2004) dances with King Arthur's Excalibur; the romantic couple in the contemporary political thriller *Indian* (Shankar, 1996) is at one point featured in Victorian attire, aboard a sailing ship. A conning episode in *Roop Ki Rani Choron Ka Raja* (*The Queen of Beauty and the Prince of Thieves*) features an Egyptian statue and the hero and the heroine dressed as a Cossack and a Japanese woman. This pronounced cannibalizing tendency often convolutes conventional aesthetics of tourism: in *Farz* (*Duty*) (Raj Kanwar, 2001)—another police drama set completely in Mumbai—a romantic segment begins in a car pound in a first world country. A huge pile of semi-demolished, foreign-made cars in this case provides the "scenic" background. In Shankar's *Nayak* (2001), a song sequence depicts the conflict between hero's public role as Chief Minister and his private duties toward his girlfriend. Here the unhappy lovers are first transformed into fairytale figures (the king and the poor peasant beauty) and then inserted into a digitized mise-en-scène of snakes and ladders, where the visages of friends and foes alike assume reptilian features. This remarkable episode ends with a series of shots showing the protagonist in the traditional attire of Hindu kings, presiding over what is, in terms of the synchronized movement of digitized figures, a modern-day military march past and show of arms. The bodies in the marching ranks, however, are those of medieval European knights in full armor.

The relationship between the out-of-frame and the immediate field of vision is therefore not that of a "whole" that can be punctually navigated through storytelling. The "outside" is a source of kinetic plenitude which continually extends objects and themes of desire without an overall map of modernist reckoning to inform them. That is, a phenomenological map with which one can track the movement of things between the out-of-frame and the pro-filmic space, relating them to history, culture, subjective biography, circulation of capital, and mode of production. More than what such random assembling finally yields in terms of representation or theme, it is the exhilarated anxiety of the movement itself that becomes the crucial factor. That is, more than the manner in which a proposed national subjectivity absorbs these shocks, it is much more pertinent to see how the boundaries of the said subject are impinged upon and percolated. More than the question of dubious origins and the *telos* of a fixated national destinying, it is the gnash of the departure itself that marks meaning. Secondly, as an outcome of this bypassing of the issues of history and production, objects often acquire mythic dimensions of a certain kind, which will be investigated in detail in Chapter 5. In short, precisely because some informational aspects of the geo-televisual come across as rootless, interchangeable signs, they can sometimes be easily assimilated into home-grown dominant myths of a revivalist national idea of being. Technology, especially, does not spell alienation and come across as an attribute of the myth of the other, as it happens, for instance, in that amusing but poignant moment in Dutt's *Reshma Aur Shera*, when the heroine identifies the transistor as "radio's baby." In contrast, I am proposing a working theorem for the geo-televisual realm in post-1990s Hindi cinema: here the disjunctive spaces, automated bodies, hurried tempos, and instruments of modernization do not spell out the specter of an Indian modernity that has finally arrived. There is no overarching narrative of the nation that sorts itself out with a realist framework of reckoning, the final exile of the idols, and the consolidation of a scientific temper. Rather, what we see is an ecology of dispersals instead of an axiomatic line of historical becoming. It is an "informatic" ecology that, as we shall see in greater detail in the final section of this chapter, is capable of housing, particularizing, and flexibly orchestrating various narrative impulses, even ones that should be at odds with each other. As a result, discursive formations that have been intimate enemies in the past can provisionally merge, separate, and then come together again. In an advertised domain of the purely speculative and the purely spectacular—where matters need not be enunciated with fidelity to logical progression or the question of historical memory— "tradition" can appear bolstered by technology, just as technology can be seen to be sacralized by "tradition." Consider, for example, the "Telephone Dhun Mein Hasne Wali" ("The Girl Whose Laugh Rings Like the Telephone") sequence in Shankar's *Hindustani* (*Indian*) (1996). It features a range of exotic animals and objects (kangaroos, penguins, emus, the sailing ship mentioned earlier). The paramount question in traversing these eclectic wonders of the world is, however, an ontological one asked in the song: "Computerko Lekar Brahma Ne Rachaya Kya." That is, what did Brahma—the divinity of creation who is one of the holy trinity in the Hindu pantheon and identified with the Vedic deity Prajapati—fabricate with the computer?

The Home in the World

In films of the past, being scrupulously Indian meant avoiding the temptations of certain Western mores: kissing in public, radical countercultures (the Hippies in Dev Anand's *Hare Rama Hare Krishna*, 1971, or *Purab Aur Paschim*), and miscegenation. From the 1990s onwards, the density and scale of such engagements assume a different dimension which makes imagining "India" as a portable state of mind a much more complex business. The "Tumse jo Kahungi" ("If I Ask You") sequence in Dev Anand's *Pyar Ka Taraana* (*The Melody of Love*) (1993) involves a stock scene in which the boy asks the girl for a kiss, which she of course refuses, despite the fact that they are cavorting in the sea in skimpy clothing. What makes this exhibition of Indian cultural discipline and sexual propriety appear much more elemental in contrast to the backdrops formed by European kissing couples in *Sangam* or *An Evening in Paris* is that it takes place on a beach in Denmark peopled with sunbathing, topless white women. Both India and the world thus enter into a general assembling stance of spectacular up-grading by which polarities between ethics and temptations become pronounced on the one hand, and the semiotic passages between the self and the other assume a critical mass and kinesis on the other. Existential and affective relationships between the land and overseas thus do not remain limited to fixated notions of *habitus* and exile, between self-definition and an anthropological-moral distinction and exclusion of the other, but the home often becomes an airy, spiritual investiture that can affectively sacralize the world elsewhere in an instant. Moreover, the cinematic picture of the home itself can bravely incorporate planetary tenacities. This is not to say that the distinction between India and the world ceases to exist, but that both irresistibly enter a metropolitan framework of cognizing space in terms of value, spectacle, way of life, and terror. The foreign city remains a domain of vice, dangerous appetites, crime, and moral relativism in which the Hindu wife can disappear into thin air, as occurs in *Prithvi* (*Earth*) (Nitin Manmohan, 1997), or scions of Indian/Hindu families can grow up to be materially greedy, spiritually impoverished sexual predators in *Aa Ab Laut Chalein* (*Let's Go Back*) (Rishi Kapoor, 2001) and *Pardes* (*Foreign Land*) (Subhash Ghai, 1997). The world at large undeniably continues to threaten the geographical nation with drugs, immorality, and terror. And yet, the heart of the nation increasingly can no longer be figured as a pastoral repose of the native spirit, one that is ascetic and devoid of materialist concerns. Compared to the films of the past, the home has to acquire a certain worldliness in order to present itself as a ceremonial/symbolic site of being in changing times. In a new dispensation of the image as a direct expression of value, the home has to acquire a cinematic plenitude of colors, textures, bodies, and objects in order to upgrade its affective strengths and emerge as an exemplary exhibit of a national-cultural heritage. That is, if we were to invert the classic Heideggerian formulation in an age in which a boundless and kinetic sea of information envelops and impinges upon the local, it is the "home picture" that becomes a matter of cardinal importance in an overall task of continuously defining the *Volk*.[58] The home can thus be "conceived and grasped as picture" only when the concept of the *Volk* and the landscape as the seat of natality undergo a necessary process of dynamic abstraction in order to meet, through relational engagements, the irresistible nomadism of our time.

I am attributing this transposed Heideggerian perspective to an "Indian" subject that has supposedly emerged at the turn of the new millennium: technologically savvy, quintessentially urban, committed to neo-liberal free market economics, yet rooted in "tradition" and fully equipped to keep India "shining." Heidegger marks the birth of the European *anthropos* in an age of modernist secularization of the Christian perspective in the twilight of the gods. The relationship with the heavens was thus transformed into mere religious experience that awaited no revelation, while the ontological void centering on being/nothingness was sought to be plugged by historiographical and psychological examinations of myth,[59] that is, one might say, largely by archaeologies and investigations of the founding myths of the nation. In contrast, our "postmodern" time comes with the strong suspicion that this sovereign human subject has entered into a state of irreparable obsolescence. Keeping that in mind, and also the usual attributes assigned to the state of postmodernity (fragmentation, the end of grand narratives, retro mode, or pastiche),[60] let us try to critically align Heidegger's formulations to the Indian situation we are studying. That is, instead of transposing them punctually, the effort will be to bring them into a state of critical adjacency, holding them as pertinent to the Indian milieu only as much as overall discourse worlds of liberal humanism and political modernity are. In doing so, I am mindful that the situation Heidegger was philosophizing was also occasioned by a new age of the geo-televisual. That is, he was locating his observations in a world marked by technological communications (he mentions the erasure of distance with the advent of air travel and radio), shrinking spaces, and collapsing skies.

Unlike Heidegger's Christian universe, various efforts toward an historical consolidation of a Hindu-normative Indian modernity was dependent not so much on secularization in a broad liberal sense, but on giving a monotheistic form to religious experience in itself. In other words, it involved the assimilation of a host of gods and innumerous lines of devotion into a single edifice of faith that could then be parlayed to the nation itself as axiomatic form. Instead of *Weltbild*, what this process tendentially yields is an "Indian picture" and a concomitant and singular "Indian" point of view. I have written elsewhere in greater detail about how this task of drawing out a discursive imaginary of the nation from a monotheistic religiosity began in the late nineteenth century.[61] It followed, to a considerable extent, an established format of securing a literary modernity for the nation. However, as it has been widely diagnosed, this process was largely incomplete, or has been perpetually gestating. It is my contention that from the 1990s onwards, the ontological question between being and nothingness, or between the earth and the sky, was to a large extent *informatized*, along with the postulates of national history or national mythography. In fact, it became increasingly difficult to distinguish between history and myth in this new realm of publicity. Being and subjectivity could be emphatically equated and advertised, without any need for them to be connected by way of narrative, history, or constitution. It is this scenario that I call a state of informatic modernization without claiming for it any kind of total explanatory power. However, once this impulse made its presence felt powerfully alongside older, already existing pastoral and disciplinary forms of *Hindutva*, the nationalist anthropology which we talked about in the previous section assumed a new form which, transposing from Heidegger, would be that interpretation of the world by the "Indian" who, more rigorously than ever, "already knows fundamentally what [Indian] is and hence cannot ask what he may be."[62]

The home and the world are thus products of an informatic assembling that merges floating signs of the former with the latter, perhaps much in alignment with, but in a manner more dynamic than, a paradoxical anthropology of the modern that seeks to pass from the merely national to a universal point of view. The result is a world picture that immediately and indistinguishably foregrounds the centripetal, expansive energies of the picture-of-the-nation within it. The cinematic texturing of the home therefore freely incorporates the manifold colors, exotica, spaces, and geometries of the world at large, often threatening to engulf the latter. Consider the model Hindu *Gurukul* (traditional school) in Aditya Chopra's *Mohabbatein* (*Love Stories*) (2000). This cinematic formation, which combines the monastic discipline of the idealized ashram with curricular protocols of British public school education, is a compact of multi-directional memories, aspirations, and tactile allures of space. The *Gurukul* is an abode of right knowledge which is not only good for India, but also best for the world. It apparently produces not just exemplary national citizens, but also the best productive specimens of men for humanity in general. In Chopra's film, the cinematic consolidation of this symbolic entity takes place by merging studio space with locations in England (Oxford and Longleat, in Wiltshire). This phenomenon of freely merging textures of the home and the world is part of an overall cinematic-spectacular style largely identified with the veteran filmmaker Yash Chopra. It has been seen not just in Yashraj blockbusters, but also in derivative and innovated forms in the outputs of houses like Dharma Productions and in the work of significant directors like Sooraj Barjatiya, Subhash Ghai, Karan Johar, and Sanjay Leela Bansali. The utopian, neo-traditional world in Barjatiya's *Hum Aapke Hain Kaun* (*Yours Forever!*) (1994) is a sumptuous mansion called Prem Niwas (The Abode of Love). This delirious image of a perfect north Indian extended family interiority is an assemblage of many things near and far: a horde of Disney characters, a group of uniformed cheerleaders for in-house cricket matches, Cola culture, chocolates, a billiards table, swimming pool, Art Deco, a plethora of gadgets, and a nursery stacked with imported toys. It includes a language environment that neatly formalizes and partitions Urdu from a highly Sanskritized Hindi that comes to occupy daily life. The former is decoratively presented through the comical *shairi* (poetry) of the stock Muslim character, while the latter takes over the ceremonial space so completely that even a group photograph is called *samyukh chitra*. The young hero Prem's room is adorned with graffiti which presents neo-conservative slogans ("I love my family") in radical 1960s-style *écriture*.

This particular scene of reassembled interiority in the wake of globalization has been repeatedly presented, continuously upgraded, and made even more sumptuous in a long series of films from the mid-1990s onwards, especially in the sub-genre known as the "marriage melodrama." Sometimes this template yields breathtakingly hyperbolic ways of organizing spaces and objects and enframing them into a comprehensive aura of homeliness. The Oberoi farmhouse in David Dhawan's *Chal Mere Bhai* (*Let's Go Brother*) is a composite visual world set in the imaginary outskirts of Mumbai, which invites bodies from the professional world (employees of the Oberoi industries) to be literally a part of the Oberoi "family." The cinematic "mansion" merges business and leisure, medical supervision and holiday time, romance and secretarial work, bossing and bride hunting, under the auspices of a particularly heightened cinematic style of ordering energies and movements, and collapsing studio space with locations both domestic and foreign. The Oberoi farm as assemblage harbors no categorical distinctions between the inside and outside. A shot of the swimming pool premises of the farm house, despite the strategic use of the telephoto lens, would lead one to believe that the private vacation house has its own Domino's Pizza outlet. In another sequence, Prem Oberoi, the younger scion of the clan, drives away from the premises in a swanky convertible. The car, as it might be guessed, travels down a road bordered by lush pastures, and finally comes to a halt in a European landscape.

Ranjini Mazumdar has brilliantly theorized these "panoramic interiors," as have scholars like Rustom Bharucha, Rachel Dwyer, and Patricia Uberoi.[63] Sudhanva Deshpande has pointed out that the turban-wearing ritual in a film like *Dhai Akshar Prem Ke* (*A Little Knowledge about Love*) (Raj Kanwar, 2000) is one among many such instances of an overall new age cinematic fabrication of "tradition" with fresh textures and ceremonies.[64] No such ceremony exists in North India. I shall conclude this part of the discussion by adding a few observations to this already impressive volume of critical commentary on the new "home." First, let me elaborate a point made earlier: that there is increasingly no ontological unrest between predicates of high capital, technologism, commodity culture, and tradition. In contrast to the dialectics between "capitalist modernization" and "feudal family and moral values," which Rajadhyaksha and Willemen correctly discern in Mehboob Khan's *Andaaz* (*Style*) (1949), in the current dispensation we have an informative or purely decorative equivalence between the two. In Khan's film, the trial of the female lead, the murderess Neeta, underlines the moral of the story: "all the mayhem is Neeta's fault for not having listened to her father when he warned her to avoid 'modern' ways."[65] The specter of modernity here—one that imperils the figure of the woman—includes Western clothes, horse-riding, tennis, parties, balls, male friends, and even the business empire that Neeta inherits from her father, Sir Badriprasad. It is therefore not just certain events and choices, but an entire mise-en-scène of the modern that is condemned. It has been widely noted that this moral discomfort with the propelling impulses of capital, like possessive individualism and the continual extension of markets, animate many classic melodramas of the post-Independence decades. In B. R. Chopra's *Naya Daur* (*The New Age*) (1957), it takes the form of a duel between a bus and a horse-drawn carriage. In Hrishikesh Mukherjee's *Anari* (*The Novice*) (1959) corporate greed results in adulterated medicine that not only kills innocents, but threatens to sever the relationship between brother and sister. In *Paigham* (*The Message*) (S. S. Vasan) and *Akashdeep* (Phani Majumdar, 1965) the tension between automation and living, human labor threatens to alienate brothers and, in a symbolic extension, tear the fabric of society itself.

Conversely, in the "marriage melodramas" of the 1990s a cinematic neo-tradition can only be exhibited once it assembles with a venerable "richness" (rather than ceremonial or symbolic "grandeur") of the times. This utopian ecology of commodity affects serves as a temporal and spatial cocoon for the anachronistic extended family, splendidly isolating it not only from the atomizing modes of contemporary urban life, but also from aspects of political economy and the profane money markets of the city. Yet this Brahminical interiority can apparently sacralize and be at ease with random geo-televisual matters only when a crucial condition is fulfilled. In the Epilogue to this book I shall discuss how these "non-protectionist" exchanges between the interiority of the home and an alluring global marketplace can be sustained only when there is an almost complete exclusion of finance capital from the assembling picture. The clutter of profane objects in the mise-en-scène can perhaps only then be instantly sacralized by certain axiomatic ceremonies of cinematic melodrama. This occurs when there is a dramatic rise of select signs from an otherwise awry field of horizontal contaminations and mergers; that is, when certain special aural and visual entities are allowed to emerge from the everyday of commodities and conspicuous consumption and immediately be invested with the iconic values. In fact, it is in these supine moments that "tradition" becomes figurable in itself, as a luminous, distinguishing feature of a singular Indian spiritualism amidst the clamor of the world market. The Disneyfied "Sunshine" summer camp in Karan Johar's *Kuch Kuch Hota Hai* is ontologically transformed when the British Union flag is lowered and the Indian flag is raised, and the portrait of Queen Victoria replaced with that of the goddess Durga. The environment is further transformed

2.4: Tradition as richness in *Kabhi Khushi Kabhi Gham.*

by the introduction of a pure ecology of sound which envelops all entities, both homely and alien, with the chorus of a remixed version of
the famous devotional song "Raghupati Raghav Raja Ram." An acute
focalization of affect engenders a panoptic point of view of tradition, from
where the manifold wonders of the world (the mise-en-scène of the film
is thickly saturated with brand placements), can be surveyed, sacralized,
condemned, taken in correct measure, or spiritually claimed. In Johar's
next film, *Kabhi Khushi Kabhi Gham*, the axiomatic extraction of a traditional point-of-view assumes truly breathtaking dimensions. When Rohan
Jaichand's (the young hero) plane begins to approach London, a montage
of aerial shots of city landmarks (London Bridge, Big Ben, the Houses of
Parliament) and snapshots of major outlets (Starbucks, Dolce Gabana,
Georgio Armani) are informed by an all-consuming sound ecology of
India's national song "Vande Mataram" ("Hail to the Mother"). We then
see Rohan pirouetting along Piccadilly Circus, with the famous urban
space itself transformed into a utopian site for the stage musical. First, he
dances with a group of Indian *Bharat Natyam* dancers in traditional attire.
Then, he sashays with a line of Western women wearing evening gowns;
and finally, cavorts with another line of Anglo-Saxon women in Indian
clothes.

Without a doubt this sequence has several layers of irony and ambiguity. *Vande Mataram* was part of Bankim Chandra Chattopadhyay's landmark Hindu nationalist novel *Anandamath* (1882). It found its first public

2.5: Outskirts of the family mansion in *Kabhi Khushi Kabhi Gham*. Rahul Jaichand returns home by helicopter.

2.6: *Vande Mataram* in *Kabhi Khushi Kabhi Gham*.

and political rendition in the 1896 session of the Indian National Congress in Calcutta and was later adopted as the national anthem of the Republic of India. In this sequence, therefore, many contrapuntal propositions and emotives are chimed together and drowned in one affective movement of cinema. One of these could be a simple question: how can the song dedicated to a singular mother, who is the seat of natality itself, be rendered in reference to an alien space? Another could perhaps pertain to a fantastic subjective "murmur"—the glimmerings of a post-historical memory: that the mother has finally given birth to a generation of sons to claim the metropole as their own.

Figures

In the films of the 1990s and after, the awry, global network of signs, stigmas, and wonders is allowed to *affectively* (and not just dialectically) converge with the previously absolutist feudal hierarchies and proprietorships of the "home." It is as if the pieties themselves must be affirmed and distinguished by freely colliding them with what used to be profane or unthinkable. This takes many forms and involves diverse splits and assemblings between lines of memory, fantasy, desire, and duty. In the light of what I said about fear of interracial relationships in the classical Hindi film, consider the transnational "Bollywood" upgrading of the often repeated set pieces that recreate the Puranic myth of Krishna, the amorous goatherd god of the Vrindavanas, cavorting with a bevy of *gopinis*.[66] The Hindi film hero has always been seen singing and dancing with the heroine and her female friends, or amidst a mise-en-scène randomly animated by female figures in the background. It is a setpiece that has traditionally assembled affects of devotion (*bhakti*) with amour, providing a carnivalesque, yet formalized conduit for the otherwise forbidden expression of sexual desire taken in a secular sense. The hero thereby assumes the mantle of Krishna, while the heroine, ironically, is made to approximate the figure of the married Radha, who is the object of the god's adulterous adventures. The errant energies of these segments—the frequently ambiguous relationships they establish between desiring bodies and institutions pertaining to family, community, and law—demand a separate analysis that is beyond the scope of this chapter. The point, however, is that in recent popular Hindi films like *Jansheen* (Feroz Khan, 2003, in the "Marhaba Marhaba" sequence) or *Jab Pyar Kissise Hota Hain* (*When One Falls in Love*) (Deepak Sareen, 1998, in the title song sequence), transnational women, covering a remarkable racial spectrum, replace the earthy *gopinis*. The erstwhile bucolic space is also virtualized and assembled with touristic and consumerist trappings.

Let us turn to what is, at face value, a much more sensational assemblage. In Karan Johar's *Kuch Kuch Hota Hain* (*Something is Happening*) (1998) the hero describes his widowed mother as "sexy" to his eight-year-old daughter. Later in the film, he wonders why the exasperated eight year old tells him that she cannot be a "wife" to him. The point, however, in these cases, is to precisely unleash a "cool" ecology of the purely associational, by which categories are uprooted from what used to be governing narratives of the self and other. The whole point of chiming the signifier "sexy" against the venerated figure of the mother is to drain it of its profane significations. When it is committed to the powerful ontology of the mother as icon, "sexy" is absolved of any other gravitation of meaning. It becomes a purely decorative signifier that, along with other such ritualistic and cool transpositions of language, underlines the fact that the mother is sexy precisely because there is no sexual relation.

Let us turn to Madhava Prasad's brilliant work on the absence of the screen kiss in commercial Hindi film in order to probe a little further this undeniably curious proposition: the sexy mother. Under the auspices of this new "globalizing" Hindi cinematic style, why does it not come across as scandalous? What exactly do we mean when we say that the mother can be "sexy" precisely because there is no "sex" as such? The culturalist proscription of the kiss in Hindi films, according to Prasad, amounts to a foreclosure of the private that is dictated by a psychoanalytic assertion of the feudal, that "there is no sexual relation."[67] The ban on depictions of sex amounts to the denial of an intimate zone of nuclear conjugality and, by extension, the prohibition of a modern notion of cinema itself, as an expressive form that has the individual and individuated desires at the heart of its operations. Prasad locates the problem in the realm of psychoanalysis; I will transpose it to a consideration of a regime of discourse that matches visibilities with articulatable statements. In line with a dominant, tendentially despotic Brahminical monitoring of culture, what is forfeited is the picture of the sexual relation as a symbiotic and equitable exchange of pleasure between consenting adults. Women can certainly be taken licitly or illicitly; they can be loved or raped, exchanged between males, impregnated, or exhibited publicly. But what can never be admitted is a social acknowledgment of the feminine body as being capable of partaking in the patriarchal monopoly of sexual pleasure. In other words, what is proscribed is female sexiness as an active principle: the image of a woman craving sexual satisfaction. Women can therefore always be objects of desire, but it is the picture of the desiring woman that must be banned. Under the auspices of this discursive regime, motherhood is the ultimate expression of a certain fecund principle of the feminine. She is the conduit for patriarchal lineage, she is the immaculate origin of life, and thus transcends the realm of appetites. The mother can therefore be envisioned only when one has already left the flesh behind; her iconicity is a pure iconicity of surfaces without subjective depth—that is, a depth that can harbor lurking demons of the oedipal kind. Since the classic Hindi film mother, in an absolute sense, can have only duty toward a composite patriarchy of the extended family or clan and not individuated longing (not even toward the father), the modern oedipal diagram of subjectivity and the triangulated Freudian psychodrama of desire is marginalized.[68] The private does not exist because there can be no sexual desire on the part of the woman to hide. The mother is eternal because her past is entirely of glorious and fecund procreation of the self as well as its meaning. It does not contain the equivalent of male carnal appetite, which can be given the name of desire.

This severe feudal proscription of the private has been challenged on many fronts in the new order geo-televisual universe we have been examining. The kiss has returned and relatively complex images of a new age urban private conjugality have irresistibly entered the Indian cinematic realm. The "traditional" Indian family home, despite its continual axiomatic status, perhaps most powerfully sustained by what we have called the "Yashraj template," has been besieged by diverse geo-televisual signatures of identity and desire from the world at large. This shifting scenario after 2004 will be briefly visited in the Epilogue. For now, I shall end this part of the discussion with a few observations. First, what can no longer be denied is the coming into being of a hermeneutic of suspicion to mediate between the home and the world. Issues of identity, propriety, or law can no longer be settled by the despotic feudal-Brahminical statement (homosexuality, categorically speaking, is a perversion imported from the West). In his reading of Raj Kapoor's *Sangam*, Prasad correctly diagnoses a principled "blindness" and "deafness" that marks the feudal patriarchal order.[69] When the father chooses neither to hear nor see the "depths" of individual desire, he forecloses it from the interiority of the home and the auspices of the community in a total sense. Power, in the Nehruvian feudal-bourgeois order was thereby exercised through the monopoly of name-giving powers and the practice of absolutist non-recognition. Increasingly, however, this is not what has been happening in the dispensation that has succeeded it. The celebration of a neo-traditional "Indianness" has not been based on a stringent refusal to name or acknowledge the geo-televisual elephant in the room. Instead, the trial seems to lie in wading through a sea of globalized pluralities, often through complex modes of erotics, pathology, and laughter, and somehow advertising a true self at the end. The principal difference is that this process of balancing the transforming old sacred with the new profane is inevitably accompanied by a hermeneutic of suspicion. If the latter is indeed acknowledged and admitted as a disenchanting modern sensibility, it is often subsequently displaced. That is, the anxiety of suspicion is introduced and then sidelined. Consider the maid Kantabai in Nikhil Advani's *Kal Ho Na Ho*. In this film two yuppie NRI men start living in the same New York apartment and even share a bed. The friendship follows a time-tested tradition of robust *dosti*, *yaari*, or *dostana* between Hindi cinema males, one that, according to Priya Jha, reinforces a mythic, masculinist vision of the national community.[70] As it happens in Advani's film, the woman (in this case the heroine, Naina) can only feature as a gift of exchange within a fraternal arrangement. However, unlike many such situations of the past, as in *Sangam* or *Naya Daur*, this male–male *dosti* is scrutinized with suspicion. The bearer of this penetrating gaze is the old maid, Kanta Bai, who is scandalized by the physical proximity of the two men. And yet, the point of hilarity is precisely her "double blindness," as it were, by which she mistakes a mirage for a mirror in relation to a masculinist bond between Indian males. Kantabai suspects that there is a hidden depth to *dosti*, an interiority of the private between the sheets, when in fact the absolute, timeless rules of the virtual community that bind the two yuppies in metrosexual New York dictate that there can be no such depths; there can be no sexual relation at all. We see the same hermeneutic of suspicion in the worried uncle's queries about his nephew's refusal to get married in Rohan Sippy's *Kuch Na Kaho* (2003). In Apoorva Lakhiya's *Mumbai Se Aya Mera Dost* (*My Friend Has Come from Mumbai*) (2003), the suspicion takes the form of a visual joke, when the servant boy kneels to tie the master's pajama strings and is seen by a scandalized relative from a particularly misleading angle. In the recent Tarun Mansukhani film *Dostana* (*Friendship*) (2008), two yuppie heroes (living in Miami this time) pretend to be gay partners in order to be able to rent an apartment and be close to the heroine, who is their mutual object of desire. The Punjabi mother of Sameer, one of the two young men, is devastated when she hears about his sexual preferences. In what is supposed to be one of the comic centerpieces of the film, she bites the bullet and wistfully conducts the traditional welcoming ceremony for her son's male "bride," Kunal.

The homosexual as an instance of the geo-televisual thus has to be absorbed and divested of its queering energies. It has to be inducted into the picture of a global urbanity as a decorative inscription of contemporary metropolitan identities and fashionable "vices." In the current dispensation of publicity, it presents an assembling imperative that can no longer be ignored. The homosexual is thus differentially jettisoned or excluded from the picture of the home by passing the figure through newer, more complex movements of pleasure, abomination, masquerade, and comic effect. Tradition can therefore no longer be fielded in isolation; it has to enter the same field of convertibility and overwriting along with the profane before it can be extracted through various modes of stylistic flippancy. The homosexual has to be epistemologically admitted before *dosti* can be distinguished from it as an essentially vernacular trope. This involves acts of controlled parlaying of queer energies into secondary characters (in Parvati Balagopalan's 2003 film *Rules: Pyar Ka Superhit*

Formula [*The Superhit Rules of Love*], for example), comic eccentrics (uncle 'Vicky' Nath in *Dulhan Hum Le Jayenge* [*I Will Take the Bride*]), child abusers (*Andha Yudh* [*Blind War*], Dayal Nihalani, 1987), or pathological villains (*Mast Kalander*, Rahul Rawail, 1991). On a more complex level, the rigorous, sacral extraction of *dosti* from an animated ecology of irresistible associations and suspicions call for a more complex worlding of "tradition" in the realm of language. This final extraction demands that a metropolitan vocabulary of identity, rights, and liberalism be allowed to negotiate, or even invade, the absolute despotic statement (true Indians can never be homosexuals) before the same vocabulary can be vernacularized and removed from the sphere of the sacred in the very act of such an assembling.

But what happens when the whole thing is no marginal matter and not only is there substance behind suspicion, but the specter of homosexuality threatens to intrude the inner sanctity of the home itself? Let us consider an example to see how the homosexual (in this case a lesbian) can be contained and jettisoned precisely through a cinematic assembling with it. In this case it happens through yet another instance of what we discussed in the previous chapter as the "alcohol assemblage." Karan Razdan's 2004 film *Girlfriend* was a sensationalist thriller that (wrongly) claimed to introduce the difficult topic of lesbianism to Hindi cinema.[71] Panned by the Hindu Right as well as feminist groups (for altogether different reasons), the film depicts a triangulation of desire between two women and a man. Sapna and Tanya are best of friends who share a house in Mumbai. Gradually it becomes clear that Tanya harbors an "unhealthy" fixation for Sapna which transcends Platonic limits. The former's "abnormalcy" is explained in this highly regressive film as the outcome of child abuse and dereliction of parental responsibility. Psycho-biography here is therefore a pathological-moral assemblage. Meanwhile, Sapna falls in love with a man named Rahul and unwittingly catalyzes a schizoid transformation in the obsessive Tanya. The rest of the film closely approximates conservative Hollywood moral fables on white middle-class sexuality like *Fatal Attraction*, *Single White Female*, or *Basic Instinct*. Most scenes of Sapphic passion in the film are either assemblages of dreams (from Tanya's point of view) or nightmares (from Rahul's perspective). However, there is one "real" event of female–female sex in the film, which is depicted as the result of a total but temporary alcoholic deterritorialization of Sapna's heterosexual self. She sleeps with Tanya after getting blind drunk. Apart from providing a ruse to explain Sapna's unnatural behavior, what alcohol does, within the melodramatic parameters of the film, is to strip the scenes of intimacy of all signs of pleasure that could later be referred back as endemic parts of the good woman's being. Sapna thus wakens from her stupor as an absolutely reconstituted heterosexual entity with no memory of enjoyment. It was thus only the body that partook in perverse pleasure and the body is seen to have neither remembrance nor desire. After the alcoholic interlude, it returns to the prison of the mind and soul, and is thus once again under the wholesome command of what the soul and mind determine to be the only principled hermeneutics of conjugality and desire for the Hindu/Indian woman.

Informatic Modernization

It is against this backdrop of aggravated geo-televisual excursions in cinema that I will now speculate on an "informatic" feature of a core, majoritarian Hinduism of the urban kind. This feature is not so much an outcome of a final resolution to agonistic battles; rather, it has to do with an *advertised* modernization that attempts to bypass historical disputes or dissipate them into fungible, rootless parcels of signification that can be neutralized in assembling with other signs. This new, publicized Hinduness does not pertain to orders, spaces, genres, and enclosures of modern knowledge, but to a diffuse though kinetic ecology of sights and sounds. With the coming into being of this latter dispensation, a more historical ideology, hitherto languishing in some agrarian feudal cow belts of north India and mid-caste, middle-class townships, entered the very heart of metropolitan publicity with terrifying gusto. That is, I am arguing that perhaps it is an urban ecology of informational Hinduness—one that is multidirectional and awry, one that works in volumes and quick saturations of significant space rather than directions, lineages, and closures—that creates a new age baseline of national being, roughly from the mid-1990s onwards. Unlike more mordant forms of Hindu nationalism of the past, this ecology has, with its supple constituents, managed to inflect mass responses to transformative matters like globalization, technology, and consumerism, and to emergencies like terrorism and war with Pakistan. More than that, it aspires to merge readily with Left-liberal concerns and missions, like vegetarianism, animal rights, or environmentalism. In contrast to the sometimes cautious, sometimes weary non-aligned mores of the past, this Hinduness has fused, in a non-obligatory manner, with mammoth and alien techno-financial engines of neo-liberalism, all the while retaining elastic powers to assert spectacularly a core distinguishing identity that is eternal. In doing so, and insisting on the latter amidst the rumble of change, this aspect of the urban Hindu—everyday, at home in the world, wedded to tradition, yet globally aspiring—seems to assume its proper sovereign form. That is because it tends, much like Guy Debord's Napoleonic figure, to monarchically direct "the energy of memories"[72] precisely at a moment when acts of remembrance and contemplation have been overwhelmed by data flows, and the grounds of communitarian belonging have been muddled. It is undeniable that older, axiomatic forms of *Hindutva* ideology and its derivatives have existed powerfully through the 1990s and have defined the political scenario by way of parliamentary mobilizations and murderous acts of cleansing. However, I am wagering that such instances can be better understood by examining their relations of contiguity with an overall fixture of informatic modernization. Such considerations of contiguity or critical adjacency enable us to view matters in terms of lines of energy, osmotic passages of affect rather than broad ideological recruitments. Despite the fact that dogma exists in perhaps more deadly forms, what is even more important is an environment of murmur—along with its regularities, habitual resonances, and terms of endearment or abomination—that precedes, envelops, and follows events of insurrection. Amit Rai has recently theorized this massified media ecology in terms of an overall machinic phylum of discourse, information, and affect.[73] It is a general sensorium of urbanity (with resident realities as well as torrid virtualities) that comes *before* the city's continual orderings into organic templates of the body politic, or psycho-political dramas of ideological interpellations. An individual can liberally have Muslim or *dalit* friends and at the same time be influenced by massified affects that pathologize Pakistan, pronounce Islam as endemically committed to terror, or adjudge caste reservations as debilitating to a spectral horizon of meritorious development of the nation. The idea of contiguity rather than positive logical purchase therefore allows us to understand, within a kinetic informational realm, the pronounced affective power of incommensurabilities, that is, when incommensurabilities have affective power precisely because and not despite the fact that they are incommensurable. The power of informatic modernization lies precisely in the fact that it seeks to reorder memory by cosmetically and spectacularly filling lacunae in tortured historical narratives.

This informatic-modernizing template of urban Hinduness needs to be studied even more across the disciplines and in many spheres (television, advertising, fashion, consumerism, news, opinion columns, journalism, festivals, fusion music, web culture). This project restricts it to cinema in a belated sense, when cinema in its classical incarnation can be seen to be moribund or heavily circumscribed in its vital socio-political functions. The cinema—or rather, the instances of a new "cinematic" —we have examined presumes an extended media atmosphere of which it is already a part. Cinema therefore contemplates its own death from the beginning of this period, assuming a spectral and airy form of the afterlife it is to lead in an ecology of dispersals. Rai has rightly pointed out that we can speak of "Bollywood" only after acknowledging that cinema has ended (*Untimely Bollywood*, 2). With these caveats, let us now embark on a theory of information as a diagram of power in our time and then probe the substance of what we have hypothesized as an Indian situation of informatic modernization.

The Information-City

Information, in Walter Benjamin's words, is precisely that which is "already shot through with explanation."[74] It is that process of circulation by which signs can be uprooted from any source of "authentic belongings" or "organic filiations" and rapidly dispersed as fungible and mobile pulses of perceptions, know-how, affects, allures, gnosis, beliefs, memories, and reportage on a global scale. Information is different from knowledge[75] precisely because while the latter consolidates truths through an agonistic navigation of difference or a dialectical resolution of problems (what Benjamin calls "explanation"), the former only scatters and makes kinetic renderings in varying densities, without any obligation to "totality." While knowledge, as a classic postulate of modernity, is always belated, the objective of information is to effect a social circulation of facts and variables in the least time possible. Knowledge is enunciated; it unfolds in historical time, in accordance with procedures of cause and effect, logical consistency, and the limits of reason. Information, like capital itself, tends to curtail the period of circulation. Unlike knowledge, information has no aspirations toward "wholes," like a unified worldview or an august compendium of values. The key thing about information flow is the abridged temporality of "surfing" it automatically demands—an instantaneity of connect and the readiness of disposal. What is crucial here is that it calls for the curtailing of intervals for contemplation, imaginative functions, reasoning, and remembrance. In Hegelian phenomenology, for instance, the proper tempering of sense certainty begins with a dispelling of immediacy. Both "I" and the "thing" are mediated presences in this relation. When knowledge arrives, the "now" is already rendered "has been," which is precisely why, according to Hegel, we are latecomers to modernity in general. It is through a dialectical process of determination and negation that consciousness accepts *responsibility* for the object as ONE.[76] This then becomes a notion through force and understanding, and finally a concept through the exercise of reason. One can understand why this model of subjective being in the world would be imperiled in an over-whelming environment of immediacy and redoubt that information spells.

Understanding information as a regime of power has nothing to do with paranoid suspicions about the use and abuse of media. One can readily acknowledge that information is not necessarily evil; it is also a revolu-tionary force that dispels hegemonic pieties and energizes social forma-tions. Information as such is an ecology that envelops city life itself. This ecology is not new, but perhaps we can all agree that it has grown critically elemental and noisy in recent decades. A dispensation of power becomes "informatic" when the speed and density of interaction—between knowl-edge worlds, founding ideas, institutions, dogmas, sciences, the dialects of common sense and social practices—become forceful enough not just to enable mergers, but to define the very rules of engagement. Hence, it is not this conspiring television channel or that ideologically motivated film that we are talking about, but a certain dynamic format of devel-opmentalist urbanity itself, one that involves disparate phenomena, big and small, like share markets, impulse-buying, and the instantaneous generation of terror and consensus. Paul Virilio, using a characteristic phenomenological hyperbole, has called information the fourth dimen-sion of matter.[77] But that is to accord it a directionality and precision like that of the projectile or the bomb. Instances of information, on the other hand, could be gestures that draw their power from many sources, from affirmations, opportune shifts, as well as negations. When Murali Manohar Joshi, the former Union Science and Technology Minister in the BJP government, made a public statement in the summer of 2001 about the apparent discovery of a 9,000-year-old "Saraswati" civilization off the Gulf of Cambay, he was challenged by the scientific community, particularly by marine archeologists.[78] Recently, former US Republican presidential candidate John McCain said that he would always prefer a Christian president for his country rather than a Muslim one.[79] His state-ment was attacked by both Muslim and liberal groups, and, predictably enough, withdrawn by McCain himself. However, perhaps we can ask whether these overtures—asserted, challenged, shifted, withdrawn—increasingly operate in global societies as pure advertised moments, as non-directional energies with a critical degree of freedom from regimes of truth and modes of historical narration. They are simply "take-aways" in an already distributed realm of memory. Their recall values, while foun-dationally questioned by science or liberal constitutionalism, have already been drawn from overall, looming environments of Hindu civilization or the Christian nation. In an informational world messages are never sent; only signals are transmitted.[80]

Under the auspices of an informatic modernization, the consolidation of a modern ethos, let us say a Hegelian modernity, as a necessary stage in history, can be bypassed or leapfrogged (in management speak) in pathways of developmental transformation. This is particularly true in the vast realm of informal negotiations in the world that Partha Chatterjee has called the zone of political societies.[81] Such formations can increasingly have technology without the holistic domain of "science," formalities of a democratic polity without liberalism. Rapid development, freeing of markets, can be accompanied by the rise of dogmatic fundamentalism. Denizens can readily adopt linguistic functionalities and procedural skills without what has been called a subjectivity of reason. They can have information without "knowledge," a highly energized affective universe without a civil society. The current Indian dispensation of cinema information in the city must be considered in that light.

Benjamin, as we know, compared the "tactile" and "distracted" reception of cinema to that of architecture. His analogy connects a mass habituation to cinema to a diurnal appreciation of buildings that takes place through use and perception, by touch as well as by sight. According to Benjamin, cinema, with its "shock" effects, seems to meet a similar "aperceptive," distracted mode of reception "halfway."[82] The great German thinker thus justifiably finds it impossible to theorize the phenomenon of cinema without a novel cartography of the industrial city itself which brings with it newer forms of massified habituation. In doing so, Benjamin enters an avenue of thinking about the city (evident in his other seminal works) that has attracted the attention of many significant twentieth-century scholars, from Henri Lefebvre and Pierre Bourdieu to David Harvey and Michel de Certeau. In an early, particularly memorable meditation, Georges Simmel speculates in "Metropolis and Mental Life" (1905) on how the individual can preserve his autonomous integrity of faculties against "the sovereign powers of society" and the "external culture and technique of life," that mark a new urban existence. This dispensation is characterized by "the intensification of emotional life due to the swift and continuous shift of external and internal stimuli" (324–5). What it disrupts is the "the steady equilibrium of unbroken customs" in small town and rural life. It is to manage this continuous flow of stimuli that Simmel suggests that denizens deliberately or unconsciously cultivate a blasé outlook by which "the meaning and the value of the distinction between things, and therewith of the things themselves, are experienced as meaningless" (330). This blasé outlook is a kindred spirit to a post-contemplative mode of habituation diagnosed by Benjamin in his essay "The Work of Art in the Age of Mechanical Reproduction" (1973).

What is immediately apparent is that both Simmel and Benjamin, working in a protracted twilight of humanism, are already pointing to a regime of energy dispensation and absorption that gives birth not just to new forms of consciousness, but also to new bodies. This regime opens a realm of immanently dynamic, affective commerce that challenges the integrity and constitution of the subject conceived classically. The awry shocks of Benjamin's Parisian traffic or the regulated temporalities of the Fordian conveyor belt have not disappeared in a so-called global "post-industrial"[83] order of things. It is indeed possible to understand a process of virtualization and informatizing, of financialization, service sector and supply-side economics without taking part (especially in relation to third world scenarios) in hyperbolic conceptions of a global "one-time-system."[84] Since we are trying to understand cinema and information as inextricably linked to the city, it is necessary first to establish a distinction between the metropolis in the modern sense, as Simmel uses it, and the metropolis in the contemporary sense we intend to promote, as a web of powerful virtualizations and ethereal energies that are redrawing historical spaces, circuits of production and circulation, resident hierarchies, and identities. We therefore intend to study the information–city couple not in isolation, but as a direct expression of the planetary command of finance capital.

I speak of a metropolitan diagram of finance and information that envelops the city with airy but corrosive forces of alteration. The cartography of the historical Bombay is still marked by some of the largest shanty towns in the world, the underworld, massive street dwelling, or the ghostly textile mills that remind us of the bloody conflict that closed them. The "metropolis," on the other hand, is an abstract diagram of an urban value system that informs the city, recasting the latter as a center for transnational managerial, technocratic, and military governance. It is thus a site for news, surveillance, security, advertising, entertainment, consumer choice, products, marketing, spying, terror prevention, war, and communications. When this metropolitan diagram informs the city, it attempts to reinvent the latter as a center for service and techno-financialization rather than industry, pushing labor into the global countryside. And yet, it is precisely at this interface that the energies of the old city can be seen to collide with a new regime of value and information. In relation to "Mumbai," an example of this would be the conflict between what Joseph Schumpeter has called the creative–destructive powers of capital that seek to prime historical grounds as pure real estate, and the city's old Rent Control Act, which obstinately prevents it from doing so in a total manner. Hence, the "metropolis," as a figure of thought, should not be considered in empiricist haste; real cities like San Francisco and Bangalore are merely dense, topological assemblages of money, technology, and goods in a worldwide web of urbanity.

An important aspect of this form of power is that it often does not aspire to a complete territorial takeover of the ground beneath our feet. Instead, it works by generating acute segmentations of space, creating provisional hierarchies and critical saturations and rarefactions of information-finance availability. More than the classic enclosed and sedentary spaces of the factory, financialization depends more on transnational mobility and suppleness, on modes of instant valorization and redundancy. In this dispensation of the informatization of social life it becomes all the more crucial to exploit the temporal and structural gap between the boundless mobility of capital and the heavily circumscribed mobility of labor. In our time, when all things solid can indeed melt into ether, the fate of national economies is determined by indices of global connectivity and bandwith, despite the fact, as Katherine Hayles so astutely reminds us, 70 percent of people in the world have never made a phone call.[85] In the "post-human" urban scenario she uncovers for us, it is not that "organic" entities (community, individuals, peoples) do not exist. However, three powerful actors—information, control, and communications—have brought about such symbiotic conglomerations of the organic and the mechanical that it would be a disabling act of thought to try to restore the former in its autonomous romantic glory.

Information power is a key component in an overall capitalist production of social life.[86] Informatization is therefore a direct expression of capitalist command and not a mediated or reflective relationship between the base and superstructure. It is the circulation of different kinds of words and images across global distances, *in the least amount of time possible*. The mechanism of *value* in such a turnover is computed according to a temporal measure, in which time *is* money. Information therefore creates value not in terms of veracity of knowledge (which is settled through belated rational debates among experts), but in terms of the abridgement of reporting time. It does not rely on modern cognitive-representational prejudices (the camera does not lie), but a machinic coda of efficiency (the camera has no *time* to lie). This is where informatization differs from what can be called news in an older sense. The latter can be accounted for as a secular verification of rumor, a process of expert scientific recoding of the world, absolving it of miracles and magic. Informatization, on the other hand, is a pure force of circulating common sense, in which the temporal logic of the bomb and that of the image coincide. Like capital, informatization tends toward the abolition of *circulation time*; it is, in fact, capital itself (and not a reflection of it) precisely because it acquires a "life of its own" by virtue of being value in serial flow.[87] Marx makes the important distinction between money as a simple medium of exchange, as in Aristotelian economics, and money that becomes capital precisely because it is in circulation. Information is thus possible when the money–image compact becomes immediately socialized value, without going through formal mediating circuits of society, law, and culture. Apart from Antonio Negri's thesis in *Marx Beyond Marx*, here I have Guy Debord's observation in mind—that spectacle is capital accumulated to the point of image.[88] Hence I am suggesting that money is *not* translated into image-commodity on the screen and subsequently returned to its original form as televisual revenue. Rather, the movement is that of money through and throughout. In the *Grundrisse* Marx makes a very important distinction between money and coin which may be instructive here: "Money is the negation of the medium of circulation as such, of the *coin*. But it also contains the latter at the same time as an aspect, negatively, since it can always be transformed into coin; positively, as *world coin*, but as such, its formal character is irrelevant, and it is essentially a commodity as such, the omnipresent commodity, not determined by location" (228). The coin that goes into making the image and the image itself are only different moments of money as value in continuous, "omnipresent" circulation. Marx calls money a "mental relation" (*Grundrisse*, 191) which can be seen to be emphatically *in currency* all the time, regardless of perceptual transformations from coin to image and back to coin, in capital's conditions of command. It is in this sense that money does not stop being money once the image is produced; as Godard puts it, there is always money "burning on screen," or as Fellini says about the ancient curse of money on cinema, "when the money runs out, the film will be over."[89]

In our time, perhaps the comparison with a Benjaminian, *flâneur*-like journey through the city is more apt for how the new urban figure absorbs or negotiates geo-televisual informatics as a diagram of worldly power. The city—with its manifold electronic terminals, data flows, image flickers, borderless connections, and varied pulsations of information—has itself become the screen. When we use this oft-repeated slogan, which paradoxically collapses the image of a lived, three-dimensional space with that of a flat two-dimensional plane of immanence, we speak, in the present continuous tense, of an imminent possibility, one that was announced in a White Paper issued by John Walker of Autodesk during the late 1980s: that the screen is the next barrier to be broken.[90] Amit Rai has insightfully located the Bollywood media assemblage in this particular stochastic, non-linear web of urban pulsations. The moment of cinema in the ecology described by Rai is an historical habitat of sensation in which critical turns take place precisely at the point where "body and population meet."[91] This is a crucial interface, a neurological phylum in which the brain or consciousness is not the master organizer of affects. Drawing from Henri Bergson, Michel Foucault, Gilles Deleuze, Gilbert Simondon, and Brian Massumi, among others, Rai unfolds a "Bollywood" sensorium of media contagions and habituations of affect at the pre-individual, sub-sensate level. It works at a pre-individual stratum, which is a mutational, generative interface between the subject and multiple populations. The human thereby becomes a permeable machinic entity that can log on to an overall ecology of durations and intensities. Consider the case of 24-hour, multi-channel television. Unlike the older, temporally enclosed institution of state pedagogy, contemporary TV culture addresses the population rather than the individual as subject, or the "people" as an organic composite of the latter. The conscientious, "normal" individual cannot watch all the channels at once. The prescribed psycho-biography of the model citizen demands that s/he sleeps, eats, propagates, and reproduces his/her labor power. Endowed with a pure Indianness of heart, the citizen can exercise discrimination in viewership, motivated by aesthetics, taste, or ideology. However, it is the population, as a gargantuan host of desires, pathologies, consciousnesses, and intelligence, that keeps the television on all the time, as a hum that traverses the interface between the individual and the demographic mass. The population, much like the city and the bank, never sleeps.

The Bollywood New/Intermedia assemblage is that which shoots along the interstice between the home and the world, and unlike the classic cinematic apparatus, is not confined to a contractual enclosure of time and space. It engages the population in their day-to-day "distracted" movements through the lanes, alleyways, and buildings of the metropolitan map, producing social meanings and kinetic fragments through inputs and applications that may be normal, schizophrenic, or even somnambulist. The city itself has extended into virtual lobes, construed by web-televisual formations like MOO virtual reality systems, Multi-User-Dungeons (MUDS), Role-Playing Games (RPGs), networked performances of myriad kinds, virtual communities with global real-time platforms, or borderless Bit Torrent peer-to-peer file sharing. These virtual segments of the city are increasingly haptic and sensuous by way of miniaturized gadgets, stereo-vision helmets, or data gloves. Katherine Hayles understands this as a post-human order in which cognitive structures emerge from "recurrent sensory-motor patterns" (*How We Became Posthuman* [1999], 155–6) and micro-identities are constantly generated with the formation of small cognitive balloons without a unitary horizon. This dispersion of public participation into scatterings of demographic energies was understood by Jean-Paul Sartre as an existentialist danger that could eclipse both the figure of the people and the individual subject. Television, for instance, for Sartre was part of that instrumentalization of society that produced a top ten list of *nobody's* tastes.[92] The informatic geo-televisual we investigated in the previous section has no one at the heart of its operations. It is tailored to no particular charter of "Indian" taste.

The Question of Affect

Rai's formulations about the Bollywood media assemblage rest on a foundational critique of Descartian humanism. What is displaced with the aid of a powerful theory of affect is the Cartesian separation of and hierarchy between the mind and the body. Affect as such, in the powerful sense Deleuze draws from his work on Spinoza, is a refutation of the general Cartesian rule: that affection (*affectio*) is directly of the body, while affect (*affectus*) refers to the mind. The mind in such a conception is not imperial but is parallel to the body. It can form images in consciousness of transitions between affective states.[93] For Deleuze, therefore, the idea is to affirm the powers of the body beyond the knowledge we have of it, and the powers of the mind beyond the consciousness we have of it (Deleuze, *Spinoza* [2001], 18–22). Perhaps the recent spate of affect theories in the neurosciences, cognitive psychology, and various disciplines of the humanities are driven by an urgent need to resituate the mind–body constitution of the self as part of, and not just in mediated relation to, an increasingly global sensory continuum of urbanity. Since we shall continue to talk about affect, about subjectivities caught between thinking or feeling, and desiring or pleasure-filled bodies, I beg the reader's patience to visit some important aspects of this burgeoning field of inquiry to arrive at a picture that is pertinent to our present purposes. It is beyond the scope of this project to map the intricacies of this contentious field. Rather, the aim will be to emerge with questions that disturb and problematize the ways in which we have, often with unfortunate consequences, understood matters of identity, representation, ideological interpellation, consciousness, and subject formation in the course of the long twentieth century.

One could begin with the brain and the question whether it is the central organ to house the "mind," understood metaphysically.[94] According to Antonio Damasio, reason operates through interactions between many neurological organizations, rather than a single brain center. Intelligence involves mapping and integrating signals from a body landscape and a feeling is a mere snapshot of that. "Nature," or any conception of it, would include all external stimuli, genetically engendered responses, and inherited social mores. The body is thus one organism of interactive bio-chemical and neural circuits (endocrine, immune, and automatic neural components), and the physiological operations to which we impart the metaphysical name "mind" are derived from this structural and functional assemblage rather than from the brain alone.[95] This idea of a self in perpetual territorializing and deterritorializing relations with the world perhaps has its antecedents. In her admirable work *The Transmission of Affect*, Teresa Brennan suggests that before the Cartesian bio-political individual came to the fore, it was common to associate feeling with atmosphere. In what should be a formulation useful for our immediate objectives, Brennan defines *entertainment* as a neurological phenomenon in which several hormonal or nervous systems (chemical and electrical) are brought into alignment, with hormones and pheromones acting as social catalysts.[96] What further complicates and decentralizes matters is the body of evidence in recent research that questions the central assumption that it is the hypothalamus that triggers or arrests the release of hormones. In the course of her general exploration of chemo-sensory processes (with a special emphasis on olfaction), Brennan points out that this scenario reveals a foundational crisis for Freudian psychoanalysis; it presumes an origin of affects that is autonomous of the (neurological) subject experiencing them. The Freudian unconscious, according to her, can be reconstituted as a theoretical fiction only as an immanent landscape that includes the voluntary/involuntary, sympathetic, and parasympathetic nervous systems.[97] The brain is an interpreter and not an originator of news and information; the unconscious extends to the rest of the environment.

In recent times, interdisciplinary collaborative projects like that between the neuroscientist M. R. Bennett and the philosopher P. M. S. Hacker have attacked, in a manner perhaps more frontal than Damasio's or Brennan's, what is known as the endemic "binding problem" in the neurosciences. It is a two-pronged attack on dualism: not only do they want do demolish the "Cartesian mind," they also foreclose the possibility of inserting the brain as a substitute for it.[98] The brain, according to them, is not to be understood as the master "scanner": it neither takes a picture apart, nor assembles one. It merely enables the organism to see a visual scene.[99] It is not an image that is reflected in the retina. The retina merely absorbs light. This information is not semantic (to be decoded by the brain), but information-theoretic. Vision is the outcome of several neuronal groups. There is, in other words, no representation: "The term 'representation' is a weed in the neuroscientific garden, not a tool—and the sooner it is uprooted the better."[100]

This radical thesis has been challenged and the jury is still out as to how the debate will be settled. Others continue to adopt positions that slightly, moderately, or starkly vary from Bennett's and Hacker's in relation to the classic models of Western subjectivity (Descartes, Hegel, Freud). While working without any desire "to be in bed with Descartes," philosophers Daniel Dennett and John Searle have contested Bennett's and Hacker's controversial thesis with the explicit purpose of returning conscious-ness to the brain.[101] Edelman and Tononi provide a highly complicated neuronal scenario comprising high-dimensional discriminations called *qualia*, which, in nascent form, are multi-modal, body-centered discrimi-nations carried out by the proprioceptive, kinesthetic, and autonomous systems.[102] And yet, while they think trying to understand consciousness relying on the intrinsic properties of certain neurons or certain areas of the brain is doomed to failure, Edelman and Tononi do provide a dynamic core hypothesis to address the binding problem.[103] No single area of the brain is responsible for conscious experience. However, as a performance is repeated, the number of brain regions employed in it becomes smaller. Edelman and Tononi are Freudians who wish to extend the scope of the unconscious. However, the provisional integration they insist on is not the coming into being of universal laws of psycho-biography; it is per-petually modified by transversal processes. Memory, for instance, is non-representational; it is more like the melting and refreezing of a glacier than an inscription on a rock (*A Universe of Consciousness*, 92).

Some novel reformulations of the human neurological system aside, are we stating the obvious here? Nobody now really believes (as Descartes did) that there is a real transaction between pure mental and material substances in the pineal gland. There is indeed no "homunculus, either metaphysical or in the brain, sitting in the Cartesian theater as an audi-ence of one."[104] And yet, the crucial question is, to what extent are we willing to push this dismantling of the classical Western subject in our thinking – that is, when we think with a "conscious" awareness that it is no longer tenable to consider consciousness as an epiphenomenon? To do so would be to exercise caution at every step of the way because, even though the integrated subject at ground level (the one whose grand historical task is to humanize nature) is announced to have gone, its inde-fatigable spirit keeps popping in through the backdoor. That happens when pious attributes of unqualified agency and pure voluntarism on the part of the human remain, even though the idol itself has vanished. That does not mean that we abandon necessary theoretical fictions of human reason, agency, identification, cognition, or moral or ideological choice. In recent times, Paul Bové has provided us with a powerful and brilliantly provocative thought experiment devoted to understanding a poesis of historical humanism that draws from Vico and Said, rather than an idealistic tradition of the West.[105] The ethical task of criticism today perhaps is simply to consider our key humanist categories as "pending" and not absolute, historical and not universally guided by the auto-pilot of Manifest Destiny;[106] in other words, thinking the contemporary calls for a relational engagement with the figure of the human as a paramount legacy of modernity, which is neither a relativistic nor a total critique. To do so is to acutely realize that the powers and qualities of conceived subjects and asserted identities are indeed actors, but not the only ones in the global atmospherics of techno–financial social life.[107] The problem with Jürgen Habermas's humanist lament about the re-feudalization of the public sphere and the incompletion of a project of modernity due to public opinion lapsing into mass opinion is that he would like to maintain a categorical division and a hierarchy between the human faculties of cognition and *technē* and those devoted to ethics and politics.[108]

Secondly, there is the body. Today, the concept of embodiment, for all its admirable deployments, is at risk of lapsing into an academic cliché precisely because care is often not taken to understand that this reconceived body has entered into a new covenant with the soul that was thought to have imprisoned it, and with the "mind" that apparently had ruled it. The "new" body in fact threatens to extinguish the soul and extend into the brain, absolving the latter from the metaphysics of the "mind." It is this body that Rai sees loitering in the contemporary Indian media ecology. Such a body resides exactly at the erotic and sensuous meeting point between the individual and the population, from which identities emerge as well as lapse back into. The body is not an organic counterpoint to the machinism of tools and technologies; rather, tools and technologies are generationally improving to be able to set up workable interfaces with the substantially more complex machinery of the body. Here perhaps we can reformulate Vivian Sobchack's rhetorical articulation of a phenomenological fear: that contemporary media culture conspires to get "rid of the flesh" and transcend the body. She calls it *ekstasis* (in relation to a being put out of its space): a feeling of "having had your everything amputated" in cyberspace.[109] This fear draws from a vigorous extension of the finite limits of the body itself, or what was thought to be the body. That is, extending one's bodily scope by breathtaking dimensions by way of a cosmic movement in cyberspace, which is a special space as Lev Manovich pointed out, precisely because it has no gravity to keep matters earthbound.[110] There is nothing, no soul or epiphenomenal consciousness, to send out of the body for that out-of-body experience. It is as impossible to leave the body as it is easy to lose one's mind.

The Question of Sovereignty

It is from these conceptual grounds that I would like to end this part of the discussion by elaborating the theme of informatic modernization as indicative of a new form of sovereign power. Let me begin by pre-empting a legitimate question: if this is a metropolitan diagram of finance-information, to what extent and to what functional degree does it inscribe the third world scenario of India? How powerfully does it determine and mediate realities in what is still a largely non-metropolitan scenario, massive enough to hold three African national populations afflicted by HIV/AIDS, hunger, and poverty? I shall readily acknowledge that informatic modernization is only one among many competing architectures of power in India. However, it would be an error to gauge its operative capacities purely on the basis of its reach in gross terms, just as it would be a mistake to account for the impact of technologization or financialization of social life in that manner. To quickly recall what has already been said: informatic modernization works through the erasure of distance, by what can be called a tele-localizing of traditional spaces. This is precisely why distance and the manipulation of that distance are important for its operations. In its various forms, informatic modernization, therefore, does not seek to occupy space or enclose it. Rather, it creates a virtual plane of abstraction and value above the grounds of history—one that can instantly valorize matters or render them redundant. It is a smooth plane in the sense that it can increasingly function without the usual barriers of culture, nationhood, or custom. It can, however, freely set up striations and segmentations of its own, by managing gradations of distance and temporality to exploit the uneven mobility of capital and labor. As people across the world, from weavers in Bangladesh to rice farmers in the Philippines, often discover in their daily existence, their labor power can be instantly valorized or rendered redundant by new market connections and flows. We are, of course, examining a very small part of this assemblage, one that democratizes desire in a scenario of stark material imbalances. "Bollywood" is an interface of cinema and information when the powers of the latter range across myriad other spheres, from news, to share market tectonics, advertising, networking, surveillance, militarization, or risk management. We are thus looking at cinema in a new electrified dispensation in which the overall visual culture is increasingly "cinematographic in its appearance, digital at the level of its material, and computational at the level of its logic."[111]

More than its current ubiquity or osmotic powers, it is the instantaneous temporality of information that can be isolated as a special concern in relation to the question of sovereignty. Information is affective precisely because it is "shot through with explanation." While taking strong cognizance of the fact that thinking is not limited to the mind, we must remember that pure affect is the absence of thinking. When durational intensities of affect cross a certain threshold of speed and density in their mass distribution, it indeed becomes a worrying matter. When information mass-produces affect, it also generates new regimes of habituation, attentiveness, and recall; it calls into being new forms of docility and enthrallment through a hypertrophy of the senses. Information thereby tends to bridge the temporal interval between word and meaning, reducing language to a set of clichés and a pure movement of common sense. The sensorium that Rai locates between the individual body and the population is the generative interface for massified affects to take hold.

In an age when the geo-televisual is informatized, what is perhaps ironically threatened is the temporal and spatial interval of neighborliness, that is, the very interregnum necessary to recognize the neighbor as such and enter into relations of learning and teleopoesis with her. Hence, unlike Arjun Appadurai, who thinks that the new "neighborliness" of the communications revolution and globalization has fostered the use of imagination in everyday lives,[112] I think the converse is true. When information becomes the defining feature of a dispensation of power, it is the temporal and spatial scope for the exercise of human creative and imaginative faculties that tends to be curtailed. The political consequences of this aspect were richly commented on throughout the twentieth century by many thinkers beginning with Gramsci, Benjamin, Marcuse, and Adorno.[113] For these European thinkers, the immediate danger to thinking in the world came, to a greater or lesser degree, from the grotesque propaganda machines of European Fascism and Stalinism, and the American culture industry. We can locate their works in the light of our times, when the span and speed of informatic flows have been augmented exponentially, and the artful modernist choice of dwelling either as a poet or an assassin has been heavily compromised by a military-informatic culture of generating instant terror and instant consensus. Speaking about his deep concerns about hospitality and the figure of the *arrivant*, Derrida has noted with alarm that it is precisely due to the *global* monopolization of "actuality effects" by information and broadcast capital that news "actuality" is "spontaneously ethnocentric."[114]

What does information do to the geo-televisual image or, for that matter, any image, cinematic or otherwise? The instantaneity of informatic procedures seeks to abolish what Jacques Rancière, following Roland Barthes, calls the double poetics of the image: the intellectual semiology of the *stadium* (information transmitted) and the phenomenology of the *punctum* (immediate pathetic effect).[115] What is thereby lost is a thought of alterity and mourning, with the image as such being engulfed by a stream of instant use and disposability. In such an order, art struggles to preserve an ontology of its own that would distinguish it from the commercial or spectacle. The circulating logic of an advertised modernization can thus easily make a mockery of the old surrealist aesthetic dream that Rancière wistfully recalls: the impossible encounter between the umbrella and the sewing machine. Godard's problem was that his montage, unlike Eisenstein's, was formed in the pop era. Rancière[116] actually marks the period between 1880 and 1920—with the eclipse of symbolism and the rise of constructivism—that witnessed the demise of the image in the wake of propaganda art. I thus open up the title of this book itself to a question of irony: is "Bollywood" the coming into being of a geo-televisual aesthetic, or the end of it?

Rancière's thesis can be immediately aligned with a long-standing question on the role of aesthetics and politics in totalitarian scenarios: how was it possible that modern technologies of mechanical reproduction and electrification of public communication produced European Fascism as one of its first grotesque world-historical spectacles? As Kafka anticipated, did the human subject finally create an Archimedean vantage point to witness humanity, but only to use it against itself? The paradox, as expressed in Benjamin's "Work of Art" essay, can be outlined as follows: mechanized mass culture in the twentieth century was supposed to "de-auratize" the work of art and make it more democratically available. However, what Benjamin perceives is a disturbing incursion of aesthetics into politics, rather than the politicization of art that could have been possible. Against the spirit of progress, science can thus be replaced by dogma and history by grotesque myths. This, for Benjamin, constitutes a "violation" of the technologies of mass culture, by which the "Führer cult" produces its ritual values of aestheticizing war and destruction ("Work of Art" [1973], 234–5). Benjamin formulates the problem as belonging to a society not yet "mature" enough to "incorporate technology as its *organ*" (235; emphasis added). The question has resonated down the decades, but increasingly in transposed forms. Do humans use or abuse technology, or does a particular technologization of metropolitan life produce the subjectivities and the responsive bodies that fulfill it?

The fear of "data made flesh" (or conversely, getting rid of the "flesh" in the organic sense) was therefore always with us. It is perhaps because of this fear that Norbert Weiner, one of the pioneering figures in the recasting of the human as a permeable machine in information ecology, wanted to restrict cybernetics to the physical sciences.[117] As we know, this did not happen and the mechanical reproducibility, control, communicative speed, and scope of publicity have been greatly enhanced since the times of Benjamin and Gramsci. The architecture of media power that was inaugurated in the latter half of the twentieth century has been called "informatics" by Katherine Hayles. In this sense, informatics would include "the technologies of information as well as the biological, social, linguistic, and cultural changes that initiate, accompany, and complicate their development."[118] Let us now broach the question of sovereignty and "informatics" taken as such more squarely with a comparatively recent, surprisingly anxious formulation by Deleuze. Our primary points of interest will be twofold. First, can we, in relation to informatics, understand the question of dominance (of which an extreme form is Fascism) in post-human terms? In other words, can there be an axiomatic and focalized majoritarian will without a dictatorial human face? Secondly, can the resultant theory help us understand (with the necessary caveats) the Indian situation of Hinduness? Can we speculate on a Hindu majoritarian will that works immanently, suffusing life and language, independent of representational or identitarian pieties and the works of caricatural dictator aspirants like Bal Thackeray?

According to Deleuze, the discourses of Fascism, as one of the dominant myths of our time, establish themselves by an imperial-linguistic takeover of a whole social sphere of expressive possibilities, that is, by a technological focalization of these energies in a particular direction. In such a conception, Adolf does not feature as the madman who abuses technology, but is himself a grotesque, spectacular production of technologism itself. In any given historical milieu there are different energies capable of generating multiple forms of thought, imaginative actions, and wills to art. Fascism destroys such pre-signifying and pre-linguistic powers, extinguishes pluralities, and replaces them with a monologue of power that saturates space with, and only with, the immanent will of the dictator. This is the moment in which the language system sponsored by the sovereign is at its most violent; it seeks to efface historical memory by myth; it casts the sovereign himself and his speech as absolute and natural. For Deleuze, this is a psycho-mechanical production of social reality, more than an organicity of community torn apart by human alienation and the incursion of reactionary ideologies, false consciousnesses, and agents.

Not that the latter do not exist or are unimportant components in this world picture, but that this technology of power cannot be seen simply as a value-free arrangement of tools misused by evil ones. The figure of the dictator is therefore not that of the aberrant individual madman, but a psychological automaton that becomes insidiously present in all, in the technology of massification itself. The images and objects that mass hallucination, somnambulism, and trance produce are attributes of this immanent will to power.[119] The hypnotic, fascinating drive of Fascism is seen paradoxically to operate below the radar of consciousness; Fascism becomes a political reality when knowledge-based exchanges between entities of intelligence give way to a bio-technologism of informatics. Information, therefore, becomes an incessant and emphatic localization of the global will of the dictator; in its seriality and movement, it can only keep repeating, illustrating, and reporting the self-evident truth of the dictatorial monologue.[120] For Deleuze, it is in this sense of the immanent dictatorial will that Hitler becomes information itself. Also, it is precisely for this reason that one cannot fight Nazism by embarking on a battle of truth and falsehood without questioning the very basis of information and its social relations of production. Hence, "*No information, whatever it might be, is sufficient to defeat Hitler*" (*Cinema 2*, 269).

I am aligning these diagnoses to the Indian situation keeping in mind two primary questions. First, to what extent can this diagram of power be pertinent to the Indian situation, not just in terms of how a computational/informatic logic can be extended to social and cultural life, but also in terms of how these are direct expressions of capital's power? Can these undeniably European theorizations teach us anything about sovereignty and publicity as they exist in the Indian situation? What exactly is the nature of the "ritual values" that can be discerned in the informatic geo-televisual matters in Hindi cinema of the 1990s and after? If it is indeed the case of a newly empowered national technocratic ruling elite exhibiting its life as artwork, how can it be grasped as a political phenomenon? Or consider the ultimate one central to this examination of Bollywood in the age of new media: can there be any information-in-the-city that is not tendentially Hindu? These are some of the questions that I shall attempt to open up rather than answer in the next chapters, beginning with a couple of cinematic narratives about information, justice, and sovereign power.

Notes

1. Richard Dienst conceptualizes "geo-television" in *Still Life and Real Time* (1995): 12. I am using the term "geo-televisual" in a different sense. For

all its merits, Dienst's project remains mired in a politics of formalism and representation which concludes that "Television establishes the mechanics of a global representation without being able to perform it" (167).

2. The term was first coined by Chidananda Dasgupta in *The Painted Face: Studies in Indian Popular Cinema* (1991).

3. See Mazumdar, *Bombay Cinema* (2007): chapter 2.

4. For critical accounts of the rise of *Hindutva*, see, among others, Tapan Basu et al., *Khaki Shorts and Saffron Flags* (1993); Shridhar Damle and Walter Anderson, *The Brotherhood in Saffron* (1987); Sandria Freitag, *Collective Action and Community: Public Arenas and the Emergence of Communalism in North India* (1990); Thomas Hansen, *The Saffron Wave: Democracy and Hindu Nationalism in Modern India* (2001); Christopher Jaffrelot, *The Hindu Nationalist Movement in India* (1996); and the essays in Rajeshwari Sunder Rajan and Anuradha Dingwaney Needham, eds., *The Crisis of Secularism in India* (2007).

5. See Marcia Landy, *Film, Politics and Gramsci* (1994) for an innovative deployment of Gramsci's thought in relation to Deleuze in the investigation of cultural interfaces between cinema, national hegemonic structures, capital, and, finally, globalization. Of special interest is chapter 8 ("Postmodernism and Folklore in Contemporary Science Fiction Cinema").

6. Antonio Gramsci, *Reader* (1988): 189.

7. By the beginning of the 1990s, India's foreign debt had risen to 70.1 billion rupees (making India third in the ranks of debtor nations, after Brazil and Mexico). The problems were quickly compounded by sharply increasing oil prices as a result of the first Gulf War, the withdrawal of foreign currency deposits, and a decline in the flow of money from Indian expatriates in the Middle East. In October 1990, the World Bank proposed a 20 percent devaluation of the rupee to redress the balance of payments.

8. See Sukhamoy Chakravarty, *Development Planning: The Indian Experience* (1987); Pranab Bardhan, *The Political Economy of Development in India* (1984); and Ashish Rajadhyaksha and Paul Willemen, *Encyclopaedia of Indian Cinema* (1999): 23–9 for an overall picture of post-Independence development in the Indian national context. For various accounts of the globalizing process in India, see John McGuire, "Economic Liberalization and India: New Rhetoric, Old Theme," in C. T. Kurien, *Global Capitalism and the Indian Economy* (1994); T. J. Byres, "Introduction: Development Planning and the Interventionist State Versus Liberalization and the Neo-Liberal State: India, 1989–1996" (1997). For a set of revisionist essays, see Parthasarathi Banerjee and Frank Jürgen Richter, *Economic Institutions in India: Sustainability under Liberalization and Globalization* (2003). Amit Rai insightfully connects this complex economic scenario to urbanity and media developments in *Untimely Bollywood* (2009): chapter 2.

9. See Rajadhyaksha and Willemen, *Encyclopedia of Indian Cinema*, 29 and 92. For political and historical studies of Indian television, see Nilanjana

Gupta, *Switching Channels: Ideologies of Television in India* (1998); Arvind Rajagopal, *Politics after Television: Hindu Nationalism and the Reshaping of the Public in India* (2001); Sudeep Dasgupta, *Hindu Nationalism, Television, and the Avatars of Capital* (2003); Melissa Butcher, *Transnational Television, Cultural Identity, and Change: When Stars Came to India* (2003); and Shanti Kumar, *Gandhi Meets Primetime: Globalization and Nationalism in Indian Television* (2006).

10. Early cable expansion from the mid-1980s (most of it illegal) was beset with problems because it involved the use of decrepit Russian satellites like Gorizont, which were not geo-stationary. In 1990, the Hong Kong-based Hutchison Whampoa Group bought ASIASAT1, then the only geostationary satellite over the Indian Ocean. This began a process by which increasingly cheap beaming facilities became available over the South Asian footprint.

11. See Vanita Kohli-Khandekar, *The Indian Media Business* (2006): 62–78.

12. Ibid., 16–17, 62–78; and Nina Sabjani "The Challenges of a Sleeping Giant" (2005): 100–1.

13. See Melissa Butcher, *Transnational Television, Cultural Identity, and Change* (2003), especially 58–78.

14. See Shanti Kumar, *Gandhi Meets Primetime* (2006): 44–5. Older habits nevertheless died hard. In 1996, after two months of deliberation, the Indian Board of Censors deemed thirty-one programs broadcast on eight channels unfit for TV. In 1998, companies with a maximum of 20 percent foreign equity were allowed to uplink from India. See Melissa Butcher, *Transnational Television* (2003): 82. By July 2000, foreign-owned broadcasters could do the same (with the exception of news and current affairs channels). In 2003 new guidelines stated that news channels could buy a 26 percent stake in Indian companies.

15. See Butcher, *Transnational Television*, 80.

16. See Gayatri Gopinath, *Impossible Desires* (2005): chapter 5; Ratna Kapur, "The Cultural Politics of *Fire*" (2000); and the essays pertaining to the "*Fire* controversy" in *Economic and Political Weekly* end-1998/early 1999, especially Tejaswini Niranjana and Mary John, "Mirror Politics: '*Fire*,' Hindutva and Indian Culture" (1999); and Carol Upadhyay, "Counter-Fire" (1999).

17. See Bruno Latour, *We Have Never Been Modern* (1993).

18. See Deleuze's elaboration in *Foucault* (1988): 7.

19. See Anustup Basu, "Hindutva and Informatic Modernization" (2008), and "The Indian Monotheism" (forthcoming in *Boundary 2*).

20. See Daya Kishen Thussu, "Hollywood's Poor Cousin—Indian Cinema in the Era of Globalization" (2002); and Vanita Kohli-Khandekar, *The Indian Media Business* (2006): 108.

21. For critical readings of "Bollywood" cultures in various diasporic contexts, see Gayatri Gopinath, "Nostalgia, Desire, Diaspora: South Asian

Sexualities in Motion" (1997); also chapter 7 of *Impossible Desires*; Sunaina Maira, "*Desis Reprazent*: Bhangra Remix and Hip Hop in New York City" (1998); Patricia Uberoi, "The Diaspora Comes Home: Disciplining Desire in *DDLJ*" (1998); Purnima Mankekar, "Brides Who Travel: Gender, Transnationalism, and Nationalism in Hindi Film" (1999); Anthony Allesandrini, "'My Heart is Indian for All That': Bollywood Film between Home and Diaspora" (2001); Mita Banerjee, "Bollywood Meets the Beatles: Towards an Asian German Studies of German Popular Culture" (2004); Sangita Shresthova, "Swaying to an Indian Beat . . . *Dola* Goes My Diasporic Heart: Exploring Hindi Film Dance" (2004); Ashley Dawson, "'Bollywood Flashback': Hindi Film Music and the Negotiation of Identity among British-Asian Youths" (2005); Ashwin Punathambekar, "Bollywood in the Indian American Diaspora: Mediating a Transitive Logic of Cultural Citizenship" (2005); Rosie Thomas and Adina Bradeanu, "Indian Summer, Romanian Winter: A 'Procession of Memories" (2006); Manas Ray, "*Chalo Jahaji*: Bollywood in the Tracks of Indenture to Globalization" (2007); Brian Larkin, "Colonialism and the Built Space of Cinema in Nigeria" (2007); Vasna Jagarnath, "The Politics of Urban Segregation and Indian Cinema in Durban" (2007) and "Itineraries of Indian Cinema: African Videos, Bollywood, and Global Media" (2008). These essays, together, present a highly complicated scenario of exchanges between cultural forma- tions, the specific nuances of which are beyond the scope of this project. David Martin-Jones, in "Kabhi India Kabhi Scotland: Recent Indian Films Shot on Location in Scotland" (2006), for instance, argues that while Scotland features as a fantasy land in films like *Kuch Kuch Hota Hain* and *Kandukondein Kandukondein*, in Rajiv Rai's *Pyar, Ishk Aur Mohabbat* (2001), it is a location for the negotiation of diasporic identity. On the other hand, Shakuntala Rao's ethnography of Indian non-elite audiences in "The Globalization of Bollywood" (2007) establishes that they do not like the NRI film.

22. By 2005, there were more than 100 multiplex screens, 225 digital screens in India, with thousands more in the pipe line. See Kohli-Khandekar, *The Indian Media Business*, 16–20; Komal Nahata, "The Future is the Multiplex" (2002).

23. See Kohli-Khandekar, *The Indian Media Business*, 122–7.

24. Ian Garwood, "The Songless Bollywood Film" (2006): 172.

25. Sudhanva Deshpande, "The Consumable Hero of Globalized India" (2005): 191–2.

26. The term "geo-televisual" is ironic in that it critically inhabits a core pre- sumption of modernism, one that, as Martin Jay has pointed out, privileges vision among all the other senses. Jay connects this to the birth of a domi- nant Cartesian rationality which, in assemblage with a linear, stereoscopic perspective of the Renaissance *Quattrocento*, birthed the "ahistorical, dis- interested, disembodied" human subject which claims to navigate the

world from a panoptic point of view. See Martin Jay, "Scopic Regimes of Modernity" (1988): 9–10.

27. Siegfried Zielinski, *Deep Time of the Media* (2006): 2.
28. See Bernard Stiegler, *Technics and Time, 2: Disorientation* (2009), especially chapter 3, 97–187.
29. Miriam Hansen, "The Mass Production of the Senses" (1999).
30. Kaushik Bhaumik, *The Emergence of the Bombay Film Industry, 1913–1936* (2001). See also Priya Jaikumar's groundbreaking study, *Cinema at the End of Empire: A Politics of Transition in Britain and India* (2007).
31. Kaushik Bhaumik, "Emergence of the Bombay Film Industry" (2001): 41.
32. The stunt and fantasy genres, richly inspired as they were by an eclectic Orientalism borrowed from Europe and Hollywood (which was then mixed with Arabian Nights fantasies, Greek and Moorish legends, and other narrative impulses in Parsee theatrical traditions), offered a range of virtual milieus. Some of them (*Bulbul-E-Paristan* [*The Bird of Fairyland*], Fatma Begum, 1926 or *Hatimtai*, Prafulla Ghosh, 1929) had imaginary settings, while other studio-construed milieus were imaginary projections of a mythic time and space marked by geographical proper names: Persia (*Shirin Farhad*, J. J. Madan, 1931), Yemen (*Lal-E-Yaman*, J. B. H. Wadia, 1933), Rome (*Yahudi Ki Ladki*, Premankur Atorthy, 1933), the Ottoman Empire (*Judgment of Allah*, Mehboob Khan, 1935), Syria (*Char Darvesh* [*Four Dervishes*], Prafulla Ghosh, 1934). These imaginary chronotopes were not always deployed for spectacular purposes. Rajadhyaksha and Willemen, for instance, point out that *Watan* (*Land*) (Mehboob Khan, 1938) was a Central Asian war fantasy about a conflict between Cossacks and Tartars, which was also a thinly veiled allegory of national assertion and independence (*Encyclopedia of Indian Cinema*, 278). It is important to note that this fantasy assemblage persists in Indian film in later decades, but with the rise of the reformist social and then the eventual consolidation of what Madhava Prasad has called the feudal family romance, it is relegated to B-and C-grade productions, often featuring second-string stars like Premnath, Dara Singh, Mahipal, and Helen.
33. Bhaumik, *Emergence of the Bombay Film Industry*, 31.
34. It can perhaps be said that the ambiguity between spectacle (white women and men playing Asian people), the authenticity of representation, and the concomitant tension between the sacred and profane pertained to the original sin of *being in cinema*, even in the mythological genre that involved a *darsanic* encounter with the gods. The figure on screen can be seen as an assemblage of polarized powers: the iconic aspect of the divine and the profane texture of the body irremediably touched by the bazaar publicness of the cinematic institution. This duality between the nativity of myth and legend and the lurid yet alien cinematic body on screen can be best understood in relation to the early female stars, many of whom were of Anglo-Indian descent or were white actresses imported from the US, UK, or Australia: Patience

Cooper, Dorothy Kingdom, Ermaline, Adele Wilison, June Richards, Violet, Pearl, Kumudini (Miss Mary), Seeta Devi (Renee Smith), Sabita Devi (Iris Gasper), Indira Devi (Effie Hippolite), Madhuri (Beryl Clayton), Lalita Devi (Bonnie Bird), Lina Valentine, Wilma Garbo, Vimala (Marcia Solomon), Vilochona (Marien Hill), and the redoubtable Sulochana (Ruby Myers). The exotic texture of the mythic figure on screen—the cinematic body was at once a compact of profane allure and intimate *pauranic* memories—was often not a secret, despite the Indianized screen names of many of these actresses. An extreme example of casting Europeans as Indian mythological figures was Madan Theatres' *Savitri* (1923, *Savitri Satyavan*). Described as India's first international co-production, this film was shot entirely in Rome with an all-Italian cast and directed by Giorgio Mannini in collaboration with Unione Cinematographical Italiana of Rome. This is what the film historian Feroze Rangoonwala has to say about this now lost film: "One can imagine how it must have all looked, with Countess Rino de Liguoro appearing as Savitri, Bruto Castellani as Yama, Angelo Ferari as Satyavan . . . and with the Indian mythological episodes shot against the cascade of Trivoli palace of Count Chiggi and the romantic grandeur of Frascati. And one can condone the film for getting a poor response in India" (Rangoonwala, *Indian Cinema Past and Present* [1983]: 51).

35. The striations in the field of the geo-televisual were both international and infranational: the idea of the home and the world shifted between the nation and global wonders, between the country as the authentic seat of being and the city of lurid, perverted attractions. Kohinoor's *The Telephone Girl* (Homi Master, 1926) was advertised as containing "nightclubs, a Turkish bath, and college life." See Yves Thorawal, *The Cinemas of India* (2000): 13. In *Gamdeni Gori* (*The Village Girl*) (Mohan Bhavnani, 1927), the star, Sulochana, plays Sundari, a village girl lost in the big bad city. The film's publicity material touted "electric trains, motor cars and buses, the giant wheel, cinemas and theatres" (Rajadhyaksha and Willemen, *Encyclopedia*, 250). The cinematic persona of Fearless Nadia, the iconic caped crusader of the stunt genre during the 1930s and 1940s was that of the Bombaywali. See Rosie Thomas, "Not Quite (Pearl) White: Fearless Nadia, Queen of the Stunts" (2005): 55. The accessories of the blonde, blue-eyed actress of Australian stock included masks, hoods, leather attire, whip, a horse called Punjab ka beta, and a car named Rolls Royce ki beti.

36. This began with the launch of the first Gujarati film magazine, *Mauj Majah*, in 1924, followed by many others. There were two principal governing impulses in an overall task of bringing cinema into line with a projected national cultural mainstream. The first pertained to Gujarati reformism and the second to a Bengali modernist commitment to realism. A symptomatic moment of this culturalist clampdown is the heated denunciation of the "alien" and Islamicate productions of the Madan Theaters in favor of the elite literary realism (of which Bengal's New Theaters would become

the chief progenitor) in the publication *Filmland* from 1931 onwards. See, for instance, the documents collected in Samik Bandyopadhyay, ed., *Indian Cinema: Contemporary Perceptions from the Thirties* (1993).

37. See Bhaumik, *Emergence of the Bombay Film Industry*, 169–72.
38. See Aruna Vasudev, *Liberty and Licence in the Indian Cinema* (1978): 78–94.
39. Ibid., 94.
40. Sibaji Bandyopadhyay, *Punar Bishoye Punarbibechona* (2009): 219.
41. Ibid., 249.
42. See Bankimchandra Chattopadhyay, *Dharmatattva* (1954): 526.
43. Sibaji Bandyopadhyay, *Gopal-Rakhal Dwandhosamas* (1991), 219.
44. Later in London, when a rude renegade Indian expresses disdain for the backwardness of his mother country, Bharat reminds him that without Indian mathematics, humankind would not have been able to compute the distance to the moon, let alone land on it. On the other hand, toward the end, when the NRI villain Omkar is asked what the West has given him, he gleefully brandishes a revolver.
45. Valentina Vitali, *Hindi Action Cinema* (2008).
46. For an insightful theoretical account of the cultural logic of adaptation in Hindi cinema, see Sheila J. Nayar, "Dreams, Dharma, and Mrs. Doubtfire: Exploring Indian Popular Cinema via its 'Chutneyed' Western Scripts" (2003).
47. Jerry Pinto, *Helen* (2006): 54–6.
48. See Ajanta Sircar, "Romancing the Rural Belle: Bombay's Love Story" (1998): 137–9.
49. See Rajni Kothari, *Politics in India* (1970) and "The Democratic Experiment" (1998). See also Partha Chatterjee's critical evaluation of Kothari's work in the "Introduction" to *Wages of Freedom: Fifty Years of the Indian Nation-State* (1998).
50. Pinto, *Helen*, 127. Pinto provides a long list of such films (92–168).
51. Prasad, *Ideology of the Hindi Film*, 64.
52. Raminder Kaur has understood the recent geo-televisual qualities in popular Hindi cinema in terms of a new Occident in the making. See "Viewing the West through Bollywood: A New Occident in the Making" (2002).
53. I am referring to what Ashish Nandy has called a "slum-eyed" view of Indian politics seen in classic post-Independence Hindi cinema. See "Introduction" to *The Secret Politics of Our Desires* (1998): 1–18.
54. See Prasad, *Ideology of the Hindi Film*, 42–51.
55. They are not the traditional seven wonders: the Empire State Building features in the list.
56. Sudhanva Deshpande, "Consumable Hero" (2005): 187.
57. Ranjini Mazumdar, *Bombay Cinema* (2007): 93–4. See also Anne Friedberg, "Cinema and the Postmodern Condition" (1997); and Jonathan Crary, "Modernizing Vision" (1997). The connection between cinema, a mechanical extension of the visual space (the diorama, the cosmorama, the cyclorama,

the museum, or the public zoo) in the age of industrial capital, high empire, and what I call the geo-televisual has always been present in film theory. Christine Gledhill has, for instance, talked about the expanding culture of the visible in relation to melodrama, and as a nineteenth-century prelude to the cinema in the "Introduction" to *Home is where the Heart is* (1987).

58. See Martin Heidegger, "The Age of the World Picture" (1977).

59. Ibid., 117.

60. The defining works are still Jean-François Lyotard, *The Postmodern Condition: A Report on Knowledge* (1979); Fredric Jameson, *Postmodernism or, the Cultural Logic of Late Capitalism* (1995); and David Harvey, *The Condition of Postmodernity* (1990).

61. Basu, "Hindutva and Informatic Modernization" and "The Indian Monotheism."

62. Heidegger, "Age of the World Picture," 153.

63. See Ranjini Mazumdar, *Bombay Cinema* (2007): 110–48; Rustom Bharucha, "Utopia in Bollywood" (1995), Chapter 5 in Patricia Uberoi, *Freedom and Destiny: Gender, Family, and Popular Culture in India* (2006); and Rachel Dwyer, *Yash Chopra* (2008).

64. See Deshpande, "Consumable Hero" (2005).

65. Rajadhyaksha and Willemen, *Encyclopedia of Indian Cinema*, 312.

66. The bucolic figure of Krishna comes primarily from Puranic texts like the *Bhagwadpurana* and the *Vishnupurana* and also latter-day texts like Jaidev's *Geet Gobinda* and the *Padabali*s of Bengal. Its associations with the radical energies of the widespread *Bhakti* movement are well known. Under the auspices of this kind of *Bhakti*, traditional caste and gender hierarchies became redundant because the entire community of devotees replaced Radha and the *gopinis*. It was a major part of Bankimchandra Chattopadhyay's early Hindu nationalist project to replace this amorous figure with the warrior Krishna of The Mahabharata who was also the sovereign articulator of the *Gita* as Word. In Chattopadhyay's recasting, the Krishna of The Mahabharata would not just incarnate prophetic intelligence like the Buddha or Christ, but would not be a retiring entity like them. Krishna would be prince and messiah all at once, and also the ideal representative of the monogamous, caste Hindu householder. See Chattopadhyay, *Krishnacharitra* (1954).

67. See Prasad, "Guardians of the View: The Prohibition of the Private," in *Ideology of the Hindi Film*, 88–113.

68. Ravi Vasudevan has called our attention to the fact that A. K. Ramnujam details a number of Oedipus-like tales for India, the closest of which privileges the mother's point of view. Ramanujam notes that the withdrawal or renunciation of the son in the face of the father's aggression is a characteristic feature of stories relating to father/son conflicts. See "The Melodramatic Mode and the Commercial Hindi Cinema" (1989), 32; also Sudhir Kakar, *Inner World* (1978).

69. See Prasad, *Ideology of the Hindi Film*, 79–87.

70. See Priya Jha, "Lyrical Nationalism: Gender, Friendship and Excess in 1970s Hindi Cinema" (2003).

71. Jabbar Patel's *Umbartha/Subah/Morning* (1982) was, to my knowledge, the first Indian film to admit the word "lesbian."

72. Guy Debord, *Society of the Spectacle* (1995): 76. On the question of cinema and cultural memory, the keystone book in my opinion is Marcia Landy, *Cinematic Uses of the Past* (1996).

73. Amit Rai, *Untimely Bollywood* (2009).

74. See Walter Benjamin, "Storyteller" (1985): 89.

75. We might think here of the three Kantian categories: Knowledge of the World (*Weltkenntnis*), Man of the world (*Mann von Welt*), and Cosmopolitanism (*Weltläufigkeit*).

76. Hegel, *Phenomenology*, 60–73.

77. See Paul Virilio, *The Art of the Motor* (1995): especially 53–82.

78. See the "Spotlight" on the journal *Frontline*: www.hinduonnet.com/fline/fl1907/19070940.htm. Accessed August 27, 2007.

79. See, for instance, www.nydailynews.com/news/wn_report/2007/09/29/2007–09–29_mccain_no_muslim_president_us_better_wit.html. Accessed September 15, 2007.

80. Katherine Hayles, *How We Became Posthuman* (1999): 18.

81. See Partha Chatterjee, *The Politics of the Governed: Reflections on Popular Politics in Most of the World* (2004).

82. Walter Benjamin, "The Work of Art in the Age of Mechanical Reproduction" (1973): 233.

83. The reference is to Daniel Bell's prophetic tract *The Coming of the Postindustrial Society* (1973).

84. See Paul Virilio, "Speed and Information" (2001).

85. Hayles, *How We Became Posthuman*, 20.

86. On this, as well as Manuel Castells' celebrated trilogy *The Information Age* (2000, 2000, 2004), see Mark Poster, *Information Please* (2007); Robert Hassan, *The Information Society* (2008); and the essays in *24/7: Time and Temporality in the Network Society* (2007).

87. See, for instance, in the *Grundrisse*: the "tendency of capital is *circulation without circulation time*; hence also the positing of the instruments which merely serve to abbreviate circulation time as mere formal aspects posited by it (671).

88. See Antonio Negri, *Marx Beyond Marx: Lessons from the Grundrisse* (1989); and Guy Debord, *Society of the Spectacle* (1995): 24.

89. See Deleuze, *Cinema 2*, 77–8.

90. Cited in Katherine Hayles, "The Seduction of Cyberspace" (2001): 308.

91. Rai, *Bollywood Assemblage*, 4.

92. See Richard Dienst's reading of Sartre and the ideas of televisual seriality and flow (Raymond Williams) in *Still Life and Real Time* (1995): 8–12.

93. Gilles Deleuze, *Spinoza* (2001): 49.

94. Consider Hegel: "It is not the brain, *qua* a *physical* part, which stands on one side, but the brain *qua* the *being* of *self-conscious* individuality. This latter as a lasting character and spontaneous conscious activity exists *for* itself and *within* itself" (*Phenomenology*, 200).

95. Antonio Damasio, *Descartes' Error* (1995): xvi–xvii. Damasio's study is based on patients in whom brain lesions have impaired the experience of feelings. He talks about the phantom limb syndrome and anosognosia (153–4) in which patients do not realize that they are paralyzed and are therefore not worried about their future.

96. Teresa Brennan, *The Transmission of Affect* (2004): 9.

97. Ibid., 77–94.

98. See M. R. Bennett and P. M. S. Hacker, *Philosophical Foundations of Neuroscience* (2003): 64–5. They point out that during an epileptic seizure, due to an abnormal excitation of parts of the cortex, the person is temporarily denied some normal capacities (memory, decision-making, emotional stances, sense of humor), while the abilities to perform routine actions are retained.

99. Bennett and Hacker deny all previous analogies pertaining to some sort of centrality of the brain here: the brain is neither a computer nor is mind the programmer. It is not a central telephone exchange and the mind is not the chief telephonist. The purposes of a person are neither the purposes of her brain, nor those of her mind. "They are the purposes of the person—and they are to be understood in terms of facts about human life, social forms of life, antecedent events, current circumstances, agential beliefs and values and so forth." It is, of course, true that without the normal functioning of the brain, everyday purposes cannot be pursued. See *Philosophical Foundations of Neuroscience*, 65.

100. Ibid., 143.

101. See M. R. Bennett et al., *Neuroscience and Philosophy: Brain, Mind, and Language* (2007).

102. See Gerald Edelman and Giulio Tononi, *A Universe of Consciousness* (2000): 157–75. Also Gerald Edelman, *Wider Than the Sky: The Phenomenal Gift of Consciousness* (2004).

103. Edelman and Tononi, *A Universe of Consciousness*, 139–54.

104. Antonio Damasio, *The Feeling of What Happens* (1999): 11.

105. Paul Bové, *Poetry against Torture* (2008).

106. I am grateful to Ronald A. T. Judy for the idea and phrase "pending thinking."

107. Here I have in mind Bruno Latour's wonderfully innovative reconceptualization of the social as perpetual assembling and dispersion of actor-network relations in *Reassembling the Social* (2007).

108. See Jürgen Habermas, *The Structural Transformation of the Public Sphere* (1991) and *The Philosophical Discourse of Modernity* (1995).

109. Vivian Sobchack, "New Age Mutant Ninja Hackers" (2001): 326.

110. Lev Manovich, *The Language of the New Media* (2002): 253.
111. Ibid., 180.
112. Arjun Appadurai, *Modernity at Large* (1996): 5.
113. We could once again, and with a deep sense of irony, recall another observation made by Heidegger. Voicing concern with how the lure of modern technology causes Dasein to lose itself through a massified familiarity with the world, Heidegger says that technology, in that sense, becomes a "A Being-with-one-another [that] dissolves one's own Dasein completely into the kind of Being of 'the Others', in such a way, indeed that the Others, as distinguishable and explicit, vanish more and more. In this inconspicuousness and unascertainability, the real dictatorship of the 'they' is unfolded" (*Being and Time*, 164).
114. Jacques Derrida and Bernard Stiegler, *Echographies of Television* (2002): 4.
115. Jacques Rancière, *The Future of the Image* (2009), 10.
116. Ibid., 18–21.
117. See Hayles' wonderful exposition in *How We Became Posthuman*, especially chapter 3.
118. Ibid., 29. Stiegler says "Informatics is the instrumental and industrial concretization of cybernetics." The word *informatique* [informatics, as in data processing or computing] was first coined in 1962 by Philippe Dreyfus to combine the ideas of information and the automatic. *Technics and Time 2* (2009): 101.
119. See Deleuze, *Cinema 2*, 263–9.
120. Hannah Arendt's memorable theorization of massified thought in *The Origins of Totalitarianism* is pertinent here.

Part II

Informatics, Sovereignty, and the Cinematic City

CHAPTER 3

Allegories of Power/Information

In this chapter, I shall connect the theory of geo-televisual informatics and the concomitant question of a national being-in-the-world to a theme of sovereignty in contemporary India. I will examine some cinematic moments that express a new metropolitan habit of thought by which state-of-the-art informatization is immediately and inextricably tied to the desired arrival of a novel regime of power. The trope of "information" becomes emblematic of a new techno-financial imagination in these cases, one that seeks epic rewriting of an uneven third world historical landscape. This picture of information/informing emerges as a direct manifestation of an ardent religiosity of development, a particular will to power, and not merely a symptom of it. Two questions are of crucial importance: first, how and for what reasons must we reconsider (in our new media age) the long talked-about nexus between axiomatic modern instruments of communication (printing press, telegraph, even the railroad) and the invention of the nation as an "imagined" time–space continuum? How do pertinent questions of production, ideology, and interest change in an era of aggravated informatics? Secondly, if the kinetic flows of information set up telescopic relationships between historical distances (the country and city, for example) how does that alter scenarios of human agency and citizenship? Let us investigate these questions by taking a critical look at some films in which "information" itself appears as a narrative theme connected to a larger allegory of the nation.

Apoorva Lakhiya's 2003 film *Mumbai Se Aya Mera Dost* (*My Friend Has Come from Mumbai*) and Shankar's *Nayak: The Real Hero* (2001) will be our primary texts. These two films, along with Aziz Mirza's *Phir Bhi Dil Hai Hindustani* (*The Heart is Still Indian*) (2001), Goldie Behl's *Bas Itna sa Khwab Hai* (*Such Are My Small Dreams*) (2002), or the recent blockbusters *Rang De Basanti* (*Paint it Yellow*) (Rakeysh Omprakash Mehra, 2006) and *Lage Raho Munnabhai* (*Munna Meets Mahatma Gandhi*) (Rajkumar Hirani, 2006) form a small batch within the annals of popular Hindi cinema that explicitly deal with an overall informatization/capitalization of "traditional" contexts. This tendency is not unique in world cinema, but perhaps in contrast to memorable instances from the

West, like Peter Weir's *The Truman Show* (1998) or Maurizio Nichetti's *Ladri di saponette* (*The Icicle Thief*) (1989), matters are not limited to anxieties about the obsolescence of individual agency or privacy in the wake of massive structures and micropunctual networks of information. In Hindi cinema, informatization comes with a messianic or apocalyptic zeal, with grander arcs of exhilaration or foreboding. Geo-televisual informatics, as a form of socially transformative power, is seen either to electrify a perpetually gestating horizon of national becoming or, in telling moments, is seen to imperil it.

In Aziz Mirza's *Phir Bhi Dil Hai Hindustani*, for instance, a tie-up between two powerful corporate media houses and politicians creates the possibility of a barbaric event: the televised execution of a man accused of terrorism. The two principal protagonists are journalists who bear the burden of a modern consciousness *qua* justice, humanity, and citizenship rights. They are aghast at being faced with a perverse danger: that a population might be converted directly to a massified public, bypassing the promised historical tryst with a consolidated national *peopleness*. That is, a commercial and populist media space (ruled only by considerations of television ratings and profit) can be created without the completion of a civil society. Unbridled and inhuman market forces can thereby alienate the nation itself from its unique humanitarian spirit (the "heart" in the film title), which would include a non-violent Gandhian compassion. It is only after we get a glimpse of the televisual-informational system as a demonic power that it is tamed and realigned to the continuing story of the nation. It is by entering the belly of the beast (invading a broadcasting station), that assiduous citizens discover an Archimedean point to address the "heart" of the nation. Through their illegal and non-commercial transmission, they reanimate the sense of "Indianness" in the enthralled, mediatized mass. In the process, they also restore the works of information in themselves to their proper ethical function: that of facilitating an ongoing conversation of the nation with itself.

Similarly, in *Rang de Basanti*, a state-owned radio station is taken over by a group of young vigilantes to speak directly to the people and make them aware of corruption and malfeasance in the government. In *Lage Raho Munnabhai* the protagonist, a reformed mafia don, who believes that he is visited by the ghost of Mahatma Gandhi, becomes a radio talk-show host to inaugurate a new public cult of national spiritualism as an antidote to profane times. On the other hand, in *Bas Itna Sa Khwab Hai* one sees the other side of the problem. The ambitions of a powerful media baron and his abilities to manufacture consent are seen to imperil what is revealed to be the vulnerable and fragile foundations of the Indian political

system. The latter is saved, but only just. The horizon of dynamic information thus promotes two possibilities: a disconcerting alienation of the
people from an abiding national *Geist* due to nefarious mediations in the
capital–media–political sphere, and, on the other hand, to effect not just
an instant and heady reorientation of the public to authentic peopleness,
but also a popular cleansing of the governmental system in order for the
national state to emerge in its authentic form.

The First Story of the Nation: the Metropolis Comes to the Village

Apoorva Lakhiya's 2003 film *Mumbai Se Aya Mera Dost* (*My Friend Has
Come from Mumbai*) tells a story in which a new historic relationship is
forged between the country and the city. It begins in a small village in
contemporary Rajasthan, which (as a voiceover establishes) used to be one
of half a million such rural enclaves in present-day India that are without
electricity. At this point, however, the village has just become a bright spot
in the nightly landscape of the region. Within days of the arrival of electric
power, there is yet another novel import into these traditional backwaters.
Kanji, a young son of the soil who had moved to the big city of Mumbai
in search of a livelihood, returns with a television set and dish antenna as
presents for his grandfather. The TV is set up in the front yard of Kanji's
ancestral home for the entire village community to watch. When it is
switched on for the first time, a roaring lion appears on the screen. The
people scream and scatter in panic. The terror here is primal, but it is
calmed very quickly; normalcy of viewership is soon established, and fear
is replaced by wonder.

   The entire rural community is fast taken in by a strange geo-televisual
universe of sights and sounds. Hari, the village barber, becomes obsessed
with the desire to throw his razors with the dexterity and accuracy of cinematic cowboys handling six-shooters. Similarly, Abdul, another villager,
lends his body movements to a mode of slow-motion/stop-motion action
choreography famously seen in *The Matrix* trilogy. Hari and Abdul thus
become quixotic figures, zapped by a magical impelling beamed to them
from the skies. Their movements are locked in an indeterminate zone of
adventure, between a primitive, earthbound rusticity and an electrified
horizon of desires, with the latter presenting seemingly limitless scope for
self-invention. Others in the village are also taken up by different vistas
of being in the world and a vast repertory of lifestyle signatures. Bodies
venture forth from an organic composite of the agrarian community and
surreptitiously or publicly flow into the many global fictions that appear

on screen. Couples indulge in French kisses and stripteases on the sly and invent the "private" as an epistemological space for nucleated desires.

The early part of Lakhiya's film can be considered to be a short fairy-tale narrative of televisuality. The affections of curiosity and laughter, of recoil and endearment, that mark the awkward rites of passage from a pre-historical state of nature to a realm of metropolitan consumption are profound in their implications. Let us return to the early moment when the villagers are scared out of their wits by the lion on the TV screen. Why is their shock such a primal one? Why does it convolute everyday cognitive means of distinguishing the magical from the technological, or reality from illusion? The crucial point here is not that the villagers have never seen a television set. It pertains to the fact that *they have no geo-televisual idea of television*, despite being inexorably tied to the city through historical modes of production, politics, and migrant labor.

Televisuality, once again, has nothing essentially to do with the instrument called "television." It involves long-distance dissemination of material images and sounds, as well as imaginative pictures of being and becoming that irresistibly proliferate through affect, knowledge, or rumor. The powers of the geo-televisual bring about transformations in local habits, existential attitudes, and psychologies. Hence, the fact that the rustic population receives the new instrument as a pure, other-worldly entity imparts a mythic dimension to their own primitiveness. The village is revealed to be not just an "underdeveloped" space, but a pure sphere of noble natality untouched by a broader historical commerce of sight and sounds. The village is *local* in an absolute sense, in being the degree zero of the geo-televisual, and therefore unstained by the worldliness of modernity at large. Within the visual architecture in the film, there is thus an immediate relationship that is established between the village-in-cinema and the television-in-cinema. The latter inaugurates history in its proper sense in the former with the first roar. The only *subject* here is the television as an instrument of power that claims the village as its own by making it televisual. As in a dominant anthropological subjectivity that resides at the heart of this cinematic depiction, it is actually not the villagers on screen who see the television on screen, but the other way round. The villagers begin to behave as they should on TV. The roar is a meditation of the self-origins of television-as-subject, when it posits an originary landscape to mythologize its own coming into being in the world. The images of the telegenic village, as well as images of television-in-the-village, are components of a metropolitan power's conversation with itself. The city thereby conquers the village as its own inverted image.

The lion's roar ushers in two reckonings of temporality. The first is that of a congealed, stultified past of the village, which subsequently is clarified to be one of absolute stagnation and despotism. The second is a little more complex. It is registered by a phenomenological trigger of time that is as if pulled as soon as the set is switched on. This is a new temporal realm in which the origins of the geo-televisual coincide with that of history itself, and both become manifest powers in this desolate landscape *only with the advent of television as part of a certain stage in planetary financialization.* That is not just any television, but television with a special connection to the market. The screen witnessed by the villagers is not that of Doordarshan, or what used to be the pedagogic institution of the older, postcolonial, welfare state. The villagers overcome a deep historical alienation in a single stroke; despite the fact that they have never been ideologically recruited as citizens, they display a remarkable aptitude for being consumers of global "infotainment." They therefore go directly from a state of natural infancy in which the geo-televisual could only be the revelations of the gods, to an historical self-consciousness forged, not by philosophy or poetics, but by *information.*

The villagers become ardent viewers by bypassing grander projects (and the concomitant obstacles) toward citizenship, civil society, and representative politics. Their ambiotic mass of affections, which had so far not been touched by the spirit of a Hegelian understanding of history as humanity's long march to self-consciousness, are directly connected to a metropolitan hermeneutic of desire. The peasant thereby enters the virtual metropole by leapfrogging the unhappy divisions and battle-grounds that have, since time immemorial, alienated her from the historical city. The flood of otherworldly images does not result in any *ontological* transformation in tastes, beliefs, lifestyles, and labor practices. Rather, the transformations are cosmetic. They do not challenge traditions or taboos. The villagers, hitherto unsteeped in national culture, take to television in earnest because their romantic innocence proves to be nothing other than a waiting to revel. They are already enframed as cinematic images of "primitive-people-who-watch-images-on-television" and as such construe their own selves according to a televisual anthropology that has already claimed them and forecast what will happen to them once they are so claimed. The self is thus reported to the self as the fascinating other. Modes of labor and distribution of objects in the village are redrawn as ethnographic motions and attributes of the museum as a metropolitan grid of intelligibility. When the young man, Kanji, does what has been forbidden for generations and falls in love with Kesar, the beautiful sister of the cruel overlord of the area, the song sequences celebrating their amour rewrite their bodies into idioms of designer ethnic ware advertisements, tourism, and cottage curiosities.

The abridged movement from pre- to post-history is already chronologically mapped in the film because Kanji is on leave from his job in the city for thirty days. Signal events in a decade and half of the career of Indian television are telescoped in that short span of time. The villagers watch the tele-serial *Ramayana*[1] at the beginning of the film; by the end, they are avid watchers of the *Mahabharata*.[2] It is contextually clear that both programs, which were initially broadcast on Doordarshan during the late 1980s/early 1990s, are now rerun on private channels. The community watches both serials with fervent devotion. This begins a transformative politico-historical process in the village, albeit indirectly, in a fit of distraction. Busy witnessing the divine exploits of Lord Rama, the villagers stop going to the local temple and unintentionally disturb a longstanding edifice of power. A new, electronic Protestantism suddenly makes redundant the traditional protocols of *Darsana*,[3] marked by graduated priestly mediations based on class, caste, and gender privileges. Tributes rendered to the priest and the temple for the hitherto restricted privilege of witnessing the gods are reduced.

The priest complains about this to the *thakur* (feudal overlord) who lives at a distance from the village. The *thakur*, however, is unable to appreciate the gravity of the situation; he sees no threat to the status quo because he too has a television set in his mansion. The patriarch, however, does not understand that he gets only two terrestrial channels from the government-owned Doordarshan, while the villagers, equipped with a dish antenna, have access to the multi-channel, private sector geotelevisual universe. It is this information gap that proves decisive in the final conflict of the film. The *thakur* gets to hear about Kanji's relationship with his sister, Kesar, and draws the villagers into a tribalistic war of honor.

Unknown to the *thakur*, even before the battle can commence, the information odds and balance of power shift away from him. A crew from Star News arrives in order to film a human interest story on the latest coming of television technology to the boondocks. The villagers are therefore able to see images of themselves on the monitor as imminent information, while the journalists sense a bigger scoop in the local intrigue and go to interview the *thakur*. The arrogant despot unwittingly declares his evil intentions in front of the camera and heckles the crew during a live telecast. He thus grossly underestimates the new system and temporality of circulating images that have already inscribed themselves into his domain. The *thakur* works under the delusion that he can deal with the crew as well as the villagers in the same manner in which he has warded off the city and the republican revolution of 1950, through a terrestrial war of barriers and besiegements. He confuses the camera of Star News with that of the old Doordarshan,[4] which he is familiar with. The camera of Doordarshan was largely a recording instrument for the archival, developmentalist state, mired in the latter's sedentary maneuvers in slow historical time, its bureaucratic impasses, legal and extra-legal censorships, and fatal compromises between ruling groups. It was thus a camera devoted more to a modernist pedagogy than to information as instantaneous circulation. Such a camera, like all other formations of a "half-baked modernity," could thus be enclosed and beleaguered within the village as a *bordered* space of absolute sovereign control. The *thakur* does not realize that, in being able to enter a virtual realm in which the local can enter into instant telescopic relations with the global, the village has transcended the earthbound territorial grounds of his dominance.

Thanks to Star News, the *thakur* has already been "reported" by the time he attacks. He thinks the battle to be waged will be at a time of his choosing, and in a space where he controls the flow of visibilities and representations through supreme prohibitions and licenses. But he does not know that a different time scheme of geo-televisual power has already reduced him to an information image on a pan-Indian TV screen: that of an abject and suicidal "backlog" of old history. His clear and present actions have been judged elsewhere. The state, in this case, merely has to cover a finite distance to connect the judgment to the fact; it does not have to establish a guilt that has already been confessed and broadcast. Informatics is thus seen to bridge the historical gap between the constitutional law of the weak liberal democratic state apparatus and the "fact" of feudal oppression. Police jeeps are seen to be on the way to bring the tyrant to book even as the latter approaches the village with his goons. And yet, the final induction of the villagers into a constitutive narrative of the nation is not a formal matter. It contains a mythic dimension, which we shall now turn to.

After much trepidation the villagers finally decide to fight a decisive battle against the powers that have oppressed them for centuries. But this revolutionary motivation is not just the outcome of people suddenly becoming aware of their rights and rising up. They are alarmed when they realize that the danger includes losing the television and hence their viewership rights. But the combined weight of superstitious fears and timeless memories of abjection and powerlessness proves to be a mental block until it is once again television that inspires them. This vital event takes place when Kesar, in a bid to exhort them to battle, asks the profound question, "What have you learnt from TV?"

If the answer was limited to an inventory of consumer objects, a boundless universe of desires, and general knowledge of the distant and alienating state, the villagers would not be galvanized into action. But it is precisely at this moment that the otherwise calendrical time architecture of television intersects with a messianic temporality. The television was on while all of this was happening. An episode in B. R. Chopra's celebrated adaptation of the epic *Mahabharata* was being shown. By divine providence, Kesar's call to arms coincides with a special moment in the telecast of Krishna's enunciation of an ethical cosmology to Arjuna, just before the commencement of the titanic battle of Kurukshetra. Krishna, an incarnation of Lord Vishnu himself, utters those memorable words from chapter 4:7–8 of *The Bhagwad Gita* while goading the Pandava prince into a just war: "Yada Yada Hi Dharmasya / Glanirva Bhavathi Bharatha/ Abhyuthanam Adharmaysya / Tadatmanam Srijami Aham / Praritranaya Sadhunam Vinashaya Cha Dushkritam/ Dharamasansthapnaya / Sambhavami Yuge-Yuge" ("When righteousness is weak and faint and unrighteousness exults in pride, then my spirit arises on earth. For the salvation of those who are good, for the destruction of evil in men, for the fulfillment of the kingdom of righteousness, I come to this world in the ages that pass").[5] Learning from Gita momentously coincides with learning from TV.

After this oracular broadcast from the heavens, the villagers are stirred to take up arms against what they had earlier thought to be a sea of troubles. The picture of informational television in the cinematic world of *Mumbai* emerges as a mythic union between the earth and the sky, when the state and all the profane powers that *this* commercial television congeals into itself (the striptease, the French kiss, finance capital, globalization, supply-side economics) can be dissolved into a singular broadcast of divine wisdom. In this critical moment, television ceases to be what Heidegger calls a technology of *enframing* (*Gestell*) that simply produces the world as picture.[6] Instead, it is now lodged between the world of history and that of the epic. Hence, it is as if the earth itself, with its cosmology of memories and eternal waiting for the gods, that comes forth to be sheltered by what is now a mythically wise television. The myriad flows of information otherwise follow an empty, chronometric plane of temporality, but what is revealed is that it is not fundamentally at odds with a messianic time that tellingly interrupts the habitual and, in an instant, reveals the true path of Dharma. One is now properly at home with television because television, as an instrument of geo-televisual informatics, has been naturalized and blessed.

The *thakur* is finally vanquished. The police arrive just in time to prevent Kanji from taking the law into his own hands and finishing him off for good. But this time, unlike the classic instances outlined by Prasad in his definitive thesis on popular Hindi cinema of the 1970s (when the police always arrived late), the formal arrival of the men in uniform signals the closure of a process of policing that was always underway, facilitated by a vigilant camera in the frontiers. A "live" epic-informatic compact between the functions of the juridical state and a Dharmic order of justice enunciated in the *Gita* had already produced a spiritual *uniformity* that could claim all bodies, with or without formal attire, as soldiers. There can be no distinction between police officers and men in plain clothes at this point, since all view the world on the same plane of viewership. The republican revolution in the village had already been underway, and it was being televised.

Lakhiya's film, therefore, collapses together different imaginations of time. It begins with a picture of the pre-modern caught between an untarnished pastoral existence and Asiatic despotism. The end of despotism, however, is not seen to be succeeded by another stage of historical *agon* in relation to a gestating third world national development troubled by questions of class, caste, or gender. Once despotism is in retreat or has finally come to an end, the villagers are seen to directly enter a virtual metropolitan realm of circulating value, as image or value as affective consumption (in an overall capitalistic production of social life itself) without overcoming the historical distances or alienating obstacles that marginalize them from the city and its political economy. The imbibing of strange, otherworldly visuals into the heart of the community takes place through affections of familiarization and laughter. But this can take place only when cinematic temporality becomes absolutely one with time for viewing television and labor time is expunged from the picture. In other words, here we are connecting matters of style and representation to a material consideration of time as money in narrative cinema discussed in the previous chapter, along with rehearsing the other distinction between the metropolis as an abstract diagram of value and the industrial city. Hari, the barber, becomes "cinematic" within this framework of image as value only when he leaves his sedentary occupation and rides a donkey with his twin razors slung across his waist. Abdul's fascination with slow motion motorizes his body in a manner more conducive to picking quixotic fights than his toils as a peasant. Other figures too, in the course of their daily duties, enter the frame only after being excused from the dirt and grime of labor, as part of the ethnographic ensemble of cinema as museum or arcade. The life of the peasants "reported" on screen follows a track in which what is "worth" reporting is determined by how, and to what extent, one watches television and identifies oneself as televisual. The freedom gained in the boondocks is indistinguishable from the right to consume metropolitan information and at once be information to be consumed by the metropolis. Unlike the socialist-realist reportage of labor and noble poverty in films like *Mother India*, or even the developmental realist account of state mobilization and the plight of dairy workers in Shyam Benegal's *Manthan* (*The Churning*) (1976), labor cannot enter the overall picture of infotainment in *Mumbai*. I am, of course, not raising this as a simple matter pertaining to a politics of representation. Rather, I am connecting it to a thought of informatic visual anthropology that came earlier. It had set up a regime of telegenic value by which, in an overall metropolitan reporting of the self to the self as other, everybody could be seen on TV and enter a democracy of desire, but not their laboring bodies. This is because this new telegenic village, by the very logic of its creation, is not an entity of documentation or realist representation. It is an entity that is to be *advertised*. When that happens, what is foreclosed is the encounter between the geo-televisual and the customary. The extinguished site of this encounter would have been the very site of historical pain, the site of limitless possibilities pertaining to what we have come to know as the geo-televisual's prompts for teleopoetic and mythopeic modes of thinking and imagining. Let us keep this paradox alive: are we really talking about geo-televisual informatics, or a situation in which informatics extinguishes the geo-televisual image?

The fantasy in *Mumbai se Aya Mera Dost* is that of an instant absolution of history (especially its unhappy aspect) and the negation, even in a basic phenomenological sense, of the laboring process. It is a fantasy of a creative-destructive redrawing of an uneven landscape by a singular homogeneous theorem of value. Within this fantasy, the image of information-in-cinema, as a "frontierist" incarnation of a new sovereign power, assumes an onto-theological character. It is clear that the hinterland and the peasantry are Disneyfied in Lakhiya's film. What is nevertheless more crucial is how exactly this Disneyfication takes place. Let us examine the relationship this kind of cinema—as a material, expressive instance of *informatic modernization*—sets up with prior modes of *veritas* in representation. Without getting into the many complex differences between historical templates of realism[7] in Indian film, we can house them within a modernist sphere of aesthetic and political concern. Subalterns never spoke in such films of the past, but one can say that they were animated by dialectical tensions between desire and interest, between *Vertretung* (rhetoric-as-persuasion) and *Darstellen* (rhetoric as trope),[8] or between semblance and representation. When figures are withdrawn from such modes of enunciation and informatized, these binaries are collapsed together. Information not only threatens to abridge or erase "distance" in a phenomenological sense, but also tends to make redundant the spatial or temporal gaps (precisely where the burden of history is lodged) between such polarities. It is able to do so because it organizes and circulates signs in a manner not beholden to writing as enunciation, which is an act of scripting a world through agonistic historical negotiations. What is thus tendentially obliterated is the historical interval between sign and referent, between the advertised anthropological profile and "reality" or any conception thereof. The peasants as information-image are airy and ethereal because they have been virtually liberated from the dead weight of the past.

On the other hand, it would be a mistake to account for this cinematic picture of informatizing a third world mise-en-scène in terms of a broad template of postmodernism diagnosed by thinkers like Lyotard and Jameson in relation to Western societies under late capitalism. That is, perhaps we are not speaking of a scenario in which "the modernization process is complete and nature is gone for good."[9] Rather, the trope of information has to assume a messianic character precisely because it has been set the formidable task of erasing the picture of the absolute pre-modern (the Asiatic despot) and inaugurating a landscape of "perpetual presents" in a single stroke, without negotiating with the *agon* of modernity. That is, information as a theme of the transformative power of capital has to *narrativize* its coming into being in a context in which nature has not gone for good, and the modernization process is not complete. Moreover, this narrative has to compress a hitherto powerful imagination of historical time in order to transform a scenario of primitive accumulation directly to one of late capitalism. The information revolution has to arrive without the mediating stage of the industrial revolution. Much like the transcendental stupidity in Francis Fukuyama's "end of history" and "last man,"[10] this story positions itself as the "last narrative." That is, it promises that after it comes into being, there will no longer be the burden of history, but simply the grand supply and consumption of things; there will be no politics, but only management. It is a story that has to be rehearsed again and again, precisely because, at every instance of repetition, it has to register the presence of the historical in the act of emptying it out. I do not intend to open a can of worms here about the problems inherent in the theme of modernity itself or the many models of progress or becoming it provides. It is enough to say that the "modern," as a sea of historical *agon* (which includes the *agon* of incompleteness itself, as in the case of India and its republican revolution), imprints its disconcerting presence through the very event of its spectral overwriting. It is precisely because of this breathtaking journey between extremities of time—an absolute pre-modern and the singular postmodern—that there are frontal encounters, not causal passages between sign systems. The long-awaited but suddenly bypassed tryst with the modern appears as a line of rupture in this violent assembling process. These observations will be useful in understanding the allegorical presented at the end of this chapter.

The Second Story of the Nation: How Mumbai can become a Metropolis

The title of Shankar's 2001 film *Nayak—Asli Hero* (*Nayak—The Real Hero*) proposes a new protagonist for the times. The film is about the genesis of a figure, from nondescript, middle-class origins to a leader urgently called for by the ground realities of the third world market in a general sense, as well as particular folk interests in the Indian state of Maharashtra. But this is no ordinary story; the title qualifies the hero, emphatically one might add, with the epithet "real." The image of *Nayak* (which means hero in Sanskrit and several north Indian languages) is thus invoked in a position of splendid isolation amidst numerous examples of stellar heroism in the pantheon of Indian mass cinema. The promise here, therefore, is that a uniquely "real" aspect of this personage will single him out from a host of "reel"-based pretenders. However, this attribute of real-ness cannot be accounted for in terms of a mimetic logic of representation or of reflection. The filmic life and works of *Nayak* are not quite "real-istic" in a humdrum, phenomenological sense by which one habitually evaluates the "truth" content of cinema. On the contrary, his actions are super-human and miraculous, often beyond the finite capabilities of the human, and frequently assuming epic proportions. *Nayak* is a cinematic construct of a special kind. He performs the Herculean labors of navigat-ing the social dredges of an underdeveloped milieu and stringing together scattered signs and totems of the world at large—MacDonald's, the World Bank, unemployment, poverty, development, third world, shanty towns, housing, clean water, corruption, politics, publicity, citizenship, conjugal-ity, values, ethics, or even the proper name "India"—into a dynamic and synergetic world picture.[11] He is "real" because he responds to what the film marks as the most devoutly desired tasks of the times.

The Traffic Jam

The life of Shivaji Rao takes a turn toward the extraordinary when he finds himself equipped with a video camera in the middle of a rush hour traffic jam in Mumbai. This Q-TV news employee was on his way to work when the hold-up begins and quickly takes over the city. A Maharashtra State Transportation bus does not halt at a designated bus stop and is pursued by an irate group. They catch up with the vehicle at the next red light and confront the driver, Sakharam Selke. However, the arrogant and impetuous Selke not only refuses to apologize, but also seriously injures a student by pushing him off the bus. Within minutes, the agitated passengers and a quickly assembled group of bus operators are poised for a showdown in the middle of the road junction. It is from this point that the accidental correspondent, Shivaji Rao, picks up his camera and starts filming. What is of critical interest here is that, from the outset, Shivaji's "on the spot," guerrilla-style news-gathering fosters a diagnostic perspective of the situation that either intersects with, or punctually corresponds to, a transcendental global perception of cinema which comes with the latter's industrial omniscience and god-like editorial intelligence. As if by magic, Shivaji always arrives at the right place at the right time to record, in proper sequence, the islands of clarity that open up amidst the bedlam. A compact between these local and global standpoints gives rise to a utopian will to narration that tends to induct into its propulsive drive all floating signs and dispersed bodies in this cinematic universe. Nobody other than Shivaji knows exactly what is happening and why. He has already transcended the accidents and fragmentary motions on the ground and composed a wholesome tracking diagnosis. Later in the film this unique gift—one he acquires as if by magic and the fruits of which he relays to the world as urgent and conscientious information—is what gives Shivaji wondrous powers of speech. He is able to speak the truth to the world, or rather enunciate it afresh and call it properly into being by addressing the chaos.

Matters quickly escalate. The bus driver, a functionary of the ruling party, is a minor figure who arrives into and vanishes from the narrative solely as a force of schizophrenic disruption. After ejecting the student from the bus for no reason, he sneaks away to make a phone call and engineer a statewide strike in protest of his fictitious molestation. A couple of top-angle aerial shots subsequently suggest that within hours the traffic jam has not only throttled much of the city's road network, but has spilled over to the countryside as well. A feverishly filmed and rapid-cut montage, with a surreal rain of sheets of paper floating into the frame from the out-of-field, imbues the scenario with tragic effects. The critical-anthropological eye of cinema—warmed with its selective gaze for detecting, recording, ordering and signifying—assembles bodies and movements into symbolic and inferential perspectives. These add up to a world picture of an urban, third world middle class denied mobility: the student who fails to appear for his exams, the man who cannot attend a job interview, the bride who is prevented from making it to her wedding, the heart patient who dies in an ambulance en route to hospital. In contrast, Selke and his fellow bus drivers appear in the pro-filmic city space as pure pathological animations from a lumpen proletarian "outside," without biography, history, or ethical habitat. In their inhuman coldness and cruelty, they are not only incapable of a minimum amount of conformity and voluntarism demanded from the citizen, but are also viciously hostile to a basic imperative of metropolitan life: that of keeping money and laboring/consuming denizens in circulation. Their violent and seditious figures are the only ones in the crowd disconnected from verbs and predicates that denote value and legitimate practice—education, occupation, or medication.

Shivaji does not miss any incident that becomes important in the task of following a dominant grammar of plausibility in narrative cinema, and donating meaning to the cinematic world even as it is being built frame by frame. He captures Selke on camera while the latter is making his insidious phone call, and also records, with unbelievable ubiquity, all the other revelatory episodes that follow, including one involving the baiting of an Islamic constable, which gives a communal slant to the conflict. Meanwhile, the unrest quickly descends into rioting and looting of shops in the precinct. In the middle of the mayhem Shivaji films two other phone calls, both made by the police officer in charge to Balraj Chauhan, Chief Minister of Maharashtra, asking for permission to use force to disperse the crowd. Chauhan expressly refuses to allow the use of tear gas, bullets, or any other measure to defuse the situation. The reasons he gives makes his interest as a political functionary amply clear: caught between four voting constituencies (students, workers, the ruling party, and opposition) which are presently at loggerheads, the Chief Minister is unable to make a "decision."[12]

A resolute application of sovereign will is thus foreclosed by a perpetual impasse between interest groups and syndicalist factions of a third world parliamentary democracy. The jam by then has become a ruinous dispersal of energy, value, and property in dire need of being reconstituted as a "city" of homogeneity and consensus. In such a situation of emergency, law-preserving forces are prevented from re-establishing a monopoly of violence precisely because the Chief Minister remains mired in liberal parliamentary protocols of "endless conversation."[13] He is always caught up in the dead center of things. He treads a finely calibrated, centrist line between a narrow spectrum of Left/Right politics and is thus unable to pronounce a categorical friend/foe definition appropriate to the context. The weak machinations of a democratic polity can be exercised in this case only by suspending sovereign power; Chauhan can maximize votes only by maintaining a catastrophic status quo in the battlefield.

Later in the film, the body of evidence mounted by Shivaji's camera is used during a televised public interrogation/trial of Chauhan. Shivaji is asked by Q-TV bosses to step in as anchor of the program *Amne Samne* (*Face to Face*) and interview the Chief Minister. The discussion, broadcast live, follows a line of inquiry oriented to a focused notion of good governance which "educated" citizens like Shivaji expect from the premier office. After pointing out that the rich are getting richer and the poor poorer under Chauhan's administration, Shivaji produces reports from the IMF, Amnesty International, Human Rights Watch, and the World Bank to show that the Chief Minister has failed to provide proper leadership in the most important area—development. The World Bank report declares that the latest installment of a loan has been cancelled because the previous one never reached the people, but was gobbled up by a circuit of bribes and embezzlement in the Chauhan ministry. Cornered by these disconcerting questions, Chauhan throws a radical challenge to Shivaji: he offers to invoke a constitutional provision and make the young man acting Chief Minister for twenty-four hours for the world to see if he can do any better.

After a lot of soul-searching, Shivaji accepts. A remarkable sequence in the film depicts him carrying out his duties in a manner that shakes the government completely. Here, in a nutshell, is what happens. Sivaji begins the day by launching a massive clean-up of the governmental machinery. He has, by then, already made a telling statement by arriving for office in corporate attire, refusing to don the Gandhian *khadi* robes widely used by Indian politicians. After that, he solves the hitherto intractable housing problem in one of the largest shanty towns, and other allied matters, through a series of decisive suspensions of personnel: the chairman of the Housing Development Committee, a government rations contractor, a doctor, and two police officers. The general tempo of decision-making and instant enforcement of sovereign will achieves a spectacular dimension when Shivaji single-handedly fights and neutralizes a group of goons and political contract killers. Toward the middle of the day, he sends a televised message to the public, asking them to collect receipts of purchase from merchants in order to ensure collection and accounting of sales tax revenues. The Chief Minister also warns unscrupulous businessmen that strong action will be taken against them unless they declare and submit their dues. Within hours, the government coffers swell with tax receipts.

Before sundown, the money has been used to create jobs and provide income opportunities to the 20,000 families in the shanty town, who, by then, have been relocated to government-funded living quarters. Shivaji then completes the clean-up process within the allotted time by suspending, by ordinance, more than 45,000 corrupt government functionaries and ministers of a dozen state departments. The list also includes the name of Chief Minister Balraj Chauhan, who is arrested at the stroke of midnight.

Cleaning up the Cinematic City

The entire sequence featuring Shivaji as Chief Minister for a day is interspersed with stylized fast-motion and iconic freezes similar to the visual style in MTV capsules. The movement of bodies through diegetic time and space is hastened by disjunctive editorial splices. Shivaji and his entourage, as figural attributes of a special cinematic cosmology, are set to an affective-symbolic rhythm that easily overwhelms the limited cartography of filmic Mumbai. A corrupt police officer, for instance, is seen sitting at his desk in full uniform when Shivaji informs him over the phone that he is being suspended. After an instantaneous ellipsis in diegetic time, the officer is shown sitting at the same desk and in the same posture, but symbolically stripped of his uniform. There is thus an inhuman acceleration of bodies and things by which narrative time breaks out of its normative metrical flow and acquires an epic maturation and thickness. The organization of space too is no longer constrained by the geometry of a determined milieu; spaces arrive as sheets afloat in a new messianic tempo of cinema, in the form of imminent stages for epic actions already foretold.

The epic dimension of this episode is at odds with a normative economy of segmented serial/analytic narration largely identified with classical Hollywood film. In terms of the latter a symmetrical relationship of plausibility should be established between the volume of work done, the time taken to do it, and the limits of human agency. As far as the "cleaning up" sequence in *Nayak* is concerned, the prescription is that there should be a sense of phenomenological adequation between the objective of cleaning up a monstrous bureaucracy, the time allotted (a single day), and the locomotive, affective, and intellectual powers of the human. But what is instead witnessed in this sequence is a hyperbolic rewriting of real time by a diegetic temporality out of bounds. As soon as the figure of Shivaji is inducted into this dynamism, he achieves a lightness of being without the lugubrious burden of third world historical conditions. The finite human attributes of his persona are heightened and transformed into an immanent image of *Nayak*—the messianic hero in the city. The image of the hero becomes a manifest leaderly will that can be dispersed immediately and universally throughout the milieu, with interactive communication between the myriad horizontal flows of social life and singular transcendence of the state. Shivaji always arrives at the right place at the right time to solve problems precisely because his body is *cinematic* in a way that is no longer anthropomorphic. He is not a reflection of a presiding human subjectivity. Rather, an epic dimension of filmic time that claims him is the only subject here. It is this temporal order that brings about dynamic compacts between man and milieu (Shivaji and the shanty town, Shivaji and bureaucratic corridors), and man and objects/instruments (Shivaji and the telephone, Shivaji and the fax machine that instantaneously circulates letters of suspension). The figure of *Nayak* is thus an ensemble of humanoid (figure, attire, gait, speech, discourse, signs of education, class, etc.) and machinic (special effects, a larger-than-life editorial intelligence that makes metrical space vanish from beneath his feet and transports him to the thick of the action) attributes. Perhaps all cinematic figurations are such, but in this case the profile of the mortal and the machinism of "cinema" can no longer be hierarchically arranged, with the first humanizing and concealing the second. Shivaji is always a cinematic android in anthropomorphic drag.

From this perspective, the film *Nayak* is a mishmash of realist cinematic paraphernalia (psychological characterization, shot/reverse-shot, continuity editing, 180 degree rule, etc.) and a primitive motorization of those same devices to an absurd level beyond historical finitudes of the human. The so-called "real" hero is thus only a pretender—a vehicle for unscrupulous wish-fulfillment through bad faith and faulty representation. Unlike the camera of Descartian humanism that always has to open out to the world in a state of doubt, the cinematic camera here, which aligns a global perspective with Shivaji's line of vision, is always imbued with mythic pregnancies of already existing meanings. But if one were to try to understand it on its own terms, Shankar's film could be seen in a different light altogether. It can be understood as a direct manifestation of thought in cinema, an autonomous force with a social reality of its own, rather than as a faithless reflection or representation; *Nayak* is thus an unmediated cinematic class fantasy. But under what conditions of epistemology, technology, and social relations of production (of discourse, cinema, ideology, etc.) can such an image-of-the-leader be possible?

The State of Information

Shivaji's entire one-day tenure as Chief Minister is broadcast live on Q-TV. As soon as the camera is switched on, it seems that the state itself is inaugurated in its proper form with the arrival of a pre-existing consensus that awaits no further stimulus: the people watch the leader watching over the people. This synergy of points of view recasts the body of Shivaji as that of leader directly and luminously incarnating the general will. He assumes the mantle of *Nayak* the leader as a bundle of energy, intelligence, and information that harbors no secrecy or dark side. We shall thus, at this point, make a distinction between Shivaji the man and *Nayak*, which is a compact between the man and the television camera.

The aspect of the common man that Shivaji displays is a force of rigorous re-familiarization of exceptional situations; when his face is inserted into the madness of things, it comes with an ontological power that immediately accords strange and new objects of the world with already designated, endearingly familiar profiles. However, that is not due to his visage alone, but because it is a visage that is *publicized*. His is a wisdom that is not merely uttered, but instantly enframed together and connected to "reality." It is this force of informed and informing governance that immediately connects signs to their referents, dissolves complexities of history to the "already said" or already remembered, and reduces language to pure functions of mass transmission. Hence, categories of thought and political action, like rights, law, or truth, are set to a trans-contemplative, accelerated application of cogent administration, without any interval for investigating, knowing, legislating, or judging. This is why in the cinematic transformation of Shivaji to *Nayak*, the usual agents of political or juridical intelligence—the ministerial cabinet, house members, or judges—need never appear. The *Nayak*'s emphatic decision-making can take place on the spot without the delay of institutional procedures and the clamor of parliamentary conversations as his actions and their victims are both caught "live" on camera.

From a messy, historical landscape, Shivaji recasts the city as a flat screen of transparent visibilities. To that end, he does not have to pronounce a new, constitutive worldview strikingly different from Chauhan's. In fact, Shivaji measures himself and the corrupt Chief Minister on the same scale of managerial capabilities and speed. They are distinguished only by their relative efficiencies and commitment to a chronicle of development already foretold. Politics for Shivaji is not a battleground of thought and action pertaining to combative readings of the world and its historical problems. Rather, it is a constant facilitating and secure management of circulating value as, and only as, capital. His "educated" and youthful governance does not extend to a questioning of World Bank proposals on the basis of the very concern that he himself states at the beginning: that the rich are getting richer and the poor poorer. He does not draft a new social contract of rights and duties; rather, he establishes a visual contract of transparency and efficiency. However, this visual contract is not suited to communicative actions and rational public conversations about different value systems and ways of life; instead, its chief objective seems to be instantaneous detection, containment, and a perpetual suspension of disorder, that is, a relentless warding off of disturbances that vex the process of socializing capital's neo-liberal command. The visual contract binds the denizens of the city into a subject–subject cycle of sovereignty[14] which, in the heat of the "live" moment, can connect statements of suspension immediately to visibilities of "corruption." The principle of seeing and being seen achieves an amusing application when a gang of criminals watch the vigilant activities of Shivaji with relish, until the mise-en-scène starts looking familiar to them and they realize that the crusading premier is approaching their neighborhood to nab them.

The instantaneous gathering of information as image is that which allows the *Nayak* to operate without delay, bypassing the disabling dialectics and plural interpretations of liberal polity. When Shivaji suspends dishonest functionaries "on the spot" and in the presence of a live television camera, a livewire circuit of immediate consensus is produced that is predicated on both faith in the epic voluntarism of the leader and an unquestionable devotion to the sufficiency of a social technology of information in itself. This is not because the camera does not lie, but because in the uninterrupted stream of direct transmission (which is seen to legitimately monopolize the flow of meaning itself), it has no *time* to lie. The *Nayak* becomes immanent through the very process of a violent compression of time and space, by which gaps between the private and the public, the law and the fact are informatized. He is thus a part of the cinematic image of information itself, and not a "representative" of it. As Shivaji keeps reminding the perturbed Chauhan during the dramatic television interview, one has to answer the facts—the live telecast is *on*, the *people are watching*. In the present circumstances, there can be no citizenship without adequate viewership.

In *Nayak—Asli Hero*, one sees a form of melodrama assembling with the techno-informatic diagram of what can be called a new metropolitan will to power. This assemblage of social bodies (the educated urban middle class) and social machines (television technology and sovereign tasks) can be provisionally called a picture of "informatic governance." This form of power does not operate through dialectical syntheses between opposites or traditional symbiotic exchanges between war and politics; instead, it works by way of forceful micro-management of tendencies, data inflows, and variables.[15] The screen–city couple can accommodate only precepts which are already predicted; it cannot harbor or recognize an event the leader has not already talked or warned about. Here there can no longer be any *potentia* for an ontological transformation of values, but only technical innovations that can keep repeating, illustrating, and calling into being what the managerial monologue has already divined or forewarned. The *Nayak*'s management is thus deemed efficient not because it *knows* best, but because it can *report* best and *act* fastest. Individuals great and small can only climb onto one or many designated demographic profiles: the criminal (the contract killers, Balraj Chauhan), the unemployed or home-less (the inhabitants of the shanty town), and the "people" (the masses who ask Shivaji to run for office). Informatic governance consists of the state's pharmacopic actions on such bodies, through measures of develop-ment aid, medication, schooling, or policing.

In Shankar's film, the passage of the figure of Shivaji into the iconic aspect of the *Nayak* happens precisely when, in the image of the "direct" telecast, the camera of cinema becomes indistinguishable from the camera of information. Cinema, of course, has assumed imperial forms in the past by many such mergers with the anthropological camera or the eth-nographic camera. But despite the obvious presence of Q-TV, informa-tization, as a diagram of power that envelops the city, is not restricted to instruments of media technology like radio, television, or print. Rather, informatic power pertains to a micro-social spread of sovereign will and calls for a novel form of habituation and conformity in what is a new mana-gerial environment. Later in the film, after Shivaji contests the state legis-lature elections and becomes *de facto* Chief Minister, he sets up complaint boxes for public use throughout Maharashtra with the promise that action will be taken within twenty-four hours to address the concerns of every letter dropped. This informing/being informed circuit of intelligence later proves crucial in dealing with a moment of danger. When the criminal stooges of Balraj Chauhan plant four bombs around Mumbai to disrupt law and order, Shivaji hears of the plot well in advance, through informa-tion provided by a network of citizens. As such, informatic governance is a techno-social horizon where the immanent monadic consciousnesses of the people instantly meet and correspond with the transcendental wisdom of the leader.

Iconic Genealogies

There are further important dimensions to Shivaji's transposition from ordinary man to leader. The mantle of *Nayak* is not the outcome of a mere formalization of capital's command over signifying processes, or of making global a neo-liberal manual of governance. The iron aspect of *Nayak* holds many other auratic qualities which endow him with an aspect of love and familiarity. It is this crucial component that prevents him from becoming a cold universal, accords him name-giving rights (he is the one who calls a spade a spade), and the right to stand outside the law and announce that no one can be outside the law.[16] These powers and qualities give him the Dharmic position of the *sutradhaar*—the one able to string scattered concerns of life and finance into a constitutive, cosmic drama of development.[17] The new leadership of *Nayak* becomes possible not only by an epistemological sufficiency of Shivaji's method, but also through the ontological *certitude* of his word. The latter force allows for a special operation of language, whereby global prescriptions for production and law-keeping are socialized in the local realm through procedures of ritualistic vernacularization. It involves the evocation of a mythic memory of *Nayak*dom that seeks to naturalize Shivaji's managerial concerns and render them holy.

One can begin with the name itself. "Shivaji" triggers memories of the seventeenth-century Marathi chieftain who fought against the Islamic Mughal dynasty and has been subsequently lionized in dominant late nineteenth-/twentieth-century nationalist discourses as the modern founder of a tragically evanescent "Hindu Rashtra."[18] The short form, "Shiva," by which the hero's parents and friends address him, recalls the creator-destroyer figure in the Vedic pantheon. In diegetic terms, Shivaji's journey from common man to anointed leader involves several gestational stages, in which his body keeps accruing particle signs from disparate tel-evisual and mythic sources. After completing his one-day tenure as Chief Minister, he is attacked by Chauhan's goons. He manages to fight them off in a digitized, hyper-real combat sequence featuring high-wired bodies strikingly reminiscent of *The Matrix*, but his clothes are burnt off and his body covered with mud. A group from the city discovers their leader the next morning and bathes him with milk, the customary way of cleaning the idol *Shivalinga* during the festival of *Shivaratri*. Later, when Shivaji goes to the countryside, the farmers recognize him and offer him the first grains of their harvest, an offering usually reserved for the gods. Later, in the fantastical "O Saiyan" ("Oh Beloved") song sequence, Shivaji appears in the traditional garb of a Hindu king surrounded by medieval European knights in full armor. It is through such non-linear, extra-constitutional modes of ritualistic vernacularization that the educated, Westernized Shivaji becomes an earthy "postulate" for divination and deliverance.

Apart from these mythic registers, there is another frame of reference for the *Nayak*'s iconic leadership. Mr Bansal is an honest bureaucrat who takes pleasure in working with Shivaji ("an opportunity to work for an *educated* Chief Minister for a change") during the latter's one-day clean-up drive. In trying to convince the reluctant hero that he should enter politics on a full-time basis, Bansal complains that it is due to a selfish dereliction of responsibilities on the part of an urban intellectual class that the country is in such bad state. The exemplary names he invokes to encourage Shivaji are indeed remarkable in their proximal application: Mohandas Karamchand Gandhi, Thomas Alva Edison, and Alexander Graham Bell. According to Bansal, the world would have been far worse off if these luminaries had chosen to stay at home and confine themselves to individual and petty interests. In his passionate articulation, these names appear as a panorama of signifiers free of any historical location. They are particularized bits of an urbane "quizdom"—semiotic pulses mobilized to create a de-differentiated specter of middle-class meritocracy and vanguardism. Shivaji is thereby invited to enter the murky world of politics as an entrepreneurial saint-*provocateur* who is the bearer of the Dharmic, rather than a mere human expert in administration. He is inserted into what is purported to be a sphere of multi-party parliamentary procedures as an "outsider" who is at once mythic, as well as endowed with pragmatic technical and meritocratic credentials.[19] The *Nayak* has to become a "manager" for the same reasons that Gandhi had to become a Mahatma.[20]

Shivaji can therefore also be considered an assemblage of authorial signatures: Shivaji the hero, Shiva the god, Gandhi the national leader, or Graham Bell the innovator. In him, the attributes of management and mythical agency are indeterminately present, without synthetically resolving their mutual tensions.[21] The figure is therefore "real" because it neither faithfully copies nor escapes (as in many commercial fantasies of heroism) from what is "out there"; instead, it claims to be able to order into being what "should be there," as a commanding cinematic image of national destinying. The-image-of-the-hero has a life of its own; it does not assert itself as reflection, with a borrowed vitality from the material universe. Rather, it is meaningful matter itself of a cinema machine that is part of an overall technologization of social life. *Nayak* is an immanent actionist class fantasy emphatically advertised, a fantasy that re-scripts the universe, brings mythic memories and cool gadgets under a new regime of information and desire, and, in the process, brings the universe to judgment.

As Deleuze and many others have suggested, a study of the unique aspect of the expressive power of the cinematic begins with the movement of the image. The efficacy of this form of power/publicity, therefore,

3.1, 3.2, and 3.3: The many incarnations of *Nayak*.

must not be gauged in terms of an abstracted, frozen architecture of propositions; that is, how *Nayak* studiously spins ideological concepts into a *constitutive* edifice of the nation in the world or to what extent that edifice is riddled with holes. To critically judge the cinematic in this way would be to dismiss it by calling it conceptually poor, simplistic, or naive. But that would be to underestimate, in a critically disabling manner, the evocative powers of such a vein of populist entertainment. A phenomenological reduction of movements of melodrama and affect to instances of the Hegelian concept would call for a primary separation of the image from its movement; that is, a consideration of the film as a series of snapshots. The creation of the positive concept in the Hegelian sense invites the subjective consciousness to absolve the object of its vital motilities and produce its corpse in a timeless theater of historical inquiry. In his brilliant Foreword to *Grundrisse*, Martin Nicholas elaborates on the formative conditions of the Hegelian concept: to have a "concept" (*Begrieff*) in the Hegelian sense means to "grasp" (*Begreifen*) or "grip" the thing mentally, to get hold of it and render it still as appropriation. (*Werke* XVIII in *Geschichte der Philosophie* I, pp. 305, 325). Lenin's comment in *Philosophical Notebooks* (*Collected Works* XXXVIII, pp. 259–60) can also be cited in this regard: "We cannot imagine, express, measure, depict movement, without interrupting continuity, without simplifying, coarsening, dismembering, strangling that which is living. The representation of movement by means of thought always makes coarse, kills—and not only by means of thought, but also by sense perception, and not only of movement, but every concept. And in that lies the *essence* of dialectics."[22]

In contrast to this form of evaluation, one might say that the power of the cinematic in *Nayak* lies precisely in the quality of movement that the filmic image brings. That is, not in how adequately it arranges propositions (like the World Bank, India, development, corruption, etc.) in punctually synthetic forms, but how it affectively orchestrates them. *Nayak* does not usher in the world by resolving the tortured dialectics of the old, but embraces it as a torrent of "presentisms" that can be encountered not through an historical consciousness, but in the way of informatic feedback loops. Attributes of modernity or doxa of tradition are never engaged in foundational conflicts in this realm. Instead, they enter into a spectacular realm of peace where rich and poor, neo-liberal management and traditional paternalism of the father, the welfare state and the World Bank are set in mutual concert. They are merely advertised through the movement of information-images.

Sovereignty as Melodrama: The "Lalloo Assemblage"

This thought of informatics-in-the-city, as a signature of development, is undeniably hyperbolic. It is, like the disappearance of circulation time itself, akin to an impossible dream of capital. As such, the fantasy of informatic governance can find cinematic form only as myth rather than as a purely techno-financial structure, through complex melodramatic assemblages between humanistic concerns, themes of welfare, and visions of terror and violence. The broad ideological purpose here, much like *Mumbai Se Aya Mera Dost*, is to present a utopian desire for a perfect telescopic relationship between an abstract global diagram of financialization and the uneven ground realities of a third world milieu. This new regime of power is announced in the film to be "post-political" because it is seen to inaugurate a system of absolute transparency in governance. It is given a humane aspect not just through Shivaji's interactions with ordinary people, but also in the city-bred, educated young man's relationship with the country girl, Manjari, which is broadly symbolic of a desire to integrate town and country in this new picture of enlightened patriarchy. The girl's traditional father finally blesses the "national couple" only when he is convinced that his future son-in-law is not a "politician."

Let us take a closer look at a moment of "exception"[23] to this overall dispensation of absolute, post-political transparency. For it is at that point that a hitherto hidden aspect of *Nayak*'s managerial stewardship reveals itself. The moment is special because it is only then that Shivaji does something as Chief Minister that is not transparently broadcast to the public. This happens after the young man reaches the end of his tether in dealing with his rival, Chauhan. After losing office, the latter had been busy trying to assassinate or discredit the new age hero, hiring hitmen from Malaysia or planting bombs in the city. Matters become intolerable when an attempt on Shivaji's life claims his innocent parents. Shivaji realizes that the "politician" Chauhan represents a pathological energy that cannot be controlled by principled management alone. He thus plans to hoist the disgruntled former Chief Minister by his own petard.

Before we go into how exactly this plan is carried out, let us try to understand the genealogy of the figure of Chauhan as an evil counterpoint to the *Nayak*. Chauhan can be understood as an instance of what can be broadly called an overall "Lalloo assemblage" in Indian cinema and public culture. That is, his cinematic figuration borrows from a caricatural typology routinely deployed in Hindi cinema of the last two decades to depict the political degeneration of the Nehruvian order. Emblematically put in place through the deployment of a certain mannered acting style, uncouth and uncivil behavior, and the use of Bihari–Bhojpuri dialects, this assemblage immediately lays out a field of inter-textual references. It grounds the figure as an anthropomorphic incarnation of those very energies that besiege the new city and prevent it from coming into being. This iconic image of perversion is largely drawn from a cult of *dehatism*[24] centered on the public persona of Lalloo Prasad Yadav, the former Railway Minister[25] of the Central Cabinet and erstwhile Chief Minister of Bihar—a state that is rich in minerals, but also chronically underdeveloped. Hailing from the lower-caste constituency of the Yadavs, Lalloo Prasad is one of many politicians in India's complex political dispensation who rely on a solid voter base maintained through tribute and kinship alliances. From an elite perspective, Lalloo is thus emblematic of a tribalistic machinery that continues to inundate rational processes of financialization. He is reckoned as a figure of obstinate antagonism that not only effects a continual, pre-modern dismantling of the parliamentary mechanism, but also wards off a global imperative of neo-liberal "development." The cinematic Lalloo is a conglomerate of affective markers pertaining to class, caste, dialect, education, hygiene, violence, totalitarianism, brutality, and myriad pathologies. A plethora of such effects can be compressed into grotesque parodies or distributed across bodies and peoples of different ethnic and linguistic backgrounds as interchangeable signs of a terrifying pre-modern specter that continues to haunt India in the new millennium. The panorama of comic villains in popular Hindi cinema based on the Lalloo prototype is indeed a vast one; examples include Bachchu Yadav in *Shool* (*Weapon*) (E. Niwas, 1999), Lakhan Yadav in *Calcutta Mail* (Sudhir Mishra), Sadhu Yadav in *Gangaaja* (*Ganges Water*) (Prakash Jha, 2003), Parshuram Bihari in *Major Saab* (Tinnu Anand, 1998), and Balraj Chauhan himself.

Chauhan's affiliation to this overall "Lalloo assemblage" is underlined from the very beginning, particularly through the acerbic wit of the government bureaucrat Mr Bansal. By the time Shivaji calls him to a private meeting to carry out his plan, Chauhan is well entrenched in the film as the figure of the "politician" who can only be a body of pure, "uneducated" pathologies. In the chamber where the private meeting takes place, Chauhan is tricked into incriminating himself. Shivaji pulls out a gun, shoots his own arm, and then throws the weapon to the bewildered Chauhan, who catches it by reflex. On hearing the gunshot, the Chief Minister's bodyguards rush in. Seeing Shivaji injured and Chauhan in an incriminating posture, they shoot the latter dead without further ado.

The private room that Chauhan had unwittingly entered thus becomes a space of sovereign secrecy and *exception* to which the camera of information is not privy. It is a non-televised operating space of a new sovereignty that declares that everything should be televised. After this founding act of violence, cinema is once again seen to resume the perpetual citation of the visual contract of the screen–city couple as normative. The cameras are switched on and a live telecast of the leader in action continues after a brief break. The exit of Chauhan is a summary elimination of a world of signs and negative energies pertaining to inertia, underdevelopment, and corruption, all compressed into his body. Chauhan is thus the scapegoat *par excellence* whose dispatch paves the way for the final transcendence of unhappy histories and a singular leap of faith. After the fatal shooting, the scrupulously ethical Shivaji is mortified at his descent into "politics," but he is reminded by the honest bureaucrat, Bansal (who guesses what has happened), that it is precisely thanks to this act that the city can be finally absolved of "politics" and merged into an endless, post-historical global administration of things. The killing of Chauhan was, like Fukuyama's Hegelian vision of the "last man," the last "political" act.

This is where the cinematic melodrama lends itself in an unbridled manner to a secret onto-theology of capital. After the exit of the scape-goat, a prophetic leadership can be uncoupled from the yoke of history and bring about a permanent miracle of progress. A seductive montage begins on screen featuring Shivaji heading a group of new age managers who are symbolically marching forward. "No Vacancy" signs in front of office buildings change to job postings as armies of fresh college graduates run towards them in slow motion. Nothing but a dry leaf falls into a now empty public complaints box. The film ends with a cinematic lap dissolve that magically transforms the pockmarked cityscape of suburban Mumbai into a digitized picture of a downtown first world metropolis, complete with high-rises and helicopters dotting the skyline. Let us dwell on the profound implications of this final shot.

Nayak as Allegory

The traffic jam exemplifies the role of cinema as a symbol machine. It was then that the city appeared for an instant in a dissolved state—the *tanquam dissoluta*. But the filmic jam is symbolic not because it reflects, in a realm of truthful subjective representation, an endemic state of affairs, but because as a cinematic bringing together of visibilities and statements, it has tried to set up an accord between an anarchic dispersal of signs and the ideological signifying process that designated the jam as diagnostic of the nation at large. We are drawing this formulation from a fragment from Benjamin: "The object of a symbol is imaginary. A Symbol means nothing, but is, in accordance with its essence, the unity of the sign and the intention that fulfills its object. The unity is an *objectively* intentional one; its object is imaginary . . . . We may not ask what the meaning of the symbol is, but may ask only how, in a realm of what objective intention and what signs, it has come about" ("Outline for a Habitation Thesis" [1996]: 269).

This objectivity pertains to a material relation of power/discourse and not a transcendental dictation of a sovereign *human* subjectivity. It has, in other words, no rational status of truth in terms of a unified phenomenology, but is the product of an elite instrumentalization of language. The latter effects an efficient, technical communication between scattered signs on screen and ideological judgments about the condition of the country: a picture of the world out of joint and an entrepreneurial exasperation about static third world realities. The only materiality here, once again, is that of a subject–subject visual contract of cinema. Cinema, in other words, is neither a window nor a mirror, but a form of discursive power in the world. As Foucault would say, it produces realities.

It is thus neither a composite intellect of a community of subjects, nor a contractual "tacit consent" of equal shareholders who designate the symbolic as such. Rather, it is the visual contract of power, which produces practices of viewership and viewer judgment, that makes the symbolic possible. Contemporary metropolitan Indian culture (of which the concept "Hindu" serves as a baseline of normalcy) is not an organic resurgence of a national being, but the result of specific assemblages, affinities, and constellations between forces of urban technocracy, finance capital, and ideology. Hence, unlike Hobbes or Locke, one can begin with the contract itself instead of its volunteering human signatories. That way, instead of trying to forge an anthropological understanding of why citizens, in their naiveté or wisdom, might agree to accord something with the status of a symbol, one can try to examine how the workings of the symbolic machine of cinema propose signs as well as the subjectivities that fulfill them: the picture of the city under duress as well as that of the middle-class messiah who rescues it.

The contentious question of national allegory in third world culture is difficult to avoid if this symbolic impulse is generalized and associated with an overall style of narration in Indian popular films like *Nayak*.[26] But perhaps allegory can be proposed as a non-narratological trope, a moment of interruption or supplementation that occurs when narration either reaches an impasse or forces a violent passage between contending sign systems. It can be understood as part of the rhetoric of cinema that always brings about a tension between the noun and the event, rather than a linear mapping of them in a schema of historicism.

3.4: Historical Mumbai being rescripted as the metropolis.

Considering allegory in this sense allows one to attend those moments of tension when a dominant grammar of cognition and plausibility fails to command the errant sights and sounds of a changing milieu. Allegory in that sense would be an event of catachresis, the body of the film itself, and not the relationship between it and what it stands for. It would not be determined in terms of a parallelism and a metonymic accord between the story of the film and the story of a singular history. Rather, allegory would be an image of ruins in the Benjaminian sense,[27] where both the film and its historical setting have merged in a situation[28] marked by colliding sign systems.

In a narrative style that proceeds through unceasing exchanges between realism and myth, the allegorical in *Nayak* in fact becomes acutely manifest only for an instant as a moment of incommensurability, when the propositional, cause–effect dialectic of the narrative is at a standstill. This is when the discourse of cinema departs from a phenomenological pretension of reflecting the world and instead becomes clearly visible as an act of writing. It is an instant of collision between pure sign worlds, one broadly part of a picture of the disappearing past as history, and the other of an imminent techno-financial future. In the final shot of the montage, allegory becomes figural at that moment of the cinematic *dissolve as special effects*, when the vanishing, slum-eaten, pockmarked cityscape of Mumbai is allowed to exist inseparably for an instant with the dazzling metropolis being superimposed on it.

Notes

1. Ramanand Sagar's Hinduized television adaptation of the epic Ramayana was primarily based on the Tulsidas's version of the epic story written around 1624. It ran for 78 weeks, from January 25, 1987 to July 31, 1988. See Vijay Mishra, *Indian Cinema: Temples of Desire* (2002). Mishra provides an insightful genealogical account of the emergence of a modern iconology of Rama in line with a scriptural tradition, centered on the *Tulsidas-I Ramayana*, which attained a pan-Indian discursive status during the nineteenth-century consolidation of a mainstream Hindu-normative nationalist discourse. See also Nilanjana Gupta, *Switching Channels: Ideologies of Television in India* (1998); Arvind Rajagopal, *Politics after Television: Hindu Nationalism and the Reshaping of the Public in India* (2001); Sudeep Dasgupta, *Hindu Nationalism, Television, and the Avataars of Capital* (2001); and Ananda Mitra, *Television and Popular Culture in India: A Study of the Mahabharat* (2003).
2. B. R. Chopra's television adaptation of *Mahabharata* was broadcast by Doordarshan for 91 weeks, between 1989 and 1991.
3. Madhava Prasad and Ravi Vasudevan have presented an understanding of the *Darsanic* as a mode of looking in which the devotee is permitted to behold the image of the deity, and is privileged and benefited by this permission, in contrast to a concept of looking that assigns power to the beholder by reducing the image to an object of the look. See Madhava Prasad, *Ideology of the Hindi Film* (1998): 75–6; also Ravi S. Vasudevan, "The Politics of Cultural Address in a "Transitional" Cinema: A Case Study of Popular Indian Cinema" (2000). On the social institution of *Darsana*, see Diana Eck, *Darshan: Seeing the Divine Image in India* (1998).
4. State-owned public television in India.
5. *The Bhagwad Gita*, 23.
6. Martin Heidegger, "The Age of the World Picture" (1977).
7. In this group, one could provisionally include a wide range of practices, popular or otherwise: the lyrical-naturalist style of Satyajit Ray, the Nehruvian socialist-realist vein of Mehboob Khan or Zia Sarhadi, or the "developmentalist realism" of a state-sponsored cinema of the 1970s in the works of Shyam Benegal.
8. Gayatri Chakravarty Spivak, "Can the Subaltern Speak?" (1988): 277.
9. Fredric Jameson, *Postmodernism or, The Cultural Logic of Late Capitalism* (1995): ix.
10. Francis Fukuyama, *The End of History and the Last Man* (1992).
11. *Nayak—Asli Hero* is a Hindi remake of Shankar's earlier Telegu/Tamil film *Mudhalvan* (1999).
12. The disgusted police officer mutters, "Kya char paise ka CM hai . . . koi decision nehi le sakta" ("What a cheap CM . . . can't even take a decision").
13. The allusion is to the Nazi jurist Carl Schmitt's critique of parliamentary liberalism, in its incarnation in the Weimar Republic. According to Schmitt,

the protocols of endless conversation and a liberal imperative of "consensus" divide the polity into a plurality of force interests and prevent sovereign power from coming into being. See Carl Schmitt, *The Crisis of Parliamentary Democracy* (1988).

14. See Michel Foucault's critique of the Hobbesian notion of the social contract in *Society Must Be Defended* (2003). Foucault talks about a subject-subject cycle of modern sovereignty (43).

15. It needs to be made clear that the diagram of power elaborated here does not amount to a systems theory *qua* modern epistemes. Rather, this mode of power is akin to what Jean-François Lyotard says about "postmodern" knowledge systems, where any increase in knowledge can lead to more uncertainty and a lowering of performance. Control, therefore, in such a situation can be exercised more efficiently through regulation of chaos—that is, by a performative management of instabilities and variables rather than a negation of uncertainty through metaphysical invocations of truth. See *The Postmodern Condition: A Report on Knowledge* (1979): 53–60.

16. See Giorgio Agamben's elaboration of sovereign power and the rule of exception in *Homo Sacer: Sovereign Power and Bare Life* (1998).

17. The *Sutradhara* is the figure of the director in ancient Sanskrit dramaturgy. See Bharatmuni, *The Natyasastra: A Treatise on Hindu Dramaturgy and Histrionics*, Vol. II, 227. As the last chapter of the treatise establishes, the *Natyasastra* is of divine intellectual origin. Bharata himself is a celestial intelligence who, at the behest of the gods, cohabits with mortals and has earthly sons. The beginnings of *Natyasastra* is traced to the mythic moment when Lord Indra, king of the pantheon of gods, asks Brahma, the preserver figure, to try a form of enunciation that is both audible and visible. The purpose was to achieve a form that could be used to disseminate divine wisdom among the general people, since the Vedas were forbidden to the lower castes. It was then that Brahma combined the four arts of speech, song, dance, and mime to create the *Natyaveda*. Bharatmuni's treatise is a descent of that heavenly form to earth, one that achieves a noble degradation when his sons mix *natya* with popular bawdy forms like the *Prahasana* and are cursed by the sages for doing so. They are, however, restored from an imminent, lowly, *Sudra* existence by the gods who declare that *Natya* (as an inseparable compact between speech, dance, music, and mime) should be a form of worship. The *Sutradhaar* in that sense is an intelligence that strings together *sattva* (light), *rajas* (energy), and *tamas* (reified matter or inertia) —the three attributes of primordial matter or *prakriti*—and casts them as manifold ripples of being as one Brahman. Its etymology can be drawn from the Vedic notion of the cosmic string or *sutra*, as delineated in Book X, verse 90:2 of the *Rig Veda*. See Richard King, *Indian Philosophy: An Introduction to Hindu and Buddhist Thought* (1999). King points out something else that may be pertinent to our discussion. Indian formal logic, as in traditions like *Samkhya* or *Nyaya*, predicates itself on grammar, not mathematics. The universe, therefore, conforms

to the grammatical structure of the sacred language of the Vedas. Sanskrit, which does not have any punctuation marks, is thus *akhanda* (indivisible) and ultimately refers to a single monistic reality, the *Sabda Brahman*. *Sutra*, as a thread or strand that traces a temporal and earthly textualization of the Brahman in time, is thus a provisional *vivarta* (illusory unfolding) which has to be submitted to the history of the universe as one sentence (*Vac*), one play, and one film (see King, *Indian Philosophy*, 47–50).

18. For a detailed analysis, see J. J. Roy Burman, "Shivaji's Myth and Maharashtra's Syncretic Traditions" (2001); and Malavika Vartak, "Shivaji Maharaj: Growth of a Symbol" (2001).

19. Unlike the archetypal Indian politician clad in traditional *khadi* attire (as in the iconic paradigm created during the Gandhian–Nehruvian moment of nationalist mass mobilization), Shivaji always wears a suit and tie. Chandra Babu Naidu, the former Chief Minister of the state of Andhra Pradesh, habitually referred to himself as the CEO of the state.

20. The importance of grand symbolic gestures and what I am calling ritualistic vernacularizations in modern Indian mass politics has been apparent right from Tilak's Shivaji Utsav at the turn of the twentieth century to Gandhi's many symbolically governed, evocative mobilizations. In this context, see Shahid Amin, "Gandhi as Mahatma" (1984).

21. As an instance of figural thought, Shivaji is not to be understood by notions of "hybridity," "excess," and "mimicry," which abound in postcolonial discourses. As I mentioned in the Introduction, hybridity, as an organicist concept, presumes a progressivist dialectical resolution to historical/narratological conflicts between East and West, or tradition and modernity, through a libertine intercourse between the master and the slave, giving rise to a new, revisionist phenomenology of the postcolonial. The trope of "excess," on the other hand, imparts a strict modular character to the manager as a structural, closed proposition of the "modern," in this case exceeded by Shivaji as the traditional name of the father. Similarly, mimicry as a category subsists on the assured regularity of power protocols guaranteed by the imperial sway of the integrated subject in the world, and a consequent, Hegelian-psychoanalytic distinction between the self and the other. Such designations would propose Shivaji only in terms of a representational schema of truth, mired in a humanistic mimetopolitic of the West.

22. Martin Nicholas, "Foreword," *Grundrisse/Karl Marx* (1973): 28.

23. The long line of twentieth-century thinkers who have directly or indirectly addressed the idea of exception in relation to the modern nation-state include Carl Schmitt, Walter Benjamin, Hannah Arendt, and (more recently) Georgio Agamben. Agamben's work—aided by the renaissance of hard-right thinkers like Schmitt and Leo Strauss in a moment of crisis of liberalism—has stimulated an academic industry on this subject. I use the term "exception" in a general sense originally proposed by Schmitt—that the state shows its true sovereign form when it suspends the constitution in order to

protect the constitution itself—in other words, when the state stops being a Weberian great administrator of things and goes beyond the law in order to emphasize that no one can go beyond the law. However, I use exception provisionally, noting that in its Eurocentric incarnation, the category takes for granted an historically consolidated (liberal) relationship between the life of the law and that of custom, which may not be true in postcolonial, semi-feudal milieus like India.

24. This word roughly means being a country bumpkin.

25. The "Lalloo assemblage" remains in place to this day, although Lalloo as an individual frame of reference has disappeared from this pathological-comic assemblage, particularly since his groundbreaking success as India's Minister for Railways (2004–9).

26. See Fredric Jameson, "Third World Literature in an Age of Multinational Capitalism" (1986). Jameson's thesis was virulently attacked, but Madhava Prasad defended it in "On the Question of a Theory of (Third) World Literature" (1997); and Madhava Prasad, *Ideology of the Hindi Film: A Historical Construction* (1998): 9. Prasad suggests that Jameson's controversial argument, that third world narratives are necessarily allegorical, has a kernel of truth to it. According to Prasad, films, like other forms of cultural production in the Indian context, have an allegorical dimension precisely because they register, in various ways, a continuing struggle over the state form.

27. Walter Benjamin, *Origins of German Tragic Drama* (1985): 178–9

28. Benjamin's notion of allegory is grounded in his critique of the romantic symbol. This disperses the paradox of the theological symbol that proposes a unity between the material and the transcendental object, but substitutes it with a relationship between appearance and essence (ibid.: 160). The disenchantment of the baroque allegory that Benjamin investigates offers a landscape of ruins where even gods have become concepts (225).

CHAPTER 4

The Music of Intolerable Love: Indian Film Music, Globalization, and the Sound of Partitioned Selves

Toward a Lyric History of India

It is almost inevitable that this discussion about the geo-televisual and popular Hindi cinema of the 1990s should turn to the song sequence. But before that, let me frame the terms of engagement by attaching an aesthetic-political question of lyricism to that of Indian nationalism. In discussing the poetry of Faiz Ahmed Faiz,[1] Aamir Mufti has posed an important question in relation to third world modernities: instead of a more conventional format of aligning categories and events into a narrative of constitution, is it possible to understand historicity as a lyrical assemblage of expressions that are obtuse and eliding in their relational meaningfulness? That is, instead of following the usual way of tracing emergent national consciousnesses through the novel form, or more specifically the *Bildungsroman* (as exemplary instances of what Foucault calls a new disenchanted prose of the modern), what can the poetic, more specifically in the form of the lyric, teach us? More than that, could this be a way to address a situation politically in a manner that does not perpetually refer back to the state as the ultimate horizon of possibilities? The turn toward the lyric could therefore be a responsible turn away from narrative accounts of a singular story of the nation as spirit and psychobiography. It could be a turn toward a crisis of meaningfulness instead of positive or dogmatic affirmations. The lyricism of Faiz, according to Mufti, is precisely that which "represents a profound attempt to unhitch literary production from the cultural projects of the postcolonial state in order to make visible meanings that have not been entirely reified and subsumed within the cultural logic of the nation state system" ("Toward a Lyric History of India" [2004]: 246). The obstinate meaningfulness of the poetic resides in avenues that have not been imperially taken over by the logico-prosaic imagination of a dominant form of becoming. The latter tries to impose a panoptic narrative of the subject (as heterosexual male citizen) that seeks to engulf all expressive powers. In a Hegelian schema of the modern, the lyrical, in contrast, would pertain to that impulse of the "irrational" in the Indian spirit, which, since the dawn of the world historical, has "produced superb gems of poetry without any corresponding advances in art, freedom, and law."[2] Mufti's invitation, therefore, is to turn the tables; it is to leave the illusory comfort of exhausted universals and unities and see if the powers of historicity are actually unleashed in the fragmenting and searing moves of the lyric.

In Mufti's Adorno-inspired reading of Faiz's poetry, lyrical abstraction is not an effete departure from the social, but the very moment at which the social becomes immanent in the *suffered* language of the poetic. In the case of Faiz, one sees a self that is "Indian" in a radically encompassing sense, precisely because it claims an historical meaningfulness and memory beyond the given borders of communal identity and the nation-state. The poetic enters the world as the pre-thought of all political divisions, like that between India and Pakistan as geopolitical entities. The lyric subject in Faiz's poetry never finds a home in the aftermath of the Partition of 1947; rather, it generalizes a state of exile, corroding all fatal and bloody demarcations between the past and the present, the home and the world, India and Pakistan. As a result, love and a painful alienation from the beloved assume the form of a political arrest of prescribed becoming, a groundless foreclosure of consummation, conjugality, and other anchors of habit in the form of citizenship (Mufti, "Toward a Lyric History of India," 248). The lyric thereby inhabits what Bhaskar Sarkar, in a recent magnificent account of Indian cinema in the wake of Partition, has described as the very "runes of laceration."[3]

Mufti elaborates that in the Sufi traditions of Urdu and Persian poetry, *wisal* is a sign for mystic union with the divine accomplished when the desire of the self becomes extinct (*fana*) in a realization of *ishq-e-haqiqi* or "true" love of God ("Lyric History," 257). Compared to this consummation, love of man is only *ishq-e-majazi*, a love that is inauthentic and metaphorical. What Mufti finds in Faiz is a secularization of this cosmic devotion, one that resolutely closes the door on the unfreedom of given homes and embattled worlds. *Wafa* (loyalty) and *junoon* (the madness or trance of poetic love) come to mean both political steadfastness and selfless abandon. They become the rational and irrational components of a being no longer enthralled and mentally enslaved by the historicist fatalism of a modern enterprise that cannot step outside the operations of the nation-state (257–8). Love becomes that which is unbound from the law and psycho-biographical procedures of identification that govern the prose of the world; it emerges as that candid expressive power that is no longer searching for form and recognition, but has become historically manifest as a catachrestic assemblage in itself. Love therefore requires no further validation from grand narratives and anthropological reckonings of the self in order to be figurable; it dismantles assiduous quests for home and belonging to inject a perverse sense of exile into the very heart of the city. Love aims to call the city itself into being as a perpetual site of love's own eventfulness. The question of *Bildung* thereby becomes irremediably complex, when we, in relation to a tormented career of modernity and enlightenment in the subcontinent, turn the spotlight on the partitioned nature of selves instead of their evanescent wholes. In our time, such thinking of the lyrical radically suspends the fatalism of an historical imagination that has recently announced its own spectacular death, as well as the universalist presumptions of a neo-liberal language of the state (and its isomorphic others) that has been going global in an increasingly terrifying manner.

Mufti's thinking is pertinent to any discussion of popular Indian cinema and its lyrical expressive qualities, not just in relation to national culture, but also its location in a global dispensation of cinematic forms. The lyrical aspect of such films is evident not just in the staple song sequences, but also in terms of a powerful poetic urge of the *Lukhnawi* Urdu culture of the north Indian Muslim aristocracy which informs manners, speech, diction, and style in many melodramatic forms and ceremonials. Lyrical elucidations and exchanges between older and newer regimes of value, between a dominant Sanskritic Brahminical culture and a radical or decadent Islamic-Urdu poetic romanticism, are important aspects of popular Hindi cinema. In the formative decades of the all-India film, this was consolidated in the hands of a group of exceptionally talented lyric writers: Sahir Ludhianvi, Kaifi Azmi, Hasrat Jaipuri, Shakeel Badauni, and Shailendra. The work of Faiz himself has regularly featured in dialogues and lyrics in countless films in India and Pakistan. The purpose here is not to engage a musicality of cinema in a dialectical battle with the classic realist text. Rather, it is to understand the lyrical as that which can infuse exiling and errant powers of language and contaminate hard artifacts of historical narration. This is not to deny history, but to question its presumed continua, which are at once useful and abusive, imperial and revolutionary.

The Song Sequence

The powers of the lyrical, especially in their modular expression in song sequences, are often at odds with a broad privileging of realist narration. On the other hand, popular generic song sequences can only rarely be accounted for as signatures of modernism; that is, as gestures to question or overcome a fatalist conservatism that, contextually, might mark some forms of realism.[4] Except in some memorable instances, as in the cinema of Guru Dutt, the staple Hindi film song sequence has been predominantly accounted for in decorative terms, as something that has not graduated to a Brechtian template of the fighting popular, even though the potential was there.[5] The song sequence thus always had a contentious status in what was a conflict-ridden field of modernity, defined not only in terms of a projected national culture, but also in those of a many armed third world anti-imperialist internationalism.[6]

There was always an overall discomfort with the interruptive, expressionist-decorative status of the song sequence in relation to ideas of plausible narration. It can be detected early, even in a reformist social like V. Shantaram's *Duniya Na Mane* (*The Unexpected*, 1937), which featured songs played on a gramophone. And yet there were other authorial sensibilities that were perhaps guided by different ideas of cultural expression. In her book on Guru Dutt, Nasreen Munni Kabir (2006) cites a telling anecdote from the autobiography of the great actor and Indian People's Theater Association (IPTA) cultural activist Balraj Sahni which is pertinent to invoke here. The incident takes place presumably in 1950, after Chetan Anand, one of the founders of Navketan Films, invited Sahni to work on their new film, *Baazi*, which was to be Guru Dutt's directorial début. The story also involves the filmic philosophy of Sashadhar Mukherjee, the co-founder, with Rai Bahadur Chunilal, of the Bombay-based studio Filmstan Talkies (established in 1943–44). Previously, Mukherjee had been a stalwart producer in Bombay Talkies, the other major studio of the era and responsible for landmarks like *Naya Sansar* (*New World*) (1941) and the massive box office hit *Kismet* (*Fate*) (1943).[7] This is what Kabir writes:

> While Sahni believed that the most important element in a film was the screenplay, he felt that Guru Dutt—influenced by Sashadhar Mukherjee's school of film-making—gave more importance to the songs. Mukherjee allegedly believed that a screenplay should be "artificial and rickety," making the viewers impatient for a song; Mukherjee thought that if the viewers were too engrossed in the story, they would regard the song or the dance as an unwarranted intrusion.[8]

Traditionally, therefore, for an artistic vanguard committed to a broad socialist-developmentalist horizon of the new republic (of which Sahni is a good example), the song sequence was the imprint of a folk or feudal culture that either had to be rhetorically enframed or formally subsumed by a superior historical metalanguage in the process of becoming modern. Since they disrupted the serial continuity of the storytelling process, musical interludes were often viewed as quaint insertions of the ceremonial or ritualistic kind in what would be an otherwise normative business of teaching, instructing, and delighting in classical narrative cinema.

Tom Gunning and Miriam Hansen have suggested that early cinema in the West had developed along many potential lines of social usage before they were erased or transcoded by a corporatist-Taylorist mode of big studio production, a style of melodramatic realism, and continuity editing.[9] In Indian cinema, and more specifically in relation to the song-and-dance sequence, a similar historical process of aesthetic reformation and normalization can be found. For instance, in early experiments with the technology of sound, narration in films like *Indrasabha* (*The Court of Indra*) (J. J. Madan, 1931) or *Kalidas* (H. M. Reddy, 1931) unfolded musically, in the form of what Bhaskar Chandravarkar has called "son-glets" of short duration, rather than through a now dominant mode of dialogue-based, propositional realism.[10] Ashoke Ranade has suggested that these lyrical formations were a continuous rather than an "inter-rupting" principle of expression, perpetually between poles of tune and dialogue, emanating from oral expressive cultures.[11] It would therefore be gratuitous to say that *Indrasabha* had seventy-one songs; instead, the entire soundtrack can be considered as a single, constitutive body of musical narration, in which interacting lyrical assemblages are inter-spersed by stylized voice incantations. The gradual suppression of this comprehensive melodic impulse, the streamlining of an often radically experimental interface between traditional forms and technology,[12] and a cultural abjuration of genres of attraction and magic (like the Phalke and Prabhat mythologicals and the Wadia stunt films), subsequently created a modernizing aesthetic clearing for various modes of narrating the nation.

Under the auspices of a modernist critical paradigm, the song-and-dance routine would therefore be an index of what Prasad has identified as a pre-emptive diagnosis of "not yet cinema" on the part of a dominant template of Western film studies. On the other hand, scholars like Sudipta Kaviraj have noted that in many cases the lyrical-abstract mode of the song sequence can harbor complexities that are far richer than the often simplistic moral fables that house them.[13] Lalitha Gopalan has insightfully read commercial Indian cinema as one of interruptions, where "song and dance sequences work as a delaying device; the interval defers resolutions, postpones endings and doubles beginnings; and censorship blocks the narrative flow, redirects the spectator's pleasure towards and away from the state." Along with these digressive impulses, "Indian popular films are equally invested in assuaging the discontinuity accompanying these cuts by resorting to generic logic."[14] Ravi Vasudevan has suggested that the pleasure of visual entertainment (of which the song sequence would be a powerful instance) can be seen to operate in a zone of in-betweenness amidst narratological propositions: "Etymologically, entertainment means 'holding between'. The cinema's work of representation performs just such an operation; its skills are used to generate fantasy spaces for its audience, spaces which are literally 'held between' phases of routine domestic and working life."[15]

The crucial issue here is the question of temporality. Which form of cinematic time can be considered normative because it approximates, in a proper manner, the architecture of historical temporality itself? The query that follows is perhaps obvious: is the arc or the principle of history in itself a settled matter? Are song sequences always interruptions in Gopalan's sense? Or do they, precisely because they suspend the linear flow of narration, sometimes bring to the fore endemic crises in dominant imaginations of history and their temporal orders in themselves? It is only from a grid of value that sets up a clear hierarchy between the two historical roles of cinema—the pictures of life in the work of the Lumières gaining aesthetic precedence over the cine-magic of George Méliès—that one can pronounce the song and dance to be an interruption in the first place.[16] At this point, however, I need to make clear that I am not trying to put in place a general theory of the song sequence. That is not possible. There are indeed numerous instances of this formal device that do not remotely acquire the specific lyrical quality Mufti talks about in relation to Faiz. Later, we shall look at some instances that do, in less radical ways, present a crisis of historical imagination characteristic of our times.

Concern with the song sequence was not merely aesthetic. From an international marketing point of view, the song sequence, along with other non-realist or mythical curiosities, was one of the major reasons why Hindi cinema, for decades, did not find an audience worth mentioning in the West, despite being popular in the Arabian Peninsula, Africa, the Caribbean, and the former Eastern bloc. As we discussed in Chapter 2, in recent times this scenario has changed, with first world markets increasingly warming to that thing called "Bollywood." Indeed, there seems to be a fresh metropolitan attitude that would suggest that popular Hindi film is not yet modern because it is already postmodern.[17] From being decorative markers of an obstinate tradition of nativity, the song sequence seems to have become an eminently consumable eccentricity—much like the non-realist action choreography of Hong Kong action cinema—in the smooth, multicultural space of planetary capital.

The song sequences are often not simple vehicles for the geo-televisual that is being investigated in this project. Instead, in exemplary cinematic moments, the geo-televisual itself reveals its lyrical character in them, that is, when it detaches itself from schemata of information that relentlessly consign the awry flow of signs to the unities of the state, the subject, the signifier, and the law. These special sequences remove bodies from the propositional flow of narratives, transport them to temporal and spatial orders that are outside a determined milieu of storytelling, and endow them with magical resources and playthings. Humanoid figures are only one type of bodies orchestrated in the dynamic sign flows that character-ize such sequences; other clusters of cinematic energy—digitized dancing effigies, animals, cartoons, expressive-naturalistic objects, totems, or emblems—regularly feature in them. Part of this autonomy stems from the traditional mode of production followed in the Hindi film industry, one that Madhava Prasad, from a Marxist perspective, calls the heteroge-neous form of manufacture, in contrast to Hollywood's usual template of serial manufacture theorized by Janet Staiger, among others.[18] The song sequences are thus often dominated by the authorship of the choreogra-pher, the lyricist, and the music director, with the overall directorial or narrational vision taking a backseat. In recent decades the song sequence has, more than ever, acquired a shelf-life beyond the film itself, through a plethora of disseminating channels – television, the internet, radio, and cell phones. This heterogeneous mode of marketing can usher in differ-ent considerations of value tied to the fashion, touristic, or advertising industries.

The Music of Intolerable Love

Let us now take a close look at some exemplary uses of cinematic musical-ity in the works of Mani Ratnam. This *auteur par excellence* of contempo-rary Tamil/Hindi commercial cinema said in an interview that his 1997 Hindi film *Dil Se* (*From the Heart*) failed at the box office because the song-and-dance sequences hindered the pace of the narrative.[19] Indeed, except for the "Ay Ajnabi Tu Bhi Kahin" ("Oh Stranger, You Too from Somewhere") number, which keeps floating into the diegesis as a message of yearning on All India Radio sent by the hero to his mysterious and eva-nescent lady love, all the other musical segments in the film take place in virtual registers of time and space beyond the direct control of narrational logic. In Ratnam's analysis, it becomes clear that he sees these spectacu-lar and ceremonial departures as achieving a *thickening* of time which, in this case, ran contrary to the lean, chronometric unfolding of the thriller format. Ratnam's concern is undoubtedly shared by quite a few contem-porary artists who have worked with popular Indian cinematic idioms.[20] It has often been the case that song sequences have been understood as a commercial imperative put in place by the overall dictatorship of the distributor class in Bombay cinema, which came into being after World War II.

The question, however, is strictly not about whether it is artistically desirable to have song-and-dance sequences punctuating the flow of narration. Rather, it pertains to a notion of propriety and measure—at what point do the musical insertions stop being complementary spectacles, assume a life of their own, and begin to destroy the basic integrity of storytelling? Further, how does one culturally define and judge such exchanges? For Ratnam, otherwise a commercially successful filmmaker especially known for his musicals, it should indeed be a strange predicament. He believes that unbridled musical departures dislocated the soul of the film, as was evident in its commercial failure. However, even if one is guided solely by that populist logic, it has to be considered that *Dil Se*, as a commercial venture, broke even and actually made a profit because the box office losses were offset by the music sales. The music of the film by A. R. Rahman (along with the picturizations), continues to be tremendously popular to this day. In the discussion that follows, I shall suggest that the song sequences usher in non-directional energies of the geotelevisual in Ratnam's film and lend irreducible complexity to what is often a faltering narrative of national geopolitics.

In *Dil Se*, Amar, a city-bred educated radio journalist, meets the mysterious Meghna, when he is on his way to an assignment in the politically turbulent north-eastern region of India. He keeps bumping into this intriguing woman during his sojourn and falls hopelessly in love with her. What Amar does not know is that Meghna is part of a terrorist outfit affiliated to a secessionist movement in the north-east, and is being trained to be a suicide bomber. Most of the song sequences accompanying the dramatic unfolding of events and revelations happen to be free, indirect visual consolidations of sublimity, terror, and desire. The musical interludes appear to take bodies out from the breathlessness of Ratnam's political thriller from time to time and allow them to inhale and imbibe energies of a certain "outside" (of naturalism, of consumerism). This is where figures leave characters behind and incubate in an ecology of the unthinkable. The visual and aural flows that we see in the sequences are not fully amenable to specific contours of subjectivity, neither that of the new age city-slicker male reporter, nor of the marginalized woman-turned-human bomb. They are assemblages that have a cinematic life of their own and can be commanded by narrative logic, anthropological imaginaries, and propositional statements or queries (what exactly do these MTV type rituals mean?) only in retrospect, as "afterthoughts" of storytelling.

The "Chaiya Chaiya" sequence comes at the beginning of the film, immediately after Amar's first, fleeting encounter with Meghna on a dark and stormy night. It begins with a discontinuous cut to the top of a train moving beneath a clear sky, in broad daylight. The song segment becomes a utopian space for fragments of anthropological spectacle, signs of ethnic chic and traditional bodies combined, and set to techno-rhythms. The hero dances on top of the train with a host of people in spotless rural attire, and a comely beauty whose figure combines rustic forms with a distinctly urban body language. Such an assemblage of camera perspectives (ethnography, heritagism, etc.) is a recurring feature in many Hindi film musical interludes featuring north Indian peasant bodies, Goan fishermen, or tribal figures. In such situations, the camera assumes both an urban, anthropological look (by which the city has historically read the country) and a perspective that incorporates such bodies into a metropolitan, post-historical virtual arcade of ethnicity. The bodies of peasants, fishermen, or tribals thus become figurable (as dancers inseparable from the dance) at the interstice between the home and the world, at once inside and outside the cinematic city. The anthropological distancing of their forms and settings, as objects of discovery and study, is offset and inseparably recombined with a vision that redresses them as part of the city's fascinated romance with itself and its projected outside. It thus pertains to the casting of ethnicity itself as geo-televisual information set in seductive cadences.

The "Chaiya Chaiya" sequence begins from a top-angle, panoptic position and injects a thick cluster of signs into the otherwise linear continuum of the narrative, ushering in a different world of desires. It provides a godly urbane look into an India passing through a peaceful interregnum that comes *between* activities of urbane journalism, and those of infranational armed conflict. The sequence allows for a momentary incursion of health, when the camera briefly assumes the seemingly *normal* task of a museumic-spectacular translation of various life-functions of the world. It is precisely this normalcy that the subsequent narrative will shock the camera out of. A transnational techno-rhythm, in assemblage with the melodic strains of an indigenous Sufi tradition and Urdu poetry, occupies the figures of peasants and fruit-sellers in ethnic dress, luminously absolving them of the dirt and grime of labor, much as with the villagers in the film *Mumbai Se Aya Mera Dost* discussed in the previous chapter. There are, of course, two sides to this feature, which can be said to be a general tendency not only of Indian popular cinematic forms, but also the myriad commerce of global communication. On the one hand, they destroy certain priestly pieties of the "local," affecting perverse contaminations and desacralizations. On the other, they can also remove from the picture the *agon* and historicity of difference (the imperial career of capital, the international division of labor, etc.). The multiple emissions of a global electronic database beamed from the skies always interact in a complex manner with memories of the earth. Faced with such a mélange of formations, one can neither fortify and protect *dictated* edifices of tradition (like Sufi philosophy or Urdu poetry) nor uncritically champion the incursive powers and qualities of a transnational recoding of culture.

The next song sequence in *Dil Se* takes place a little later in the narrative, after Amar tracks Meghna down to her village and declares his intention to marry her. It is important to note that, at this point, neither he nor the viewer has any knowledge of Meghna's identity as a terrorist. Hence, the title track sequence that follows is an anticipatory coupling of affects of violence and love, one that again crosses an economy of subjective narration *qua* the point of view of the unsuspecting protagonist. The song sequence "Dil Se" combines different visual diagrams and motifs: the realist narrative, the steadycam shots of CNN-style battleground reportage, a transnational consumer lifestyle of advertising, tourism, pearl necklaces, a spinning basketball on an empty court, designer gowns, and the constantly reordered body of the woman. This is a tremulous visual style that Ratnam used in his previous political thrillers, *Roja* (1992) and *Bombay* (1995). A mobile, probing, investigative camera vision characteristic of transnational on-the-spot newsgathering is "quoted" in both films. In *Roja* it is such a steadycam that "raids," with dazzling speed, the idyllic village of the countryside, and reveals the den of terror at its heart. In *Bombay*, the CNN-style, on-the-shoulder camera captures, in a live-wire and awry fashion, the madness of the communal riots. This camera of information is thus inevitably a camera of emergency, by which the city instantly monitors and detects the objects of its worst fears, and restores itself constantly into a consensual mass through measures of militarization, aid, and policing. In the title track of *Dil Se* we see such ominous steadycam shots informing and recasting the milieu in which passion is lyrically declared. The simulated movements of newsgathering (the sense that the world is somehow, somewhere, out of joint) are thus foreboding devices here, portentously orchestrated with touristic and infomercial set pieces. These disparate visibilities come together to effect a utopian transfer of the female body from the intriguing figure in black to a totem of a globalized middle-class desire. In doing so, it also secretly prepares the affective ambience for the pending revelation of the profile of the terrorist.

The "Dil Se" sequence figurally invents an intimate space of the couple (about to be denied by the narrative) and inserts it into the public domain of violence. Music, in deterritorializing bodies from their realist milieus, affects a visual consolidation of desire that is already foreclosed by the ethical universe of exemplary storytelling: the citizen cannot fall in love with the terrorist. As surreal incursion, musicality liberates signs and bodies from the vertical control of narration to bring about a postulated expression of romance, as opposed to a "real" depiction that is already rendered impossible by word of law (the state in this case has a greater claim on the woman's body than the man's). The term "postulation" is once again being used in the etymological sense of prayer, which becomes a secular heresy precisely because it figurally establishes a desire not commensurate with an ethical substrate of nationhood. But there is another question that needs to be discussed: is it forbidden to fall in love with a terrorist simply because it is against the spirit and letter of the law?

Love here is an anarchic power because it threatens to introduce a terrible divergence of paths between the destiny of the citizen and that of the state. As we know, in the Hegelian conception of the civil society and the rational state, human (heterosexual) love is a unifying middle term which sets up an organic bridge between spirit and substance, between the particular and general interest, and between individual reality and universal essence.[21] Love is, therefore, that which (as a force secondary to reason) animates a perpetually gestating ethical life in a manner that prevents it from becoming a cold universal. This is because the ethical life propounded by reason cannot merely be a formal entity; it must, at every point, be in an *organic* relation to the immanence of social processes. The vertical emergence of the modern rational state (as a formal expression of that ethical life) has to be a synthetic move of the selfconscious spirit of history, and not the tyrannical imposition of a cold and distant architectonic. Partha Chatterjee, in his "against the grain" reading of Hegel in relation to Indian nationalism, points out that for the great German thinker, love, to that end, had to be necessarily telescoped into the modalities of the bourgeois nuclear family. Chatterjee argues that an understanding of Indian nationalism, on the other hand, calls for a conceptualization of love in relation to the community rather than the couple.[22] Apropos *Dil Se*, the peculiar nature of Indian nationalistic formations, by that token, would already delegitimize the lovers because their nuclear desire contravenes the ethics of their respective peoples. In Amar's case, it is a Hindi-speaking north Indian one that dominates the pan-Indian state scenario, while for Megha it is one that is marginalized and outlawed from the very center stage of Indianness. Let us follow this Hegelian theme a little, not as truth, but as a powerful fiction of modernity that intersects with worldly discourses about the nation-state and its becomings at large.

Once again, the three constitutive precepts of subject, unity, and law are at stake here, but in a hierarchical order of rational consideration. The trial for Hegel was to absolve a spiritual union between the family and the state from the contingencies of legal contracts that launch the political in Locke or Montesquieu. Law—constitutional or moral—in other words, is not the ultimate question. In the spiritual journey of selfconsciousness toward a rational and organic unity of things, it is merely a necessary but formal moment of isolation from the whole,[23] just as the constitution is a mere formalization of a folksy covenant of the nation–state, or moral precepts in Kant and Rousseau are externally dictated categorical imperatives. For Hegel, the absolute right of ethical consciousness is such that the deed will be nothing else but what it *knows*,[24] not what it unconsciously flouts in terms of the letter of the law. In a world devoid of oracular wisdom, the guilt of Oedipus must be foreclosed through an historical consolidation of private property, governing institutions of civil society, the bourgeois family, and, of course, the modern state that supersedes the tragic antinomies between human and divine law. The absence of these conditions of the modern can expose society and property to the libidinal duress of illicit love which can extend to the primal fear of incest. In this context, let us remind ourselves of an observation made in the Introduction in relation to Hindi cinema and India's "incomplete modernity." From an anthropological perspective drawn from Hegel, one could, for instance, say that the common lost-and-found themes of such films are not modern not because the finding is implausible bordering on the miraculous, but also because relations of property, historically evolving social life, and patrimony are not settled enough to effect a scientific prevention of incest. It is only a Dharmic dictation of fate, a mythical injunction of blood that naturalistically ensures that the brother long separated from the sister does not fall in love with her.

The problem in *Dil Se* does not involve the extreme possibility of incest; Meghna is not Amar's long-lost sister. The problem is restricted to the fact that he has betrayed an organic brotherhood of citizens in falling in love with her. To understand the heart of this problem, we need to clarify how this Hegelian model of modernity—perpetually afflicted by the duality of fallible, earthly contracts and an irresistible, cosmological spirit of world history—intersects with and departs from diagrams of desire in the third world milieu of *Dil Se*. The question we can begin with pertains to a psycho-biographical baseline of ethical narration: to what extent, at each point of the story, does Amar *know* about Meghna's identity, and how does that knowledge alter his moral being? Is Amar's "crime" on the same lines as Oedipus's—the result of a tragic absence of knowledge in an atomized and individuated world vision?

That is clearly not the case. In Ratnam's film, Amar's frenzied quest for Meghna continues even after he comes to know of her secret. It is interesting to note that the only time he is ready to give up occurs early in the film, when she lies and tells him that she is married. Once he learns that this is not true, he pursues her to the bitter end, despite discovering that she is an enemy of the nation, and even after the law declares him to be a collaborator and disgraces his family. The prohibition of the legal order is not enough to dissuade Amar; he does not find his attraction "unnatural" (it is neither incest nor a contravention of the territorial rights of another man—Meghna's fictional husband) despite being avowedly against the dictates of the state as well as the patriotic clan he comes from. We thus get a glimpse of a disconcerting new age, "urban" conjugal desire that is not afraid to pit itself against both the not yet modern third world nation-state and the self-contained ethical universe of the feudal extended family. It is an invitation to an elsewhere, where reality is not defined by these two entities.

The story of a fatal and obsessive quest of the citizen-professional is energized by the elemental star aura of Shahrukh Khan and a lyrical motorization of bodies, objects, and nature itself. A central motif of apocalyptic fatalism is established and thematically resonated in the lyrics of two songs in the film—the title track and the "Satrangi Re" ("The Colorful One") number. *Dil Se* is cast as a journey through the seven shades of love, as elaborated in ancient Arabic literature—*hub* (attraction), *uns* (infatuation), *ishq* (love), *aqidat* (reverence), *ibadat* (worship), *junoon* (obsession), and *maut* (death). This trajectory of lovelorn unbecoming departs from the *Bildung* of the modern, in the process flouting state- and society-sanctioned ideas of conjugality. We get a glimpse of what the latter can be through Amar's brief flirtation with "home," in the form of an engagement with Priety, the girl chosen by his family to be his bride. This scenario of an idyllic interiority of the feudal extended family suffers a secret subversion when it is suddenly infiltrated by the forces of war. Meghna and one of her accomplices take advantage of Amar's infatuation and use his home and family to find temporary refuge from the law. Amar introduces her to his unsuspecting family as a distant acquaintance who has come to the city in search of work. Next, as part of the terror plan, Meghna uses Amar to get a job as an All India Radio correspondent. At the same time, Meghna's cold and efficient commitment to the cause of "terror" is also disturbed by the ardor of Amar's love. Her figuration in the film perpetually takes place in the realm of the inscrutable, in between patriarchal formations of the old and the new, with signs of affection indeterminately distributed between communal love for her disenfranchised people and her sublimating desires for Amar, the yuppie innocent of the city.

4.1, 4.2, and 4.3: Utopian conjugality in the age of terror: a series of stills from the "Satrangi Re" number.

The debate that takes place when Amar finally confronts Meghna toward the end, after learning of her true intentions, is perhaps not important in this discussion. What can be noted in passing is that the dialectic between the historical legitimacy of the nation-state and the outraged search for justice and law-destroying violence by the marginal is left suspended in the showdown between the naive citizen and the hardened terrorist. In the special urban sensibility that governs *Dil Se*, there cannot be a last-minute intervention by the state or a cosmic order to finally unite things. After the unfinished interaction, conjugality can only proceed fatally, in the stark landscape of the pre-/post-political, where god is neither absolute nor has achieved a modern death; he simply has nothing more to say. In *Dil Se*, love consummates itself through an obstinate voluntarism of death, when Amar and Meghna blow themselves up with the explosives intended for the terror act. The illegitimate couple thus overcome the fear of death that is presumed by most modern political philosophies of a Hobbesian social contract or a self/other dialectic of lordship and bondage. Suicide, as a perverse, yet supreme achievement of modernism (as Benjamin would say), deterritorializes a unitary cosmology made up of a behavioral logic of modernity and an economic-governmental one of modernization.[25] It prevents the encounter between law and life and takes love "elsewhere." Death, in other words, becomes the utopian "other side" that Amar searches for when, after coming to know of Meghna's identity, her past, and her iron-clad filial obligations, he pleads that they should run away to somewhere that is distant from both—the violent geopolitics of the nation-state and the proprietorship of warring extended families and communities.

The problem of love in Ratnam's film has to be located in a cleft that perpetually opens up between the universality of a philosophical discourse of modernity and demographic modalities of the population state. Amar naively pleads with Meghna to disarm and take herself else-where, *when her identity itself is constructed by the nation-state in terms of a fundamental relation of war.* Here it would be opportune to recall that the totality of the Hegelian rational diagram invoked earlier comes with a necessary rejoinder: Meghna cannot be loved within the scope of an egalitarian homogeneity that constitutes *peopleness*; as a minoritarian presence, she can only be an object of *toleration* and *suspicion*. She can be accorded civil rights (which are always contractual and contingent) pertaining to representation and juridical forms, but *ethically speaking* she can never be a citizen.[26] Like the Quakers, Anabaptists, and Jews of the Prussian state which embodied the culmination of history for Hegel, in her case, civil recognition by law as an entity to be preserved or

punished does not amount to an entry into the ethical family–state composite. Meghna is always foreclosed from entering the former as a site
for individual love, and the latter as the repository of patriotic love. It is
this presumed organic unity between the family, the "people," and the
state that, in the Hegelian universe, dialectically presides over a myriad
field of interests and finally renders ethics as *custom*. Meghna's legal
rights can ensure her inclusion within the national fold only through a
process of tolerated, differential exclusion.[27] Her aspect of terror unfolds
at the very liminality of that tolerance, when her shadowy presence and
insidious homelessness makes her drop out of the monitoring radar of a
malfunctioning population state.[28] As a result, a question of law cannot
be mitigated by a benign, majoritarian unfolding of everyday lives and
everyday desires; *it can never be customary to be in love with Meghna*. The
debate about sovereignty, as far as her profile is concerned, is always
to be restricted to the rule of exception. On the other hand, had Amar
married his family's choice, Preity, there could have been, in terms of a
unitary national-communal spirit, the possibility of diffusing the formal
inclemency of law, that is, rendering love not only legal, but also indistinguishable from life itself.

Love in *Dil Se* thus remains a tragic pathology in terms of narration as
supreme ethical instantiation of national life. In the course of the baroque
death drive that unfolds in the realistic storytelling, the song sequences
open up luminous intervals for the visual consolidation of an unremitted
desire, a picture of love as an otherworldly life without political status.
The lyrical pathos of these sequences informs the dramatic build-up of
events, infusing it with the semiosis of an *intolerable* love that can manifest
itself only musically in a world of prose. The body of the woman, perpetually crisscrossed by contesting patriarchal forces, lends itself to various
catachrestic geo-televisual ensembles of signs. It is motorized as part of
an overall assemblage of desire that is always deporting itself to a mythical
"outside," into the pure immanence of a visual utopia that can come only
after national geopolitics. There is, however, more to this escape. The
woman, as pure form of desire claimed by song and dance, seems to be
figurable only when her body is assembled with spectacle as metropolitan
value in itself, that is, only when it is temporarily absolved of its location in unhappy history and terror, and transposed, in a state of supreme
lightness of being, to a field of global relations of commodification. The
narratologically impossible picture of the terrorist as the beloved becomes
apparent only as advertised spectacle. The woman-in-cinema as a result
assumes the form of unbridled, immanent production values (the dancing
body, the fetish body, the fashion body) in a neo–liberated mise–en–scène

no longer weighed down or mediated by statements and visions of an historically defined situation.

The song sequences exert an ontological pull that removes figures of desire from an embattled geopolitical milieu of the nation-state, but this "outside" can find expression only as a never-never, transnational arcade of lifestyle signatures. Commodities and vectorized time-space modules thus arrive without the historical procedures of labor and production, and an agonistic process of *becoming* tends to be flattened into a vision of the post-historical freedom to consume that is always arriving. This seems to be the only dream that desire for Meghna and the thought of the outside can conjure up, beyond the fatalities of identity, beyond founding questions of life and death, and beyond the nightmare of the malfunctioning third world nation-state. Intolerable love thus enters into a secret affiliation with a class fantasy of neo–liberation, one that is so primal that it is close to nature itself, not yet sullied by any historical handiwork of the state. Unlike the poetry of Faiz that Mufti studies, the lyrical powers of cinema in *Dil Se* exiles loving bodies from identitarian bloodbaths in the unhappy battlefield of national geopolitics, only to weakly advertise them in a virtual realm of transnational metropolitan desire. It is in the realm of a tortured poetics of cinema that information-images of a capitalist globalization appear as belonging to a utopian other side of suffering. If this indeed is an idealist yearning for cosmopolitan peace, it cannot be distinguished from the marketable desires in the metropolis.

However, it would be wrong to conclude that such groundless recoding of historical bodies and locations into batches of spectacles completely exhaust the semiotic energy of these interludes. In strange ways these primal expressions of an intolerable love that cannot be distinguished from a global market which is perpetually arriving are also capable of destroying sedentary and enervating pieties of the already given. In the "Satrangi Re" ("Oh My Lover") sequence, we see the militarized grounds of Ladakh transformed into assemblages of travel cinematography, exotic, eroticized dance movements, and urban motifs of bondage and ritualistic masochism. The pressures of a geo-televisual nomadism of desire cannot always be contained within the parameters of an assumed subject—for instance, the oedipal one that is central to the modern. The sequence ends with the dancing figures of Amar and Meghna striking the pose of Michelangelo's *Pietà*, with Meghna as the Virgin Mary and Amar the martyred Christ.

As I have suggested in the Introduction, the so-called indifference and non–obligatory nature of song sequences need to be understood in terms of *disjunctive* relations with the narrative, as qualitative and expressive

entities which affect narration through osmotic and capricious flows of
semiotics (as a system of signs), rather than through a constitutive dialectical participation in an overarching, synthesizing movement of semiology
(as a system of language). This postulate can be illustrated by a couple of
moments from Ratnam's two other films on political conjugality—*Roja*
(1992) and *Bombay* (1995). In the first, the "Rukmini Rukmini" sequence
comically brings about a disjunctive synthesis between a new urban code
of the sex relation with what Prasad has called the monitoring gaze of a
not yet modern, but no longer feudal moral guardianship.[29] The idea of
privacy for the newly-weds is a precarious historical proposition in the
cinematic milieu of *Roja*, where the agrarian extended family is shown to
be dominant.[30] The family–community is not dismantled, but loosened
from its earthy moorings and spectacularly deterritorialized in terms of
affect. The young and old of the village jocularly take part in the traditional practice of peeping into the nuptial bedchamber. The monitoring
gaze of the feudal—the historical foreclosure of the space of the private—
begins to be mitigated and formalized by a series of musically activated
rituals. Everyone gossips, sings, and dances to celebrate the bridal night in
this song sequence. The traditional bodies of middle-aged village matrons
are unhinged from laws and memories of the folkish milieu and trans-
muted through a groundless application of MTV musicality and laughter.
They are re-publicized as bodies in kinetic oscillation between discursive
poles of traditional moderation and modern chic. In becoming chaosmic
figures, caught in limbo between the composite body of the community
and the individuated persona of the West, the dancing matriarchs break
new ground. They create conditions for the nuclear couple to emerge in
the narrative in an affective realm, in which attributes of the feudal (the
profile and attire of the village woman) and those of the modern (the pelvic
thrust and the techno-beats) are not historically resolved, but indeterminately present. Musicality is thus that which vibrates in and renders
rhythmically fuzzy the gap between the priestly statement of the absolutist
country and the clamorous prose of the liberal city. It is only after this rite
of passage that the couple can cut the proprietorial cords of kinship and
leave for Kashmir, which is at once an earthly paradise for honeymoon as
well as a professional battleground for combating terror.

A similar thing happens in *Bombay*. The newly-weds are at first
besieged by communitarian obligations, which require them to lodge the
children of a visiting family inside their bedchamber. It is only after this
comical delay that the neighbors themselves take the initiative to give
them privacy for a long-awaited bridal night. The politically sensitive
inter-religious marriage between the Hindu boy and the Muslim girl

(who have eloped from their rural, familial stations to the anonymity of the big city) is consummated in an interesting manner. The woman had hitherto been constructed in the narrative as a furtive, *burkha*-clad figure in traditional-agrarian mode, and also, in the "Kannalanae"/"Kehna Hai Kya" ("What is There to Say?") song sequence, shot in the Indo-Saracenic-style Tirumal Nayak Palace in Madurai, in terms of a man-nered, courtly dancing body drawn on Islamic-aristocratic lines.[31] In contrast, in the "Humma Humma" number, the depiction of conjugality inside the bedroom is interspersed with a carnivalesque and libertine dance that takes place in the neighborhood premises, now discontinu-ously transformed into a sound stage of the MTV musical. The seductive techno-beat rises to a crescendo and in the course of its trajectory claims not just the bodies of the dancers—who are dressed in a mishmash of styles, assembling the *niqab* (veil) to ostensibly "sexy" dance costumes of an "alien" kind—but also that of Shaila Banu, the young bride. The body of the Islamic-rural woman begins to sway intermittently to the music, as part of a playful precoital overture, and is gradually "de-marked" of its attributes of tradition: the psycho-biographical qualities of coyness, "lack of exposure" due to a strict, Islamic upbringing in the rural backwaters, and sociological ones of body language and attire.

It is thus the deterritorializing affect of music that carries her over to an urban epistemological fold where a liminal image of private, "con-sensual," and secular sex relations becomes possible. She undresses as a musical automaton and lets her body be claimed by a new patriarchy and its nucleated desires. The mating ground between religions is secured not in a realm of cosmopolitanism after the *agon* of historical becoming, but in a plane of *consuming* the music of metropolitan globalization. Shaila Banu, in other words, *is*, because she is capable of consuming. In that, like her husband, her neighbors, and the carnivalesque visitors from the nearby red light district, she has discovered an originary plane of being capable of holding the temporalities of the ancient as well as the modern regimes. This is a paradoxical moment in which a pre-modern tribalism of religious conflicts and prejudices is offset by an emphatic *primordialism* of consumer desire. The latter arrives non-temporally, in an instant when it reveals itself to be always, already there, without graduated historical measures of enfranchisement, education, or culture. The semiotic affects of this pageant-like number percolates into the narrative, as diffuse energy rather than propositional logic. Subsequently, as Shaila Banu settles into domes-ticity and motherhood, her figure lends itself to a "metro-normativity" defined by naturalized practices of urban Hinduization. She no longer wears the *burkha* and is no longer seen near non-vegetarian food.[32] The song sequence thus retroactively envelops her "Muslim" self into a rural "pastness" that is overcome by an historically inevitable progress to urban conjugality.

Interesting song sequences in Hindi film are not moments of simple representation, the coming into being of simple good or bad ideological constructs. They are instead complex movements of power, tribulations on the battlefield of constitutive languages and errant vernaculars. The informatic-lyrical powers in such sequences are those that globalize the body in a manner that has the betrayal of the "self" (as a national-local precept of being) as its limit. The self is thus partitioned because it perpetually threatens to enter avenues of desire and fascination on the other side proscribed by home. They should not be judged simply on the grounds of what they communicate, in terms of a baseline of address taken in the subjective sense; instead, it would be critically rewarding to understand them in ways in which they problematize communicability itself in the world.[33]

Notes

1. See Aamir Mufti, "Toward a Lyric History of India" (2004). A more elaborate version of this essay appears as chapter 5 of his monumental *Enlightenment in the Colony: The Jewish Question and the Crisis of Postcolonial Culture* (2007).
2. G. W. F. Hegel, *Philosophy of World History* (1975): 102.
3. See Bhaskar Sarkar, *Mourning the Nation* (2009) for an insightful account of mourning and crisis of memory in relation to partitioned selves. "Runes of Laceration" is the title of the second chapter. Sarkar brilliantly theorizes why post-Independence Indian cinema was always haunted by Partition even though there was an overt conspiracy of silence concerning it—something the historian Gyan Pandey has described as an almost willful "collective amnesia" of almost four decades. See also Pandey, "In Defense of the Fragment" (1992).
4. In arguing for a comparativist framework for cinema studies, Paul Willemen has noted that, around 1900, Indian intellectuals and artists resorted to realism in order to question the established order. At the same moment, guided by an isomorphic "questioning and critical purpose," Western artists and intellectuals forged modernism. See "For a Comparative Film Studies" (2006): 98–9.
5. See Ashish Rajadhyaksha, "Neo-traditionalism: Film as Popular Art in India" (1986): 57–9.
6. The various journalistic and academic instances of this tendency are too numerous to list. Consider, for instance, the formal description of the popular Indian film forwarded by Arun Kaul and Mrinal Sen in the *Manifesto*

of the New Cinema Movement: "a mechanical business of putting together popular stars, gaudy sets, glossy color, *a large number of irrelevant musical sequences* and other standard meretricious ingredients." *Close-up*, 1 (July 1968): 37 (emphasis added).

7. According to Rajadhyaksha and Willemen, "Filmstan's style arguably had the largest impact of any studio on later independent commercial film-making in Hindi." See *Encyclopedia of Indian Cinema*, 96.

8. Nasreen Munni Kabir, *Guru Dutt: A Life in Cinema* (2006): 42.

9. See the essays by Tom Gunning— "'Primitive' Cinema: A Frame-Up? Or the Trick's on Us"; "Non-Continuity, Continuity, Discontinuity: A Theory of Genres in Early Films," in Thomas Elsaesser and Adam Barker, eds., *Early Cinema: Space, Frame, Narrative* (1990): 95–103, 86–94. See also Miriam Hansen, *Babel and Babylon: Spectatorship in American Silent Film* (1991).

10. Bhaskar Chandravarkar, "Growth of the Film Song" (1981).

11. Ashok Ranade, "The Extraordinary Importance of the Indian Film Song" (1981).

12. See Geeta Kapur, "Mythic Material in Indian Cinema," and the two seminal essays by Ashish Rajadhyaksha on early Indian cinema: "The Phalke Era: Conflict of Traditional Form and Modern Technology" (1987) and "Neo-traditionalism: Film as Popular Art in India" (1986).

13. See Sudipta Kaviraj, "Reading a Song of the City—Images of the City in Literature and Films" (2007).

14. Lalitha Gopalan, *Cinema of Interruptions* (2002): 179–80.

15. Ravi Vasudevan, "The Cultural Space of a Film Narrative: Interpreting *Kismet* Bombay Talkies" (1943): 172.

16. Gopalan's critical energies are directed toward a dismantling of this very normative of cinema. She uses "interruption" as a rhetorical trope rather than as a positive concept.

17. See Wimal Dissanayake, "Globalization and Cultural Narcissism: Note on Bollywood Cinema" (2004).

18. See Madhava Prasad, *Ideology of the Hindi Film* (1998): 42–5; and Janet Staiger, "Hollywood Mode of Production to 1930" and "The Hollywood Mode of Production, 1930–1960," in David Bordwell et al., *The Classical Hollywood Cinema* (1985).

19. Cited in Gopalan, *Cinema of Interruptions*, 136.

20. Ram Gopal Verma, who has emerged as a prominent *auteur* figure in the world of mainstream Indian cinema in the last decade, seems to express a similar modernist anxiety about an incomplete participation of Indian cinema in a transnational urban aesthetic. Noted for his daring experiments with inherited forms, Verma devised his 1999 film *Mast* as a self-reflexive Hollywood-style musical that foregrounded and critically commented on its own excesses and utopian energies. The film was thus purported to be a contemporary visitation and reinscription of a traditional, indigenous genre. On

the other hand, for his 2002 film *Darna Mana Hai*, Verma revolted against what can be called the "dictatorship of the distributor" and decided to delete the song sequences from the final cut. The musical track was thus marketed independently through audio cassette and CD sales, while the film (a horror flick) was released in theaters without song numbers.

21. See Hegel, *Phenomenology*, 265–74. Also *Lectures on the Philosophy of World History: Introduction* (1975): 99–100.

22. Partha Chatterjee, *Nation in Fragments: Colonial and Postcolonial Histories* (1993): 230–1.

23. Hegel, *Phenomenology*, 25–61.

24. Ibid., 281.

25. Fredric Jameson, in a valiant attempt to resuscitate modernity as a trope of political polysemia rather than as a concept, makes similar distinctions in *A Singular Modernity* (2002).

26. Hegel, *Philosophy of Right* (1967): 168–9.

27. The allusion is to Georgio Agamben's study of modern sovereignty in *Homo Sacer: Sovereign Power and Bare Life* (1998).

28. Michel Foucault has theorized late modern governmentality in terms of altered sovereign practices more attuned to the flexible management of populations, rather than to the creation of "peoples" through discipline and a cultural pedagogy of citizenship. The birth of biopolitics as such presumes the population state, rather than the territorial one. See "Birth of Biopolitics" and "Security, Terror, and Population" (1997).

29. Prasad, *Ideology of the Hindi Film*, 53–113.

30. This is established earlier in the film through a meticulous depiction of the rituals and protocols that go into the finalization of the arranged marriage, During the only prenuptial meeting between the hero and his originally intended bride she confides that she is in love with another; the hero chooses to marry her sister (without asking her) instead, in order to save social embarrassment for all. The whole thing is presided over by the entire community from a distance.

31. Gopalan, *Cinema of Interruptions*, 131.

32. An early sequence in the film shows her dressing fish.

33. See Giorgio Agamben, *Means without End: Notes on Politics* (2000) for an understanding of the cinematic as a politics of gesturality.

Part III

Myth and Repetition

CHAPTER 5

Technopolis and the Ramayana: New Temporalities

Introduction

This chapter begins with a discussion of how a primary mythic impulse of defining a nation-in-the-world acquires special tenacity amidst a new and turbulent techno-financial image universe. I shall look at how myth can be "worlded" in such a scenario, and in the next chapter at how mythic material and a concomitant notion of return can be repeated in film after film, but each time with a different sense of occasioning. From many available suspects, I have picked a science fantasy for the first task, keeping in mind that, as discussed in Chapter 2, the period under discussion witnessed the gradual demise of the all-India film and the introduction, into the A-production bracket, of decidedly transnational genres. Since the 1990s, erstwhile major formats like the *dacait* (bandit) film and the rural melodrama that fashioned some of the greatest box office hits (*Mother India*, *Naya Daur*, *Ganga Jumna*, *Sholay*) have been gradually relegated to B- and C-status or regional industries, while others like—sci-fi, horror, or sensationalist crime thrillers have been upgraded. However, let me quickly preface this analysis of the interface between myth and science fiction by pointing out a couple of more recent developments and declaring some necessary caveats.

Popular Hindi cinema today has its own superhero genre, consolidated largely by Rakesh Roshan's *Koi . . . Mil Gaya* (*I Have Found Someone*) (2003) and its 2006 sequel, *Krrish*. The first film was inspired by Steven Spielberg's *E.T.*, but what can be noted in passing, as part of an overall consideration of how alien themes are Indianized, is that here the inhabitants of outer space respond to the resonating signal, transmitted to outer space, of the singular Vedic mantra, *Om*. In the second film, the protagonist inherits the magical powers originally bestowed on his father by *Jadoo*, an entity from outer space who is a cross between Spielberg's alien and Lucas's Yoda from *Star Wars*. However, it is symptomatic that Krish's journey toward becoming a high-flying caped crusader in the metropolis begins in a bucolic setting in India, where his innocent antics and his very name invoke mythic memories of Krishna, the god of Vrindavan, as depicted in the Mahabharata and the *Vishnupurana*. These films were followed by *Drona* (Goldie Behl, 2008), with the protagonist once again named after a bulwark warrior in The Mahabharata. The patriarchy's name-giving powers are a small part of what is, overall, a complex process of claiming the works and wonders of a global order for new age Hindu spiritualism and a constantly revised horizon of mythic becoming. This is precisely what we will explore, with the caveat that mythic invocation in itself is not negative or regressive. Under the auspices of what I have called postulated resolutions in Hindi film, such appeals to popular traditions of piety can often have radical implications. My second caveat is that, if the long-standing mythic impulse in Hindi film has garnered new qualities of ontology and ambition in the age of the geo-televisual, there has also been a simultaneous emergence of a new will to realism,[1] a baroque turn away from the horizon of postulation, toward disenchanting, fragmented assemblages suffused with novelizing and pathological energies of the changing city. This can be seen in the gangster genre, which I shall comment on in the next chapter.

Epic Melodrama

In "Epic Melodrama: Themes of Nationality in Indian Cinema," Ashish Rajadhyaksha identifies three strands of cinematic realism in the complex and variegated field of Indian cinema: the modernist, the statist, and the avant-garde.[2] He notes that due to an overall equation between realism and certain "objectified values and symbols" of rationality, science, and historicity, an ontological ground was prepared early on for what he considers to be a significant change in Indian film ("Epic Melodrama" [1994]: 57). That is, apart from the general emergence of humanist or socialist-realist efforts to secure Western-style urban-industrial hegemonies in the national context, what he finds more important is an overall cognitivist valorization of realism. The code of realism, however, did not arrive with absolute powers to transcode and historically enframe diverse artistic expressions. Realism as such was frequently decorative, devoid of a rational, meta-discursive status accorded to it by the Hegelian–Lukácsian aesthetics of the West. This non-totalizing cognitive valorization—of a realism that is topical to the beholding eye, but does not spell a complete universe of godless truths and individual or class consciousness—facilitated a generic shift. In the horizon of a new India that was fitfully urban and fretfully modern, the reformist social of the 1930s (including the Prabhat "Sant" mythologicals like *Sant Tukaram* or *Sant Dnyaneshwar*) gradually gave way to an idiom of social melodrama (Rajadhyaksha, "Epic Melodrama," 67–8).

Rajadhyaksha suggests that the introduction of sound technology in Indian cinema in the early 1930s inaugurated two thematic mutations in what he calls an already there aesthetic bridge between the mobile, emblematic qualities of the screen and the cosmic pull of the mythic image in transcendent repose. First, it gave rise to a variety of allegories of the traditional in order to overcome the formal/technical problems of finding a verbal analogue to the Phalke mythological. In these allegories, religious-mythological icons or popular saints were replaced by figures from reform literature cast in dominant social values.[3] The second shift was more crucial; the icon was increasingly replaced, not by another, but by a *narrative structure* ("Epic Melodrama," 64). Hence, once a panoptic perspective—in which the tangible, here-and-now inscriptions of film always submit themselves to an epic imaginary—was in place, the mythological could undergo generic shifts without the immanent presence of the icon. It could be substituted, among other things, by a mythic national being, largely furnished by a primary imagination of the ideal woman. The narration of the nation-as-mother was thus undertowed by an otherworldly pull, despite its cosmetic realist front.

The birth of what Rajadhyaksha calls the all-India film in the studio productions of Bombay Talkies and Filmstan in the early 1940s was predominantly conceived in accordance with this narrational tendency. In the "social," therefore, secular attributes of the mise-en-scène never really combined to form an autonomous cosmology of their own. The gods animated the screen from beyond, commanding the familiar world in it as an environment of blessings and curses rather than allowing it to be presented as a battleground of history. The realist textures of the cinematic image, to a great extent, remained formal signs of a degraded, fragmentary world continuously restored and reclaimed by powerful ontologies of being as Dharmic, or being as nation. The studio films of the Bombay Talkies largely rode this non-subjective phenomenology while assembling an analytic-dramatic style of Hollywood with the manifold decorative typologies of Indic traditions ("Epic Melodrama," 64–70). This is what paved the way for what Rajadhyaksha identifies as the proto-modern cinematic creation of *Tradition* in the 1950s—a schema of narrating the nation aligned with Nehru's "third way."[4]

Digital Inscription and the Mythic Depths of Time

I shall now turn to how this founding imagination of national becoming is "worlded" in a contemporary, digital, geo-televisual universe in Mani

Shankar's 2004 film *Rudraksh* (*The Seed*). In the register of space, the film inducts a transnational, infinitely varied world into the sovereign sphere of an Indian destinying. In the dimension of temporality, it seeks to envelop the transformative energies of the present order with a figure of time that is *sanatan* (the eternal). The project, however, is to understand a *habit of thought* rather than investigate, for its own sake, a particular film that, apart from being a box office flop, is also particularly unsatisfying aesthetically. Mani Shankar's film provides a few telling examples of commerce between an ideology of present-day metropolitan *Hindutva* and the paraphernalia and practices of globalization. It pitches itself on a plane of language that can be of critical interest in understanding an overall dispensation of a Hindu normative metropolitanism in the contemporary Indian situation. *Rudraksh* is interesting precisely because of its hyperbolic banality, its delirious generation of clichés through new age common sense of urban Hinduism. The common sense here is, however, aligned to a paradoxical folklore of what I have been calling informatics; it is emphatically *advertised* rather than dialectically resolved or agonistically proposed. As a result, the text has to absolve itself of all depths and striations of language and maintain a rigorous and austere stance of informatic, geo-televisual narration, one that pronounces the newly emergent manifold novelties of the universe as nothing but part of a becoming already remembered.

The film begins with a voiceover from the depths of time. Amitabh Bachchan's rich and somber baritone reminds the viewer of a terrible advent already foretold a long time ago by ancient Puranic scriptures. The remembrance is about the imminent return of the demonic *Rakshasha* clan which has intermittently plagued mankind since the dawn of creation. Indeed, the voiceover implies that the history of the world itself can be understood as a relentless, triangulated battle between the *devas* (gods), the *manavas* (humankind), and the monstrous and Negroid *asuras* (of which the *Rakshashas* are a part) who periodically emerge from the dark underbelly of hell. According to the cosmogony delineated by the holy seers of ancient times primarily belonging to the Samkhya and Yoga schools, the first group is an evolute of *sattva* (the element of truth); the second of *tejas* (energy), and the third of *rajas* (the primal force of darkness).[5] The voiceover invokes the authority of the scriptures to say that thousands of years ago, after the demise of the last great *asura* king, Ravana, at the hands of Rama, the godly Aryan prince of Ayodhya, the forces of the netherworld had experienced a protracted twilight. But the seeds of an inevitable resurgence were buried deep in the womb of time, waiting for an opportune moment. Mani Shankar's film begins exactly at the hour of this regeneration.

When the voiceover commences, the camera opens out to a pure CGI-generated visualscape, conducting a winding journey through verdurous gloom to a strange, distant dawn. The movement ends with the declaration that the slaying of Ravana, the demon king of Lanka, not only spelled the temporary end of the reign of the *rakshashas* on earth, but also inaugurated what is, as per a Puranic timeline, the present *Kali* yuga. The camera then launches the present-day narrative by cutting away to another landscape, a picture of some ancient city ruins which is a painterly compact of analogue visuals and graphics. The voiceover introduces this space as Yala Lanka, the now derelict, once magnificent capital of Ravana. The year is 1990 AD, and the ground of a mythic battle between good and evil is seen to have been transformed into an archeological site where human beings, headed by an international group of researchers, are committing the hubris of excavating a primeval past. One should pause here and try to fathom the forbidding dimensions of time that is invoked. If Rama's monumental deed marked the end of the *treta* yuga, how far back in our habitual, linear reckoning of temporality must one travel to comprehend the ambitious scope of this archeological operation? Indeed, the question cannot just be of interest in relation to the film itself, if one keeps in mind the catastrophic events that have taken place in the theater of Indian politics centered on the historicity of Rama's birthplace.[6] Apart from fearful outcomes in the domains of cultural nationalism and sovereign power, the query has also militantly resonated in academic domains of history and archaeology.

Temporality

In her illuminating monograph, *Time as a Metaphor of History: Early India* (1996), Romila Thapar visits and challenges a long-standing Western presumption that the only concept of time known to early India was cyclic. She sets herself the task of demolishing the assumption that the unity between Chronos (time) and Clio (history) in the Greco-Roman world, one that founded an historical temporality of the state, was non-existent in Indian civilizations until the modern age. Thapar dispels a *categorical* separation between the cyclical and linear orders and suggests that they can combine in myriad ways in different forms of humanistic, statist, astronomical, theological, and eschatological thinking. She begins by recalling Mircea Eliade's observation that cyclical modules of time in the Indic tradition are often so massive that they render human activities in the world quite insignificant (*Time as a Metaphor of History*, 5). Inhabiting a temporal plane through an existential of the everyday, therefore, may be akin to walking the earth itself in a manner that casts the immediate local ground beneath one's feet flat, although beyond the far horizon it curves down to its planetary roundness. Time (*kala*), as a grand compass that is beyond immediate existence or immediate memory, is indeed that which gives birth only to abolish.[7] It is a formidable task to comprehend its looming appetites and the unfathomable scope of eternal returns that it calls into being.

The notion of cyclical time is said to have originated from diurnal regularities in nature, in the form of the synodic month, the lunar fortnights or the seasonal cycle of the year. In early Vedic literature, this came with an accompanying notion of *rta* as a cosmic imperative of rhythmic regularity and predictability (Thapar, *Time as a Metaphor of History*, 10). The yuga astronomy of the fifth century AD emerged as a compact between a scriptural cosmology of *Brahman* as being and a mathematical computation of stellar bodies, primarily instigated by Hellenistic ideas. It is this crucial commerce between worlds that opened up an entirely new universe of time reckoning, an epic extension of the powers of *Yuga* infinitely over and beyond the manageable diurnal movements of the sun and the moon. Thapar suggests that in this system *kalpha* (the longest unit of time, consisting of 4,320 million years), was derived in later centuries from Puranic scriptural sources. The resultant time reckoning was elastic, beginning with instants of humanly controllable time, like the blinking of an eye, and then arching out to the infinite temporality of the *Brahman*, crossing the timespans of the forefathers (*pitrs*) and gods (*devas*) on the way (13).

Manu's *Dharmasastra*, like many similar scriptural authorities, proposes four *Yugas*: *krta* (or *satya*), *treta*, *dvapara*, and *kali*. The first— *krta*—lasts 4,000 years with 400 years of twilight preceding and following it. The next three ages suffer a progressive reduction of 1,000 years from each, and a corresponding reduction of 100 years in the two twilight periods. *Treta* thus spans 3,600 years (3000 + 300 + 300), while *dvapara* and *kali* total to 2,400 and 1,200 years respectively. The grand total of 12,000 years constitutes a *mahayuga* (age of the gods), and 1,000 of these form a single day of Brahma, with the night being of equal length. A similar description of the four ages appears in the *Vanaparvan* of the epic Mahabharata, with the *krta* yuga returning at the end of *kali*. The cycle of the four yugas is a cosmic imagination of time informed by a perpetual understanding of Dharma being in a state of progressive decline. It is said in the *Vanaparvan* of the Mahabharata that in the age of *kali* the cycle is complete and the world turns upside down as a result. Hence, this is the age of *mlechchas* (rule of lower-caste kings); the eclipse of the Brahminical order is complete at this point, and the warlike *ksatriya* caste is stripped of its virtues (Thapar, *Time as a Metaphor of History*, 14).

The concept of the four ages was further elaborated in the body of texts known as the *Puranas*, which Thapar dates to the mid-first millennium AD (14). There is indeed a greater, almost dizzying play with numbers in these texts. The 12,000 years that made a godly epoch or the *mahayuga* in Manu and the Mahabharata are treated as divine years in the *Vishnu Purana*. A conversion of that span of time to human years calls for a multiplication by 365. As a result, *kali*, the smallest and the most degenerate of all ages in the cycle, assumes a gargantuan span of 432,000 years.[8] In terms of the sombrous weight of time that Mani Shankar's film *Rudraksh* alludes to, the momentous feats of Rama the godly king during the end of the *treta* age would thus be at least 864,000 years before even the commencement of *kali*, since the *dwapara* age came in between.

The point is not to look at the forbidding scope of these temporal modules in terms of a positive arithmetic of worldly or eschatological computations. As constituents of a mythic, "deep" time, they envelop the historical as forces of memorialization as well as destinying, rather than calibrated becoming. The time of *kali* is thus not to be identified with the here-and-now profanity of the present (which may include temporary triumphs and carnivalesque interregnums). Rather, it is a mythic postulate that curves into the finite presentism of not just individual consciousnesses, but also institutions of history and the state. The curvature of time is that which bends into a non-metric and groundless utopia both before and after the perpetual present that stretches as far back as archeology and the other sciences can remember or as far out as they can foretell. It is therefore time that cannot be tracked or traced; it can only be recalled to absolve the profane and render it sacred. *Kali*, like the ages that precede it, is a *figuration* of time, rather than a measure of numbering numbers. As an imagined postulate of degeneration it has clear implications of social power, particularly when its attachment to naturalistic, Brahminical ideologies become clear, but what is immediately noteworthy is that such notions of deep time also abound in the staunchly anti-Brahminical Buddhist, Jaina, and Ajivika texts, where it is stated that if the here-and-now is an order of *dukhkha* (endurance), it is a return of the bygone that will deliver believers from Brahminical oppression. In her monograph, Thapar illustrates this by citing a beautiful figure of time from the *Samyutta Nikaya*: "if there is a mountain in the shape of a cube, measuring one *yojana* [in various measures, a *yojana* ranges from two and a half to nine miles] and if every hundred years the mountain is brushed with a silk scarf, then the time that is taken for the mountain to be eroded by the scarf is the equivalent of a *kalpa*" (*Time as a Metaphor of History*, 16).

Rudraksh of course harbors no such radical anti-Brahminical pretensions. The recall of the mythical in this case does not pertain to a utopian affirmation of an end of unfreedom, but to what we can call a Brahminical "ritual," which is appended immediately to a statist administration of terror and crisis. One can, for the moment, cast ritual in the specific Vedic sense Thapar draws from *Satapatha Brahmana, Atharva Veda,* and *Rig Veda*: "where [the ritual] is meticulously observed, it suspends the performers of the rituals into a threshold condition where only the parameters of their time-reckoning prevail" (*Time as a Metaphor of History*, 10). In that sense, the cinematic ritualism in Mani Shankar's film pertains to a restoration of the world by replenishing its nihilistic and empty time consciousness with a messianic figure of temporality. The proper battle against terror is the righteous battle of the Ramayana remembered and renewed. In this cinematic-ritualistic evocation of a founding myth that redeems an errant reality, the act of recall becomes congruent with the frenetic surveillance, policing, and deliverance of a global emergency. An actionist affirmation of Dharma becomes one with the address of "terror" as a dogmatic prescriptive of neo-liberal statism.

One can, at this point, return to the particular place where the belly of the earth holds the seed of a monstrous power. The film opens to a dusty and grey archeological site that, in the organization of its mise-en-scène features, follows a regular, Orientalist visual texture established by Hollywood, perhaps most famously by the *Indiana Jones* and, to a lesser extent, *The Mummy* trilogies. Here one meets Bhuria, the chief labor contractor of the site. Referred to later in the film as a coming from Bihar, he is uncouth, corrupt and displays a bestial sensuality. The physicality, speech, and attire of the long-haired and unshaven Bhuria endow him with tribalesque indices of identity; he also wields an anachronistic leather whip in his interaction with the workers, in what is ostensibly the democratic dispensation of modern Sri Lanka. Bhuria, therefore, in terms of a racial aesthetics established early on and maintained throughout the film, is a *mlechcha* (untouchable), a dark-skinned non-Aryan who would be king. His female companion, Lali, too is initially presented as a tribal girl with a simmering, diabolic presence. Both are thus well equipped to inherit the *tamasic* (dark) mantle of Ravana.

Two incidents start a chain of events that soon assumes titanic proportions, in terms of a spatial span of the universe as well as the eternity of time. First, the archeological team excavates a totemic statue. Then the statue, which is of the ancient god of the *Rakshashas*, begins its nefarious ministrations in stealthy silence, picking Bhuria as its chosen one. The latter begins to wake from unsettling dreams which are the result of a long-pending call of evil on earth. Once he is under the spell of a strange mantra that keeps resounding in his head, Bhuria searches out and steals a mysterious amulet hidden inside the statue of the *Rakshasha* god. This amulet is the *rudraksh* (seed) that holds Ravana's power. The scenario then flashes forward to Mumbai in 1993. The city at that point is burning, with the communal riots that followed a few months after the demolition of the Babri Mosque by Hindu zealots on December 6, 1992. Bhuria appears and instigates both Hindus and Muslims on their murderous intent. Next, one sees Lali in the year 1995 as a chic urban woman who has lost all memory of her past existence and has been transformed into a deadly assassin for hire.

A series of quick time ellipses chart the diabolical careers of the malevolent pair over a decade. Bhuria and Lali undergo significant morphological and behavioral changes during these years. The former loses his long, unkempt tresses; his hair becomes colored and spiked, and his skin tone assumes a bleached whiteness. Lali too is continually recast by different signatures of metropolitan style; her attire is sometimes that of the dominatrix, sometimes that of the punk, often that of the leather-clad, serpentine killer. The nefarious couple grow to mythic dimensions of evil by a relentless, informatic accumulation of a global armada of signs and skills. The affective creation of the face of wickedness proceeds through "unreal," trans-social evolutions; it is a coming into being of the iconic demon, which gathers diabolical strength precisely when it keeps crossing the borders of psycho-biographical plausibility. The lower-caste, uneducated, and bestial figures display an inhuman acquisitiveness toward the riches of the world. Not only do Bhuria and Lali transform the scale of their desires and practices, they also display a disconcerting comfort in using instruments of finance and technology—cell phones, expensive cars, gadgets, weapons, and communicative media. The *Rakshasha* becomes geo-televisual. Translated into the immediate racial aesthetics of Aryanness and caste, it also means that the *dalit* is poised to inherit the earth.

The rise of the pair from petty thieves to global figures of evil involves not just rewriting their cinematic bodies, but also removing them, in phases, from an historical mise-en-scène to a pure virtual landscape that, in itself, is a mythic creation of technology. A scene set in Mumbai in 2004 shows Bhuria and Lali in surreal grounds, contemplating their future. The digital inscription here imparts a special mythic ontology to the filmic image of the demonic. The space qualifies as a fitting habitat for otherworldly evil precisely because it is not the result of an old cinema that used to be a perfect image analogue of the given world. Special effects, in being able to absolve the camera of its realist proclivities, effect a total removal of the banal here-and-now from the screen and dispel all phenomenological doubt in the medium. The iconic dimension of evil, therefore, involves a painterly operation of cinema as technological ritual. The stage of an impending battle between good and evil becomes a pure mythic locale, unmediated by the world as it is.

The Sacralization of Special Effects

Instead of a dialectic and *agon* between a boundless mythical imaginary and a degrading realism of cinema that Rajadhyaksha notes in relation to early Indian cinematic mythologicals, what we have is a relationship of adequation between the two, a new visual aesthetic that implies that technology itself had to undergo rigorous development before it could garner capabilities to be equal to the task of giving birth to a mythic cinema in a true state-of-the-art sense. Unlike the apparatus of classical narrative cinema, where special effects intervened in the phenomenological exchange between the camera and the world only as attributes of deceit or décor, here earthbound matters can be totally mythologized. Now the earth itself is claimed, with all the other powers of the cinematic (the camera, computer technology, mise-en-scène, actors, costumes, lights, or the celluloid base) into a comprehensive ritual of invoking Brahman through a narration of myth. The paraphernalia of technological imprints, therefore, become exhilarated; they bask in the ontological glow of mythic remembrance. Once Bhuria and Lali are lifted out of the historical streets of Mumbai, they cross that "threshold condition" and enter a zone where only one reckoning of a time-beyond-time can prevail. They leave all their social identities behind and emerge as true, updated versions of the *Rakshashas* depicted in the *Puranas*.

A similar power of evocation can be said to govern the visceral realism of Mel Gibson's 2004 film *The Passion of the Christ*. "Passion" is a postulate of technologistic realism here, along with being a destinying power that informs the three orders of human time. This is because within the film's ontological parameters, it can be said that cinema itself had to undergo a protracted period of maturation before it could make the picture of the Passion visually and aurally adequate to the fearful eternal it represents. *The Passion of the Christ* is a cinema of the skin and therefore a cinema of tactile entrancement, a nerve-wrenching commitment to the picture of Holy Passion. The technical vigor of its terrible sights and furious sounds seeks to stake an ontic claim greater than any common idea of cinematic veracity. The claim is that of being able, at last, to cinematically locate the earthly body of Christ in that augmented sovereign sphere of mercy and pain which Foucault, perhaps with a chuckle of irony, would describe as "the juncture between the judgment of men and the judgment of God."[9]

The Aryan Brahmin

While Bhuria plots his satanic schemes, the forces of good are introduced in the film, with the advent of Gayatri, a scholar from the University of California, who researches the paranormal. She and her assistants encounter several fraudulent godmen before homing in on an eccentric young man named Varun who works as a "genuine" miracle healer during the day and as a bar bouncer at night. He also has a third profession, as a martial arts instructor who combines physical combat techniques borrowed from the Far East with a brand of Indian spiritualism. Varun (played by Sanjay Dutt) is a tall, fair, "Aryanesque" north Indian Brahmin, highly qualified to emerge as the arch-antagonist of a dark *mlechcha* like Bhuria (played by Sunil Shetty, an actor with pronounced Dravidian looks).

Gayatri's handycam, which records one of Varun's magical cures, arrives as a humdrum, here-and-now counterfoil to the cosmic cinematic camera. The latter, as we have seen, is capable of absolving special effects by appending them to a grand ritual of invoking a mythic temporality. On the other hand, Gayatri's recording instrument, as a camera within the film, serves as a doubting, Cartesian documenter of scientific truth. Within the mythic frame of the cinematic, the video machine thereby becomes a profane counterfoil to the cosmic camera; it can trace and track happenings only up to the point where they pass into the mysterious outside to Western epistemology. When the paranormal unfolds before these skeptical lenses, earthbound matters of science are gradually absorbed by a universe of belief. Gayatri's handycam records the miraculous event when Varun cures a woman of skin disease by assuming the pain and the symptoms on his own body within minutes, even as they disappear from his patient. Later, Gayatri and her team, equipped with computational and medical instruments, monitor alterations in Varun's metabolism when he is in a meditative state. As he ascends to a plane of thought inaccessible to ordinary mortals, his blood pressure and heart rate drop below life-sustaining levels. A scan of his hypothalamus and deep cortex shows that he is exploiting more that 70 percent of his brain capacity (humans usually use only about 1 percent). All of this is accompanied by an alarming and inexplicable rise in electromagnetic radiation around his body. Gayatri concludes her investigations by declaring that Varun is in a state of *samadhi* which comes with a complete immersion of the self into thoughts of the *Brahman*. When this happens, the cosmic energies of the self, as distant ripples of a singular being, are able to abstract themselves from the prison of the body. She ends this phase of her research with the observation that "science," for the present, cannot explain the phenomenon just observed.

Translation

When Varun emerges from his meditative trance, he underlines his return to a world of appetites by attracting a soda can with his telekinetic powers. The moment of product placement on screen coincides with yet another demonstration of the miraculous. A relaxed Varun then begins a series of discussions with the diligent Gayatri. These utterances—scattered throughout the film and interspersed by spectacular encounters with evil—set up a geo-televisual field of translation, by which the postulates of a so-called old world "tradition," as well as the paraphernalia of state-of-the-art development, are re-publicized in a different realm of value. Varun, the new age Hindu, provides Gayatri with a new vocabulary of the metropolitan, a novel lens through which to view the manifold wonders of the world. Varun says that his telekinetic and telepathic powers are the result of a connectivity that comes from the immanence of Brahman itself—a plane of heavenly intelligence he calls the *swapna akash* (the sky of dreams), which, he explains, is a "divine internet," But unlike the earthly one, it is not just spatial; the *swapna akash* is a realm that incarnates all registers of time—the past, the present, and the future at once. Varun says that it is indeed what Einstein called the quantum domain.[10] Beneath this sky of comprehensive and singular intelligence, there can be nothing geo-televisual in either a practical or a philosophical sense; all visibilities and events are already towed and informatized by a monotheistic order of meaning. Later, Varun describes the *rudraksh* of Ravana's demonic powers as a "multi-dimensional hologram." The powers of this new age translation and reckoning thus aspire to create a spiritual summit of authority from which all planetary goings on can be surveyed by a Brahminical language gone global. On this plane, tradition is no longer caught up in an agonistic, contradictory relationship with modernity. Rather, particulars of tradition are seen to be enhanced by the instruments of the techno-modern, just as the latter are given their true purpose by the ontological powers of the Brahman. To recall a theme introduced in Chapter 2, the dialectic between *shoshtro* (weapon or dross matter) and *shastra* (scriptures) seems to have been resolved in a new order of things.

Hodology

Later in the film, Gayatri and Varun see the first traces of an already manifest evil on earth. They go to investigate an interned madman who is a survivor of Bhuria's diabolical ministrations. The patient keeps uttering a strange gibberish that Gayatri records on tape. This gabble is seen to be accentuated by the phonetic roots of what is described as a *rakshasha* mantra ("Rah . . . tadim tadim") first implanted in Bhuria's brain and then disseminated in the world through him. The word *Rakshasha*, the film explains, comes from the root *rak*, which is the phonetic source of all evil powers, just as *Om* is the primal word uttered by Brahman. Speaking the mantra has devastating effects because, like all precise projections of sound, they change the harmony of forces and forms in the cosmic order. In the Vedic schema, there can be no punctuations in the Sanskrit language precisely because the universe itself is one unfolding sentence, which begins with the originary, primal breath of Brahman. Uttering the word in its acute phonetic quintessence is therefore at once rewriting the world through the unleashing of originary energies. This is what distinguishes the mantra from the commonplace sentence or prayer.

When Varun tries to read the mind of the patient, he has his first telepathic contact with Bhuria. The camera zooms to the crazed person's left eye when Varun looks into it and then, in an uninterrupted sweep, proceeds to a journey into the recesses of his troubled mind. Cinema thus crosses the phenomenological threshold that divides the external from the internal cosmos; the camera forays into a timeless, metaphysical interiority that the other recording instrument—Gayatri's handycam—cannot penetrate. This internal universe is once again a pure CGI-generated mise-en-scène, in which the inner space of the brain, depicted through a flow of signals inside the optic nerve, merges into a suddenly opened-out interstellar space. This space then leads to the platform of the meeting, which is like a massive pendant suspended in the universe. There, the incarnate spirit of Varun meets the spirit of Bhuria. This is a tryst that was always already remembered as well as foretold; it takes place neither in the past nor the present, but in the very thickness of time itself. Bhuria at this point tempts Varun to join him, for he is convinced that he has finally met the man who has the mental powers to help him tame the powers of the *rudraksh*. The interview begins with Varun in regular north Indian attire with a designer accent, while Bhuria, once again in his long-haired

5.1: Bhuria and Varun in battle.

tribal incarnation, is dressed like a medieval Indian king. Varun refuses Bhuria's mischievous offer and challenges him to battle. The fight sequence that follows sees him transformed into a sleek figure in war paint and his adversary too into a peculiar transnational combat figure wielding a samurai sword. The battle ends with a determined Varun vanquishing his own internal demons. He defeats Bhuria and throws him from the battleground into the deep portals of time within his own meditative mind.

Let us, however, pause and reflect on the grand zoom through the interiors of the eye of the patient to the battlefield of the internal cosmos. This sequence can be understood as a cinematic hodology,[11] which assembles several disciplinary meanings. In psychology, following the work of Kurt Lewin, it pertains to paths in a person's "life space." In brain psychology, hodology is the study of the interconnection of brain cells; in philosophy, the psychological definition can be extended to the interconnection of ideas; and in the discipline of geography it could mean the examination of paths. The meeting between Varun and Bhuria is the culmination of an assembled pseudo-hodology of the cinematic which spectacularly combines several realms of time, space, matter, and memory. The zoom begins in the realm of the "real" and ends in the cosmos of myth. In doing so, it discovers a telepathic path that bridges incommensurables in the order of secular knowledge. The journey into the mind of the patient merges with a cosmic journey to an epic destination beyond time and space. An individual case of trauma connects with a powerful remembering that transcends all finitudes and earthly durations. Brain matter and the limits of medical knowledge pass into sacralized images of the beyond; technology itself finds an instant path to belief.

Vedic Computation

Later in the film Gayatri and her team discover that the *rakshasha* mantra has the capacity to mutate the genetic code of mice. Within a very short period, the animals evolve as an aggressive species. It also becomes clear that this strange incantation has unholy effects on both mice and men. One of Gayatri's fellow researchers falls under the spell of the mantra and is transformed into a dangerous assassin controlled by Bhuria. After that, Gayatri and Varun travel to a Vedic monastery, *Trishakti Pith*, in the Himalayas to meet Varun's father, the venerable *Adhipati*. The sage correctly identifies the diabolical source of the sound structure. He describes it as a "spiritual virus," which is first implanted in a man's brain, then spreads throughout his being, transforming him into a demonic entity. The *Adhipati* launches into a detailed phonetic analysis of the recorded soundbite, in an effort to abstract the seed mantra from the noise. An instrument is required for this. The holy man dares not perform the task within the portals of his own mind, since the mantra can corrupt even the noblest of souls. He thus takes recourse to what he calls a *ganayantra*, a Sanskrit word meaning a computing machine (from *ganan* – to count). When the *ganayantra* is introduced amidst the Vedic paraphernalia that adorns the antechamber of the secluded monastery, it is revealed to be nothing other than a state-of-the-art Apple Mac. The *Adhipati* announces at the conclusion of his research that the mantra does not belong to any of the four Vedas. The *Akhanda Puran* however informs him of the etymological roots of the *rakh* sound and of the once existent but now lost *Rakshasha Veda*.

The peace and tranquility of the monastery are disturbed when Bhuria, who has now assumed the face of globally omniscient evil, launches a whirlwind attack on the sacred place and kills the *Adhipati*. Following that, Varun and Gayatri begin a long and arduous search across the subcontinent for the villain. The tracking and detection of evil become a journey not just across geographical space, but also, as before, into the inner mythic space of Varun's mind. The events, as depicted on film, assemble tropes, typologies, and visual and editorial styles from an overall playground of globalization and world cinema—the generic formats of the Orientalist action adventure, the Hong Kong high-wire martial arts choreography, the sci-fi flick, the detective film, the texture and visual idioms of

5.2: The *Adhipati* of *Trishakti Pith* with his *gananyantra*.

transnational consumer advertising, video games, and the travel film. The centerpiece of this investigation is another meditative voyage, in which Varun returns to the moment of his father's murder and interrogates his father's assassin at the site of the slaying itself. But Bhuria is no common foe; his counter-forays into the mind of Varun sets up a Rashoman-like play of perceptions—a shadowy battle of truth and falsehood, light and shadow. During this quest, the lineage of detection, reasoning, and inference that take place in empty, calendrical time is always impressed upon and curved by a mythic, sacralizing temporality. Time in *rudraksh*, unlike in the adventure movie or detective thriller, is always a curvature rather than a lineage. It harbors neither suspense nor revelations; it functions as the power of an inhuman memory which casts the tale as a chronicle foretold ages ago.

Global Terror and the Vedic Sublime

By the time Varun pieces together Bhuria's history and his complete profile of evil through a cosmic connectivity of the universe (the *swapna akash* or divine internet), his enemy has gone from strength to strength. The ominous shadow of evil has long crossed the boundaries of a national crisis and assumed global dimensions. Riots and unrest, as a global swell of rejuvenated *rakshasha* power, have spread to cities in India, China, the US, and other Western countries. The global insurrections of disorder, however, are not caused by religious strife, political economy, trade disputes, or international relations. They fan out as a gigantic wave of unreason and terroristic energy amenable to only one description that Varun provides—a "world war" between humans and *rakshashas*, the base, negroid entities that are evolutes of dark *tamasic* matter as described in the *Bhagwad Gita*. Bhuria, at this stage, is capable of marshalling all the worldly powers of science, finance, and technology toward this end. He has taken over a host of television channels and radio stations. The worldwide dissemination of a multitude of sounds and images is seen to be increasingly accentuated by a singular resonating frequency of the *rakshasha* mantra.

Hence, once again, there is a terrifying and humbling glimpse of the impossible, when the many horizons of a planetary geo-televisuality are claimed, in a total manner, by a solitary ontology of epic evil. Manifold forms and multiplicities of global urban life are, in the process, seen to be telescoped into a page or footnote of the book of the cosmos. This is where the mythic curvature of time, which at once abolishes the pluralities of historical space and restores them to a destinying, comes into its own. No matter where Varun goes, Bhuria sends him messages through the media. Varun notices that the television in his room changes channels of its own accord. The fragmentary sound- and video-bites are already threaded by a cosmic articulation; they add up to a message in which Varun is invited to a tryst with a destiny larger than himself, or anything of this world. The restaged battle of the Ramayana, filmed again and again in various forms in popular Hindi cinema, ups the stakes from a national to a global register. If the world is at risk, it is only a techno-financial enterprise that is blessed and guided by a neo-Hindu authority that can save it.

The final battle between Bhuria and Varun ends predictably enough: good triumphs over bad. It does not merit discussion, apart from the fact that in the age of *kali*, when the gods are in retreat, the only way Varun can defeat Bhuria is by transforming himself into the *rakshasha* state. Varun is told to do this at a crucial moment by no less than the spirit of his dead father, the venerable Pandit Ved Bhushan, former *Adhipati* of the *Trishakti* monastery. It is only by assuming a demonic state that Varun is able to turn the powers of the *rudraksh* against Bhuria. In a general apocalyptic drive toward darkness that marks our age of *kali*, evil can only be overcome by exercising it differentially, through a strategic manipulation of the overall, abiding rise of demonic powers.

Conclusion

It is now clear that Mani Shankar's new age mythological does not cast tradition (the story of the indigenous self) and modernity (the story of the world) as overarching metanarratives locked in an agonistic battle. Rather, signs of tradition—the Vedas, the Puranas, the *kundali*, or the *swapna akash*—become pliant and are brought into a state of informatic orchestration with those of the techno-modern: the internet, the brain scan, Einstein, the quantum zone. Informatic orchestration is a specific production of publicity and power; it is erotics without concrete sublimation that takes place without the gravitas or the anchoring pressures of grand narratives. Hence fragments and pseudo-signifiers of Vedic spiritualism can be brought into a relation of proximity and translation with scientific markers of quantum physics and medicine; mythic visions can be cinematically assembled with the mise-en-scènes of archeology and science fiction. Tradition and modernity are neither at war, nor resolved to a state of peace. They are instead entreated and combined as fluid and mosaic packets of affective spectacle that *disjunctively* come together and disperse in the screen-city.

The end effect of this informatization is precisely the bypassing of "science" in finding an instant bridge between a projected technotopia and memories of mythic revivalism. It is in this context that we can situate the banality of *rudraksh* as a habit of thought in a larger imaginary horizon of an urban, postmodern *Hindutva*. It pertains to precisely that emboldened stance of translation that allowed the former physicist and current Hindu ideologue Murli Manohar Joshi to declare, in his address to the World Philosophers' meeting in Geneva in 1998, that in an overall climate in which many Western scientists were using language that approximates the sayings of the (Hindu) sages, it should be understood that the holographic concepts of holistic reality (astrophysics or neuroscience) were first given to the world by Eastern philosophy,[12] more specifically Lord Krishna in the *Bhagwad Gita*. The three *gunas* (qualities) of *sattva, rajas*, and *tamas* have been regularly promoted by the Hindu Right as ancient Hindu understanding of the three subatomic particles. The story of the nine avatars of Vishnu (excluding the yet to appear Kalki) from marine, amphibian, and land animal incarnations like *matsya* (fish), *kurma* (tortoise), and *Varaha* (boar) in the *Satya* yuga to progressively humanoid forms of Rama (*treta*), Krishna (*dwapar*), and Buddha (*kali*), has been said to encapsulate Darwin's theory of evolution.

Much like the evangelical debate around creationism in the United States, these discourses have been militantly sounded in quarters of governance, in state and civil institutions of science and pedagogy. Meera Nanda's investigations and debunking of such phenomena have been especially significant. At the beginning of her book *Breaking the Spell of Dharma* (2007), Nanda cites a news item that appeared in the BBC World

News on May 14, 2002, which stated that amidst the dangerous military buildup along the border with Pakistan, the BJP-led Indian government assigned scientists the task of developing technologies of biological and chemical warfare inspired by *Arthasastra*, a Sanskrit treatise on war and governance by Chanakya written more than 2,000 years ago. The projects included developing from a formula of herbs, milk, and clarified butter a meal that would sustain a soldier for a month, methods for inducing madness in the enemy, camel skin shoes cured with serum from owls and vultures that would enable soldiers to trek hundreds of miles without fatigue, a powder for night vision made from fireflies and the eyes of wild boars, and the manufacture of invisible and indestructible airplanes (*Breaking the Spell of Dharma* [2007]: 9–10).

The powers of the kind of new age metropolitan *Hindutva* publicity we see in *rudraksh* create an informatic plane, a project of new age memory, where mantras of Brahminism can fuse with metropolitan common sense, techno-quizdom, and habit. It is no longer solely about vertical pedagogic stances of narrative cinema, but also about speedy, horizontal distributions of the decorative and the banal in the mise-en-scène. If we can talk about *rudraksh* in relation to an imagistic ecology of Hindu fascism, we may do so only by understanding the latter as not necessarily a subjective or an identitarian one (although such expressions exist), but that which is part of an overall informatics of terror (the *dalit*, the countryside, the Muslim), the high-caste/high Hindu normalcy of the capitalizing city, and statist militarization. In this ecology, especially in its instantiation in the form of sovereign power, an adequation of power/information rearticulates, transposes, or even supplants the power/knowledge template that Foucault attributed to modern societal formations. This advertised and spectacular *Hindutva*, which is at once a specter of modernization, does not seek to rewrite the world in depth; it simply seeks to set the rhythm and the tenor of all speech and expressive energies. The power of the film's pristine naiveté draws from its enthralled fascination with its own coming into being in the world. It grafts faith onto the post-historical, technocratic, virtual context that has made its own production possible. *Rudraksh* is about techno-aware religiosity which announces the world itself as techno-aware and therefore irresistibly religious.

Notes

1. I am grateful to Moinak Biswas for this phrase and insight.
2. Ashish Rajadhyaksha, "Epic Melodrama: Themes of Nationality in Indian Cinema" (1994).

3. See Rajadhyaksha's reading of *Gunasundari* (*The Good Woman*) (1927) a perennial social melodrama of Ranjit Studios which was remade in 1934 and again in 1948 ("Epic Melodrama," 64).

4. Nehru described his own paradigmatic dispensation of the Indian postcolonial order as a third way, "which takes the best from all existing systems—the Russian, the American, and others—and seeks to create something suited to one's own history and philosophy." Cited in Sumita Chakravarty, *National Identity in Indian Popular Cinema* (1993): 29. It is important to point out that in making his argument about neo-traditionalism, Rajadhyaksha is not suffering from any formalist bias. The problem for him does not have to do with the fact that the reformist heroism of new citizenship inevitably follows the path of saintliness, or that historical agency is perpetually overcoded by pre-modern forces of mythic origin; rather, it has to do with the eclectic dominance of a variegated ideology combined in this secularizing process. Far from turning out to be a "fighting popular" in the Brechtian sense, the all-India film, for Rajadhyaksha, was a passive revolutionary assortment of Brahminical doctrines and weak postulates of liberal constitutionalism. As a result, he concludes, "what could have been a decorativeness alive with magical transformations now became a loose chain of attractions designed to attract the spectator's pleasure" ("Neo-traditionalism," 59).

5. See, for instance, the *Bhagwad Gita*, chapter 14: 5–16. See also chapter 17:9: "Men of Rajas like food of Rajas: acid and sharp, and salty and dry, and which brings heaviness and sickness and pain."

6. The obvious reference is to the protracted battle over the historicity of Rama's birthplace in modern-day Ayodhya launched by the Sangh Parivar. The Ramjanambhoomi movement peaked on December 6, 1992 with the destruction of the Babri Mosque and continues to this day in the form of the Hindu combine's demand for a Ram Temple on the same site. For a perceptive account, see Tanika Sarkar, Sumit Sarkar, and Tapan Basu, *Khaki Shorts and Saffron Flags* (1993).

7. Krishna tells Arjuna in chapter 11:32 of the *Bhagwad Gita*: "I am all-powerful Time which destroys all things, and I have come here to slay these men. Even if thou dost not fight, all the warriors facing thee shall die."

8. Thapar points out that, according to some scholars, the number 432,000 could be of Babylonian origin, combined with the Greek epicycle theory (1992: 15).

9. Michel Foucault, *Discipline and Punish* (1977): 46.

10. Werner Heisenberg would be more apt here, but this is only one of the many factual errors the film makes. At one point it even confuses the sequence of the four yugas.

11. "Hod-", a prefix meaning "pathway": hodology, hodoneuromere. See *Mosby's Medical, Nursing and Allied Health Dictionary* (2002), www.xrefer-plus.com/entry/3042663. Accessed March 18, 2007.

12. See Murli Manohar Joshi, "Role of Science and Spirituality for World Peace" (1998).

CHAPTER 6

Repetitions with Difference: *Mother India* and her Thousand Sons

Introduction

I will open this discussion with a few more observations and questions about Rajadhyaksha's theory of the "epic melodrama." The objective is to further complicate the notion of mythic impelling, to historicize some such instances, and to understand how exactly and through what pains the ontological constant of Dharma can be upheld amidst the duress of modernization or financialization. The task, in other words, is to find a working theory of telling and retelling the mythic, of repeating the same amidst a sea of differences. The point is also to take a fresh look at what has long been identified as the Hindi "formula" film in academic and popular imaginations. Commercial Hindi films periodically recycle old stories. Novelty in such cases seems to lie not so much in unexpected turns of events or psychological shifts, but in localized energies of episodic presentation (dramatic exchanges or comic interludes), innovative lyrical assemblages in the song sequences, and the transfer of milieus. I shall begin with a hypothesis: perpetual newness of the old does not pertain to static and absolute structures of mythic governance, but in the complex historical *occasioning* of myth. In other words, it is not so much dependent on why one should tell a story that everyone knows, but by what ingenious method one can tell the story now and make it exemplary once again.

Let us keep in mind what we learned in the previous chapter: that time in Hindi cinema (and many other Indian cinematic traditions) is a curvature rather than a lineage. It is the curve that ensures that the Dharmic order, though occasionally eclipsed, is inevitably reinstated. The alienation of industrial production, disenchantment of modern consciousness, and atomization of urban milieus are thereby mitigated by a groundless utopia that opens up both before and after the fact of history (the thought of the *Satya* yuga of the Brahminical gods which once was and will be again). As we noted in the Introduction, this can perhaps be seen most emblematically in the proverbial "lost and found" narratives of Hindi cinema, perfected by practitioners like Manmohan Desai and

Nasir Hussain. In each such case, it is the mythic and infallible course of Dharma as a cosmic theodicy that curves around the vicissitudes, accidents, and catastrophes of the profane and ensures that the lost is found once more. Because the overall flow of time follows a curve, at every finite instant it is an assemblage of powers of the calendrical and the cyclic.

But the exhilaration of these groundless restorations is tempered by an apocalyptic imagination of primal loss.[1] In the classical form of popular Hindi cinema, authorial views often declare that the instruments and works of the world are *maya* (illusion); the present age, after all, is that of the *kali* yuga, in which the righteous castes have lost their virtues. The fact that earthquakes visit diurnal life (Yash Chopra's *Waqt*), or Partition can destroy the ethical composition of the home (Desai's *Chhalia*, 1960) are evidence of that. What is noteworthy is that the state itself is frequently inducted into this overall specter of disenchantment in a world turned upside down. The schema of mythic embroilment in the order of the profane is a complex process that does not necessarily end in an unqualified affirmation of heavenly or earthly restoration. The resolution of such narratives, in the form of a makeshift resuscitation of the state, family, and a Hindu-normative national community, are more often than not weak and unstable formalisms. Mythic intervention and restoration remain temporal curvatures precisely because this impress of time cannot close on itself and render the world whole. It remains besieged by lurking historical contingencies.

The "formula" does indeed pertain to ritualistic recalls of mythic memory in relation to the experiences of the present. It is through an understanding of "recall" that the notion of the ritual (the social or familial act of reading aloud the Ramayana) and that of narrating myth on film (or admitting a general mythic impelling in the secular works of cinematic narration) can be brought into a relationship of sameness. This is, however, repetition with difference. The stories are the same not because they share a sequence of events and group of personages, but precisely because they resonate differently in diverse milieus and historical situations. Secondly, the power of unending absolution accorded by a unique ontology of being can also be used to address the less-than-ideal workings of the state. The paramount power of the nation as the ultimate custodian of life and values can be repeatedly invoked (sometimes at the expense of the state, if the state fails to live up to that ideal) just as the gods are continuously prayed to and affirmed under different testing conditions. Thirdly, what makes matters even more complicated is the fact that there is no singular, monotheistic horizon of myth. As we shall see, it is also Dharma that constantly threatens to split itself, pulled by contesting forces of custom, law, and lived life.

Mother India: Repetitions of a National Monotheme

When we broach the question of repetition, as a relentless echoing of a core national being, we are thus inevitably asking a political question. What exactly is the nature of this being? Is it singular or eclectically derived? How does it relate to the formal equities of liberal democracy? Is there a being at all, as a positive, identitarian idea, or is there only nostalgia for one? Rather, is there, after a point, any need for an organic-social presence of the idea, or are a nostalgia industry and its massified yearnings enough for a new statism? It would be a grave mistake to say that formats of repetition in Hindi cinema and their generative planes of affect have always been propelled by a fundamental Hindu ideology. One can point out many cinematic invocations of multivalent legends that refute the streamlining procedures of any nationalist mythography. This is particularly true of the Indian context, precisely because the dogmatic Hindu nationalism that we speak of has always struggled in the course of its modern discursive formation with the polyvalent richness of the cultures of devotion it seeks to claim as its own. Modern *Hindutva*, from its earliest birth pangs, has struggled to recast the religiosities under its command into a monotheistic edifice which can be parlayed into a unified stance of commitment to a homogeneous Indian/Hindu state.

This monotheistic imperative of the nation has been lately registered anew in critical thought with the renaissance of the Nazi jurist and thinker Carl Schmitt at what has been seen to be a particularly acute moment of crisis in the political legacy of classical liberalism. These circumstances, it seems, have called for a rethinking of the manner in which Schmitt called the liberal bluff by famously declaring that all modern political concepts were transposed theological ones. The state, with all its artifice of reason, could thus be rendered possible only after what he calls the concept of the "political" has been settled.[2] Here I am suggesting a deeper study of the Schmittian notion of the political as a fundamentally monotheistic calling, as a mythopoetic spiritual automaton that enables us to talk about the people, nation, and state only after "friends" have been categorically distinguished from "enemies." For Schmitt, this unitary impelling can have religious dimensions as in Anglican England, Lutheran Germany, or Catholic Spain, but more importantly it has to give rise to a monotheme of identity that may be based on race, an ideological worldview (like Russian Communism in his day), or ethnicities of various kinds. It is only after this secret onto-theology of the modern state is established as a precondition that one can indulge in seductive liberal measures of pluralism, toleration, and difference. Fundamentally, therefore, the citizen is an acolyte.

I am putting this question in critical adjacency to the question of a single cinematic horizon of Dharma that is supposed to preside over narratives of the nation. This is not because Schmitt's diagnosis offers any essential truths about the human condition and how and why humans form nation-states, but because this monotheistic imperative has been registered in various discursive efforts to define a consolidated Hindu self and to format an Indian modernity in line with a dominant model of liberal constitutionalism. I am juxtaposing Hindu and India, not to render them identical, but to echo a greater concern: even if one were to justifiably separate a mainstream Indian nationalism from dogmatic *Hindutva*, to what extent does the former share a stratum of normativity with the latter? Simply put, Schmitt's queries in terms of a vital Indian nationalism, and a consequent "strong state-economy," would be: can one ever speak of a secret Indian monotheism? We can add a few more: when religiosity *qua* religiosity becomes central to the question of the nation-state, can it assume any other form than one powerfully put in place by a broad Judeo-Christian tradition? That is, what happens if the culture in question has strong eclectic and polytheistic tendencies? The question, much in the Schmittian spirit, that ideologues of the Hindu Right might ask is: if the country is to have a working nationalism rather than an endless parliamentary clamor of identities, can it be anything other than a Hindu one? To inhabit this terrain of statist thinking and critiquing it immanently is also to understand the dangerous consequences of consigning all powers of thinking to the nation-state as the final artwork of being.

The story of a Hindu nationalist consciousness that has been perpetually gestating and, directly or indirectly, in its softer, more moderate forms, dominating the Indian political horizon is too broad and too complex to outline here. It has its roots in the colonial Indology of the late nineteenth century and was discursively carried by the first generation of nationalist intellectuals like Bankim Chandra Chattopadhyay and Bal Gangadhar Tilak and taken up and remarkably recoded as a form of cultural nationalism by Vinayak Damodar Savarkar. Extreme articulations of Hinduness were tempered by broader assimilative culturalist endeavors like the aesthetics of Ananda Coomaraswamy, the philosophy of Sarvapalli Radhakrishnan, or even the anti-caste, anti-modern patrimonial ideology of Mohandas Karamchand Gandhi. In terms of a general gloss, we can say that this terrain bore the marks of a founding *agon* that comes from the efforts to harness a range of monotheistic, polytheistic, atheistic, monistic, pantheistic, panentheistic, and henotheistic beliefs and practices into a single edifice of faith. This massive undertaking called for the epistemic privileging of the *Bhagwad Gita* as the Holy Book that could that could serve as a gravitational imperative, one that could give a substantive and unified shape to a vast field of awry devotions.[3] In terms of social power, it also meant potentially creating and privileging a uniform Brahminical patrimony that could absorb the errant pieties of literally thousands of regional cults that were generated first by the *sramana* orders (Buddhism, Jainism, and the now extinct *ajivika*) and then by the radical strands of *Bhakti* down the centuries. From the perspective of political economy and the demographics of the population state, it was central to the historical consolidation of the idea of Hinduness in the first place.

This volatile sphere of religiosity and the concomitant question of a mythography of the self as the cornerstone of the nation and its state undeniably left a lasting imprint on popular culture as a whole and Hindi cinema in particular. This was particularly evident in the cinematic expressions of what is called a Nehruvian sensibility toward secularism and tolerance. For instance, especially during the 1950s and 1960s, it was through a relentless Urdu poetics of dying selves that Hindi film complicated the question of being (which is at once a question of language) when the state was trying to articulate itself into existence through an engineered, highly Sanskritized Hindi that took over radio, and then television. Cinematic Dharma always registered the different pressures of historical meaningfulness and memory in its relentless constituting. The Nehruvian format of state secularism that came into being during the 1950s was largely a catastrophic balancing act, a passive revolutionary overwriting of this elemental field of counteracting energies. A celebrated "national integration" number like "Allah tero naam, Ishwar tero naam / Sab ko sanmatee de bhagwan" ("Your name is Allah, your name is Ishwar / Give all good sense, oh God") in *Hum Dono* (*We Two*) (Amarjeet, 1961), while admirable in its "secular" values, is also potentially a monotheistic reordering of both Allah and Ishwar, and a consigning of the faiths commended by these entities to a singular Sanskritized Bhagwan who, in this film, commands the fortunes of individuals in love as well as countries at war.

The critical points of inquiry can therefore be summarized as follows: if the narration of myth can be taken as a cinematic ritual of recalling a time beyond measure, how can this be understood as a question of sovereignty? What could be the political dimension of repeating the ritual of cinematic storytelling in the context of a formal nation-state that is supposedly not defined by Hindu-normative sovereignty? What about the occasions when invocations of the mythic are not necessarily statist or impelled by Hindu ideology? If a discourse of constitution is always striving toward acquiring a lonely language (one capable of absolving the massive historical strife of the Indian milieu, dispersed along class, caste, gender, religion, language, region, and ethnicity lines), to what extent must it persistently borrow or try to borrow from a secret monotheism? How has this overall modern process of inventing a tradition changed in the current geo-televisual-informatic scenario? To get a picture of this complex arena, we have to see how myths are *occasioned* in the contemporary.

We shall undertake a study of difference and repetition in popular Indian cinema, selecting a famous story that has been tirelessly retold in Indian films. The plot that was first witnessed in Mehboob Khan's *Aurat* (*Woman*) (1940) has been recycled, in various historical settings, involving a range of cultural formations and social identities, in a body of films across the decades. Undoubtedly the benchmark was Mehboob's own 1957 retelling in *Mother India*. This was followed by *Deewar* (*The Wall*) (Yash Chopra, 1975), *Shakti* (*Power*) (Ramesh Sippy, 1982), *Mazloom* (*The Oppressed*) (C. P. Dixit, 1986), *Naam* (*Name*) (Mahesh Bhatt, 1986), *Falak* (*Stone*) (K. Shashilal Nair, 1988), *Ram Lakhan* (*Ram and Laxman*) (Subhash Ghai, 1989), *Jeevan Ek Sangharsh* (*Life is a Struggle*) (Rahul Rawail, 1990), *Agneepath* (*Path of Fire*) (Mukul S. Anand, 1990), *Aatish* (*The Mirror*) (Sanjay Gupta, 1994), and *Vaastav* (*Reality*) (Mahesh Manjrekar, 2000). This is by no means an exhaustive list and does not include remakes in regional languages. It would be pertinent to track this temporal and spatial journey of the mother and her sons from its early agrarian moorings to the industrial metropolis. We shall earmark four films for special attention: Khan's *Mother India*, Chopra's *Deewar*, Gupta's *Aatish*, and Manjrekar's *Vaastav*. Together, these occasions of recall form a spectrum that covers both timely and untimely moments of the nation–state, from the birth of the free republic to the age of uni-polar globalization, and in terms of space, spirals out from a nondescript village in north India to Mauritius, Switzerland, and beyond. The process of perpetual recall can also very easily absorb ambiences and narrative impulses from elsewhere, as can be seen in the socialist-realist motifs and the naturalist landscapes of *Mother India* which remind us of the late Dovzhenko,[4] the *On the Waterfront*-style crime-infested dockyards in *Deewar*, or the story-line and action choreography of John Woo's *A Better Tomorrow*, which inspired Gupta's *Aatish*. By visiting such chronicles of the mother, one can see how the external powers of the world invade or tour the home, and also how a primal, uterine picture of interiority can morph in dynamic ways to embrace or recoil from the planet and its animated skies writ large.

Mother India

Mehboob Khan's *Mother India* was made in the early days of the new republic; India had entered the second five-year plan; APSARA, the first nuclear reactor in Asia outside the Soviet Union, had just been commissioned at Turbhe; the country was about to witness the dawn of the television age. All this was apart from the ongoing grand public sector undertakings of Nehruvian development, via mechanization of agriculture, steel plants, and hydroelectric dams. In Khan's 1957 Oscar-nominated epic, the mother is a rural peasant named Radha who battles monumental odds to singlehandedly bring up her two sons, Ramu and Birju. They, however, follow different paths in life. Ramu grows up to be a model farmer of the new age that has been ushered in, while Birju emerges as an unruly and tempestuous young man. This young rebel, unlike his brother and the rest of the village community, is not ready to endure the profane and wait for the long cycle of the Dharmic to run its course and rectify the injustices of the present order. Birju thus does not have the patience or forbearance to understand that justice is a cosmic principle beyond the agency of the human, that it is only an infallible appetite of *kaal* (time beyond measure), which can destroy the old and create the new. While such a belief declares that all the wicked and tyrannical powers of the world, no matter how strong, will inevitably fall to the movement of Dharma; it can also dictate that the weak and the exploited should submit to the grand cycle of things by perfecting limitless patience. This is expressed in the song "Duniya mein hum aaye hain toh jeena hi padega, jeevan hai agar zaher toh peena hi padega" ("If we have come into the world, we have to live, if life is a poison, we have to drink it"). In erasing this code of endurance, in taking matters into his own hands as it were, Birju thus rebels not only against the law or hierarchical order of society, but, it seems, against an ontological constant of Dharma itself.

The entire film is told in flashback, with Radha remembering her past life just before she inaugurates a dam that has been built in the vicinity of the village. The story proper begins with a lap dissolve: when the old mother of the village is garlanded, the scene shifts to a moment many years ago, when the young Radha, as a demure, blushing bride, was being garlanded by her husband during the marriage ceremony. The narrative then proceeds with the subsequent depiction of Radha bearing three children, an accident that leaves her husband disabled, his leaving in shame for an unknown destination, the death of her infant daughter, and her heroic struggle to bring up her sons. A mythic gathering of energies is witnessed at a key moment toward the end of the film, when an infallible ethical order achieves a total resonance in this peasant community plagued by the greedy and wicked moneylender, Sukhi Lala. The rebel Birju, in order to wreak revenge on the Lala (who has been responsible for the ruin of Radha's family and many others), abducts his daughter from her marriage ceremony. It is Radha who runs after her son, begging him to stop. She says that Roopa, being a daughter of the village, is her honor as well as the honor of the rest of the community. It is an absolute dictum of Dharma that under no circumstances can honor (*laaj*) be sacrificed. The determined Radha picks up a gun and stands in the path of her reckless son, who ignores her pleadings and says that as a mother she will never shoot her own son. Radha declares that she is the mother not just of Birju, but of the entire village. When Birju brushes her aside and begins to ride off into the horizon, she shoots him down.[5] She rushes to him and embraces his body as his life ebbs away. As Birju's blood gushes out between her fingers, the second lap dissolve in the film completes a temporal cycle, matching the outpouring of blood to the waters bursting out from the sluice gates of the dam Radha has just opened. The accumulated affections of blood, fatality, and toil thus momentously merge into a picture of development in the new republic. The powers of the allegorical in this case pertain to a temporal landscape that discontinuously brings together—as a relation of haunting rather than constitution—an arc of nationally destined progress with an abiding instance of upholding the eternal.

The moment of modern naissance is thus yoked to a profound one of sacrifice, when the community can preserve Dharma only by a terrible withdrawal of its own boundless antagonism. The monstrosities of outrage and anger that had emerged from historical relations of class exploitation, hunger, poverty, and hardship are reclaimed by a purportedly Indian spiritual order, one that can assert itself in the lusty but unforgiving field of the historical only as a dim and weakening ontology. The figure of the mother is an abstract diagram that combines a firm but endearing rusticity of speech and gait with a geo-televisual attire borrowed, according to Moinak Biswas, from socialist-realist visualizations of Gorky's Mother.[6] This cinematic mother is an entity that combines a diurnal naturalism of the earth with the principle of the womb as the ontic repository *par excellence*, one that is not just fecund with resources and values, but is also capable, in a moment of epic crisis, of withdrawing its violent offspring from the orbit of the profane. Indeed, in this allegorical world, the new republic has to be blessed by the mother in order for it to emerge as a legitimate patrimony, because it is she alone (and not the distant state) who stands on the sovereign moral ground to demand both sacrifice and martyrdom.

It would, however, be simplistic and truly sacrilegious to consign the implications of the mother's sacrifice to a unique biography of the nation in development. This disjuncture, as Biswas points out, is established early in the film when affections of wistfulness and loss surround the mother's figure in the title sequence, which features her moving across an agrarian landscape being gradually taken over by machines of industrial production. The rumble and drone of the new (tractors and combine harvesters) are counterpoised with the signs of sorrow that fleet across the face of the mother. The close-up here is not *of* the face as Deleuze once reminded us in a different context,[7] but *is* the face itself, as an expressive plane that combines both powers—of a helpless humanoid profile, as well as of the changing aspect of a land tendentially drifting away from its founding spirit. The peace between the enduring land as mother or the mother as land, and the living and dying community of historical sons is thus perpetually an unrestful one.

This remains true of the manifold instances of the mother's "return" in popular Indian cinema. The profundity of her appearances from time to time must not be judged by a calibrating scale of historicism, one that reduces history to a formal measure, by merely cataloguing events as a continuum of causes and effects, with a clearly identifiable overture and conclusion. The return of the mother is not to be understood anthropologically, in terms of semblances between the biographies of Radha in Mehboob's *Mother India* and Sumitra in *Deewar* (Yash Chopra, 1975). Rather, the return is a special assemblage of a mythic tenacity of time and the image of the mother that stakes an umbilical claim to the messy plenitudes of the historical. The return, therefore, is not accomplished when the ordinary peasant woman in *Mother India* or the simple mill worker's wife in *Deewar* performs extraordinary tasks; it is accomplished when these tasks are placed in an invagination of deep time. This is when the story stops being one of exemplary individual commitment to law or honor and becomes one in which the fallen and degraded mechanism of human law or conflict-ridden perspectives of honor are absolved in an instant by the sudden opening out of an altogether different sky of meaning. Once the woman, as a primary imagination of the national form, is endowed with such *potentia*, it becomes possible to rehearse her return in different situations and milieus, with varying degrees of strength and weakness. As we shall see, the monotheme of the mother as nation is often a weak ontology; it can be directed both toward and against the state. Moreover, this theme is never identical to a secret theology that the nation-state aspires to, although it might be in a state of proximity to it. This is true even of *Deewar*, perhaps the most statist of all the films discussed here.

Deewar (*The Wall*)

Deewar in many ways is an Emergency film, just as *Mother India* is a Nehruvian one. It was released when the fault-lines of the great Indian ruling assemblage and its passive revolutionary consensus model had become extremely tensile. The tempestuous years of the mid-1970s were a period of unraveling the Congress system and the overall Nehruvian template of the Indian passive revolution.[8] In the wake of the Nava Nirman movement in Gujarat and Bihar, rising food grain prices, and violent student and labor unrest throughout the country, the Prime Minister, Indira Gandhi, declared a State of Internal Emergency in 1975, suspending the constitution and concentrating unprecedented power in her hands. All opposition leaders and thousands of intellectuals and activists were imprisoned and the state recast itself as a populist dictatorship. It was in this volatile atmosphere of anger, disenchantment, and foundational violence that the melodrama of *Deewar* is worlded.

Yash Chopra's 1975 cinematic landmark tells the story of Sumitra and her two sons, Vijay and Ravi. The family is forced to migrate to Bombay in abject poverty when Sumitra's husband, Anand, abandons them and runs off in shame. He is a trade union leader who betrays the cause of the workers to corrupt capitalists when his wife and children are abducted and held at gunpoint. The people of the small town, unaware of the circumstances, are unforgiving. A group of drunks catch little Vijay one day and tattoo the words "mera baap chor hain" ("my father is a thief") on his left hand. Once the family is in Bombay, Sumitra starts work as a construction worker and Vijay as a shoe-shine boy and then as a brooding dockworker, haunted by the shame of his father's cowardice . Ravi is sent to school.

From this point, the paths of the two brothers take divergent trajectories, toward and away from the mother. Vijay turns to crime and launches a spectacularly successful career as a smuggler; Ravi becomes a police officer. The latter comes to know of his brother's exploits and the source of his suddenly acquired wealth from the state itself. He is given a file containing information about Vijay's criminal career and is assigned the task of bringing him to justice. The file alters the configuration of the domestic order in a way only news provided by the state can. The melodramatic construction of the home, with the mother at the center, had hitherto been cast along pure uterine lines, with no intelligence, except that of the state or god (since in the fragmented life of the city the community is no longer figurable) able to percolate it. This is precisely why the mother and Ravi himself had stayed in Vijay's luxurious bungalow without a shadow of doubt. Truth had earlier been settled frontally, when the mother, before moving from the shanty town to the comfortable house, had asked Vijay whether he was doing anything that he ought not to be doing. Vijay had replied that he was not doing anything that he *thought* he should not be doing.

It is the revelation of the state that introduces an intolerable relativization of truths in the supposed uterine completeness[9] of the family order. With the police report, the "home" registers the presence of an historical out-of-field whose forces have already destroyed its ethical composition. The revelation introduces a disconcerting "depth" of modern schizophrenia and novelization of values emblematically presented in the film as the tattoo imprinted on Vijay's arm. Interestingly, this "depth" was not produced years earlier, when the father had betrayed his trade union. For Sumitra, her husband's act was a price paid in the order of the profane to protect the family. The principled patriarch had then paid his dues by taking his public dishonor elsewhere and not staying in the unsullied interiority of the home. Voluntary exile was, therefore, the thing to do; the ultimate act of endurance and sacrifice under extreme conditions. In the present case, however, the horizon of meaning is split between what the patriarchal order has already stated to be the thing to do, and what the schizoid individual *thinks* should be done. Vijay, in suggesting that his actions are justified by his state of historical and social orphanhood, challenges the ethical totality of the interior world fostered by the presence of the mother, as well as the father in the form of the vermillion mark on her forehead.[10] The news of Vijay's criminal life destroys the innocence that the mother had invested the home with. She leaves the house with Ravi after telling Vijay, "You are my son . . . my own blood . . . how did you write on your mother's forehead that her son is a *chor* [thief]?"

A critical understanding of sound itself as image is important to gauge the epic gravity of these utterances. They are frontally spoken, with the mother (deputizing for the legitimate patriarch) turning away from a commonplace exchange between individuals, as if to withdraw the look from the disturbed world and focus it in the direction of an out-of-frame, but perpetually there horizon of eternity. This direct look *over* the camera destroys a naturalistic/voyeuristic organization of the filmic apparatus, extending the cinematic horizon itself toward a metaphysics of the Dharmic. The linear, dialectical parlay of propositions and counter-propositions is suddenly arrested and held in the static, as Rajadhyaksha says,[11] with the sound of the utterance rising to the surface, as if leaving behind the clamor of a multitudinous reality. It is in such moments of epic transmission of judgment that the mother can transcend her psychosis of maternal love and guilt—her history of exploitation, insecurity, and

6.1: Sumitra and Ravi confront Vijay in *Deewar*.

privation—and abolish the vicissitudes of the profane in a single stroke. This absolute declaration withdraws the tainted son's right to home (the mother leaves the house, but home is where the mother is); his re-entry into that fold of repose is declared to be possible only after he has purged himself by submitting his body to the justice of the state. But of course, in the cinematic assemblage of iconic declarations vehicled by historical humans, such transcendences can never completely overwrite the abiding pain of endurance. As Prasad's psychoanalytic reading of the confrontational scene in *Deewar* demonstrates, the mother's (and Ravi's) epic look away from the dialectical exchange with Vijay is always in tension with the historical mise-en-scène. The almighty utterance of the just and the iconic faciality of the human medium are tinged with the inevitable sadness of maternal loss and knowledge of the son's social disenfranchisement. "The sequence shows Vijay's exclusion from the oedipal enclosure, as brother Ravi (Shashi Kapoor) occupies [within the frame] the place of the father, beside the mother (Nirupa Roy). The mother goes along with the phallic imperative, punishing Vijay with her righteous defense of law, but when alone [foregrounded in the frame] with Vijay [receded to the far depth of the background], she is racked by guilt."[12]

The moment of epic recall, one that binds *Deewar* to *Mother India*, happens later in the film when the recalcitrant Vijay is considering a surrender in order to return to the mother. This happens after his mother recovers from a serious illness and his girlfriend, Anita (a bar dancer with a heart of gold), tells him that she is pregnant with his child. Vijay calls his mother to tell her that he will meet her at the temple where she worships. The prodigal and erstwhile atheist thus expresses a desire to surrender to the mother and to God before handing himself over to the law of the state endorsed by them. Fate, however, cruelly intervenes when Anita is murdered by the henchmen of Samant, one of Vijay's long-standing enemies. Enraged, Vijay once again goes on a killing spree, finishing off the culprits in a fell swoop. The mother hears about his rampage just as she is getting ready to go to the temple for their meeting. When Ravi dons his uniform, she hands him his service revolver with the words: "Goli chalate waqt tera haath na kape" ("May your hands never shake when you shoot"). She then says that she will keep her side of the bargain by going to the temple and waiting for Vijay: "Aurat ne apna kaam kiya; ab ek ma apne kam karne ja rahi hain" ("A woman has done her duty; now a mother is going to do hers"). Sumitra is able to effect a moment of mythic recall because she is able to punctually and uncompromisingly equate the Dharmic postulates of womanhood with the categorical imperatives of the law-abiding citizen. Her iconic status lies in a willing instrumentalization of the self to the preeminent cause of the state—in honoring the state's sole right to decide on the exception and monopolize violence. She is "Mother India" precisely because she does not allow motherhood, as a private realm of affection and desire, to come between the interests of the family and that of the state. She is able to imagine her sons as a brotherhood of citizens already consigned to martyrdom and sacrifice in a world in which principles of Dharma are inseparable from the dicta of the state.

Sumitra's exemplary status as the "mother" the nation needs in times of strife is underlined by a contrasting mother figure we see earlier in the film. She is not named, but can be described as the "mother of a thief and the wife of a schoolmaster." This takes place when Ravi is in a state of emotional turmoil. He has just been given Vijay's police file by his superior officer, but he is not sure that he is up to the task of arresting his own brother. On his way home, Ravi spots a boy stealing something and running away. He apprehends the boy after shooting him in the leg. On discovering that the thing stolen was only a loaf of bread, the contrite policeman visits the boy's family to offer his apologies. The boy's mother presents him with a bitter complaint that comes from a relational perception of reality; she says that Ravi should first arrest the unscrupulous wealthy, the rich thieves, and black-marketeers before punishing the poor and the unemployed who have few options in life. The principled schoolteacher, however, in an epic sweep, inducts all relativized realities into an absolute statement: all thefts, whether big or small, are nevertheless crimes. It is after this utterance by a surrogate patriarchal authority that Ravi gathers the strength to take up the legal battle against his own brother. The schoolteacher's exemplary lesson squares the Dharmic with Ravi's formal duties as a cop. The "mother of the thief," on the other hand, fails to do exactly what Sumitra will do later. Instead, she chooses to evaluate the transgressions of her son and the malfunctions of the state on the same plane of justice.

In the case of Sumitra, the absolute obedience of the citizen—coming from a stance of devotion that encompasses life as well as death—becomes indistinguishable from a dutiful endurance of the acolyte/patriot. The primordial uterine order that motherliness evokes is the site of perpetual births and deaths that continually sacralize the life of the here-and-now under the auspices of *kaal*. This call of Dharma is still at one with the lesser, more profane task of consigning faith in the state in an hour of emergency. In between the primordial moment of conception and the recall to that same uterine order in death, the body has to suffer the rigors of karma in intermediate worldly existence, but in a manner in which truth can lie only in instrumentalizing oneself for martyrdom or sacrifice. This is the crucial point of repetition as well as difference between the moments of Radha in *Mother India* and Sumitra in *Deewar*. While the former wields the weapon herself in order to preserve the ethical composite of her "national community," the latter announces that the "timeless" ethical mass can be singularly vehicled in a degraded world only by the law of the state. In the absence of the father, she deems it proper to hand the gun over to a police officer.

In *Deewar*, a melodrama of disaffection against the state is therefore overcoded at every point by the myth of uterine recall. After the formal handing over of the gun and its firing (when Ravi shoots his brother) the energies of rebellion incarnated in Vijay are subsumed in a body of affections pertaining to motherliness and divinity. Vijay, fatally wounded, arrives at the temple to die in his mother's arms. He refuses to surrender to the state and potentially save his life by getting medical help. The state can enter this melodrama of familial interiority only as Vijay's "mother's son," the police officer Ravi. This is when the state itself assembles with a powerful body of filial affections and stops being a cold and distant entity in an overall, derelict landscape of absent fathers and orphaned children. Forces of devotion can then be recalled to the state only by using the mother as an all-powerful conduit, an entity that lays an unquestionable ontological claim on the bodies of warring sons. Vijay dies with his head on the lap of the mother who has been calling him back from a messy historical battlefield to a ground of natality. This recall of the mother, which births the sacrificial body as well as nurtures it for martyrdom, emerges from a love that is larger than life and greater than death itself. And yet this is a spiritual assemblage that can be parlayed to causes of the existing legal order only provisionally, and always precariously. In *Mother India* this was established through affections of wistfulness and nostalgia that surround the mother when she appears in the landscape undergoing industrial transformation. In *Deewar*, this dissonance inheres in the form of the stoic and enduring mother who is called on stage by her younger son, Ravi, to receive a medal. It is pertinent to note that the film begins as well as ends with this scene, with the entire story told in flashback, loosely enframed within the perspective of the woman.[13] The aspect of the mother here is an *absent-minded* one. It is from this state of distraction that the narratives of unrest and conflict in the patriarchal order are launched in each case, as memorials of a mythic natality that has been forgotten or ignored by the state and its archives. The pull of preoccupation must be understood in a larger sense: mythic recall occupies the temporal gap between the formal recognition of the state and an act of deep commemoration of which only the mother is capable. The cinematic staging of the mother's recollections, which form an instantaneous stroke of memory for her, takes place over two hours of diegetic depiction on screen. Her remembrances cover only a few minutes of "real time," when she stands on the dais to be congratulated. It is this "in between" amplification of the instant of uterine recall that allows the momentousness of sacrifice to be brought into critical adjacency with the formal ovation that takes place when the stage of the state is set.[14]

Aatish (The Mirror)

Sanjay Gupta's 1994 film *Aatish* was another instance in which the story of Mother India and her two warring sons was repeated with contextual differences. The film arrived in an Indian milieu that was witnessing a rapid incursion of transnational finance and consumer goods following Manmohan Singh's groundbreaking budget of 1991. Gupta's film thus arrived in the globalized, geo-televisual Indian environment we are focusing on in this book. It provides a telling moment in which the mother is capable of voicing a truth precisely by distancing herself from a symbolic horizon of the nation. *Aatish* begins with a title sequence that establishes the mother as different from her illustrious predecessors. She is already a widow; a garlanded photograph of her late husband shows that he was a police officer. When a local hoodlum attacks the helpless mother, her adolescent elder son, Baba, kills him in order to protect her honor. After that, interestingly, it is the mother who initiates her son into a life of crime. She delivers Baba from charges of juvenile delinquency by placing him under the extra-legal protection of the local crime boss. Under the paternal care of the latter, Baba grows up to be an exceptionally talented operator in the underworld. He and his friend, Nawab, flourish in the counterfeiting business, smuggling, and other criminal trades. Baba, however, stays away from home with his mother's blessing and approval so that his tainted shadow does not fall on his younger brother, Avinash, who goes to school and then joins the Police Academy. The making of the model citizen is financed by crime at every step; Baba accepts his first contract killing the day the dues are paid for Avinash's admission to college.

The mother recognizes that Baba had to commit his first murder to save her life and her honor; he had to continue on the path of crime to provide sustenance to the same family he has *voluntarily* exiled himself from. Her perspective is thus remarkably different from Radha's or Sumitra's. This becomes clear during a conversation she has with the adult Baba early in the film, when he visits her. The mother says that now that the family is anchored in the city, with a house full of comforts and young Avinash is set for life, it is time that Baba completes the home by re-entering it. What is remarkable, however, is that this proposed return would be one without any settling of the debts of crime with the state. The story proper thus begins when the journey through the degraded world outside is almost over, with Baba embarking on what will be his last operation. By then, he has fallen in love with Nisha, a beautiful florist. It is during this phase that a conspiracy hatched by Sunny, a minor member of the gang, delivers Baba to the police. After Baba's true identity as a powerful crime lord is revealed, Avinash comes to confront his mother in a scene reminiscent of the memorable one in *Deewar*, in which the mother and Ravi had confronted Vijay.

In *Aatish* the young police officer comes home and is surprised to see his mother praying for the happiness of *both* her sons. The interaction between the indignant and idealistic son and the worldly-wise, long-suffering mother combines the over-the-shoulder shot/counter-shot model with the occasional turn away for a frontal broadcast of the

Dharmic utterance. Such moments of epic repose are, however, not only staggered by a conflict in the viewpoints of the mother and her police-man son, but also placed in a temporality of danger by inserts, in parallel montage, of hooded assassins arriving to attack the home. The ethical settlement of questions is thus an event that is perpetually imperiled by the violence of the outside. It brings about a polarization between Dharma and the interests of the nation-state. When the incensed police officer/son demands Baba's expulsion from the familial order, the mother refuses. A surprised Avinash wants to know how the mother, being *adarsh* (the ideal personified), could ignore the norms of *desh* (country). She replies that, for a mother, her son is *desh* itself; Avinash should tell *his desh* to declare that all starving mothers should smother their children. It is with this reason-ing of the Dharmic that the mother absolves Baba of a cardinal accusation: he is not a *chor*, no matter what the state says. The mother is acutely aware that her home in the city is never a zone of ambiotic purity; it is merely a perpetually threatened refuge from the violence of the city. The home is no longer imaginable as the thought of a pristine outside to the city's political economy of differential illegalities and the questions of survival therein, of the mother's honor and the bare life of her sons. It is sponsored by Baba and what he does, for home without protection money is only a "refuge." For that reason, it is now the mother who thinks that her outlaw son is not doing something he should not be doing.

This profound conclusion closes the door of the home on the abjectly formal law of democratic fathers. Unlike *Deewar,* where the ontic state-ment of motherhood had curved around the state and excluded the son, here the curvature of deep time congeals all thoughts of the nation (*desh*) as being around the son that has survived *despite* the ineffectiveness of the legal order. There is no longer any commerce of "emergency" between the uterine-ethical domain of motherhood and the formalism of the state; the mother instead suggests that it was Baba who has acted in a true sover-eign spirit by allowing the family to survive in spite of dire calamities. It is now the mother and not the state that stands outside the law to declare that the only law recognized inside the home is inextricably tied to the home's sustenance and replenishment. These are the final sentiments the mother expresses before she is shot dead by hired killers who invade the house now left unprotected by Baba. The violence of the city thereby not only continues to exert pressure that takes matters to the very limit of endur-ance, but finally penetrates the very heart of the uterine system.

Apart from his mother's unconditional blessing and a standing offer to return home, the cinematic trope that places Baba's rebellion in a different realm of values altogether is his romantic liaison with Nisha. Unlike the women of dubious repute (the prostitute in *Deewar*, the bar room singer in Ramesh Sippy's 1980 film *Shakti*) who entered into doomed relationships with the outlaw in the past, Nisha is a "respectable" orphan who lives by herself in the city. She also gets the chance to consolidate a legitimate conjugal relationship with Baba. The moral law that defines and blesses the union is once again one that has separated itself from the charter of the state. At one point Nisha is aghast when she witnesses a brutal murder committed by Baba in broad daylight. However, she returns to him after being convinced by a plebian Mumbai community that is present in the film that her lover is not he who kills, but he who *sacrifices* for the sake of his family and friends. In this case, Baba was dispatching a contract killer who had been hired by his enemies to kill Avinash, the conscientious police officer. Baba and Nisha's romance is established lyrically, in the course of a few song sequences, as a powerful machinery of affections that forecloses the legal out-of-field. It occupies and flourishes in the very gap that has already opened between the judgment of state law and the fact of "public" justice imagined by the community in the street.

Love here is a formidable assemblage of new urban inveiglements that form a cinematic picture of a life worth living. It becomes a convergence of amorous desire, communal blessing, and an abundance of fantasies, commodities, and geo-televisual informatics: gorgeous locations, expensive clothes, and foreign-made cars. Much like *Dil Se*, love can be made incarnate only when an abstract emotional tempo comes together with a lyrical advertising machinery of global production values in the mise-en-scène. The latter is to be understood not as a reflection of the industrial necessities of (realist) narrative cinema, but a non-obligatory coming into being of production values *qua* production values. That is, the relationship between exchange value and use value in the realm of spectacle here is not governed by a paramount question of fidelity to narrative or milieu. Romance is figurable as a form of life worth living only as an unmediated, depthless aesthetic rapture of money burning on screen.

However, unlike *Dil Se*, the affects of choreography and movement are not clustered around a founding torment of partitioned selves. That is, the citizen cannot fall in love with a terrorist, or, in terms of a core, Hegelian idea of national identity, it can never be *customary* to be in love with a woman whose community roots preclude her from the national majoritarian mainstream. The powerful invocations of masochistic desire in the dance movements of *Dil Se* and the themes of self-extinction in pursuing an intolerable love are affections tied to the conundrum at the heart of that story of the nation. On the other hand, there is no impossible love in *Aatish*. Despite Baba's formally illegal status, it is a community of Mumbai that declares that it is customary to be in love with him. As a matter of fact, under the auspices of this spectacular celebration of love, there are no distinctions between the policeman and the outlaw. Avinash and his girlfriend inhabit the same realm of affect in the same song sequence, although in separate cutaways. The brothers are estranged, but the picture of a life worth living remains constitutive. The incorruptible police officer, Avinash, can be seen to handle and consume material goods which are clearly beyond his pay scale. The historical city of Mumbai gives way to an undefined transnational space of lovely beaches, water scooters, and expensive night clubs. In such scenes the screen becomes a pure transmission of informatics that precludes not just the ethics of the old national state, but also an uneven landscape of production and labor. In this spectacular and groundless shareholding of a transnational class fantasy, there can thus be no distinction between use values and exchange values, between a legally doomed love and a moral conjugality, or between licit money and illicit money. The love of the outlaw as well as the police-man is consolidated in Mauritius as a pure outdoors—a space beyond what used to be the looming, sheltering sky of the state and its fragmented Nehruvian-Gandhian ethical mass.

The uterine melodrama in *Aatish* is already withdrawn from a legal public order when the mother dies after issuing a call to Baba to return to the family home but without the mediating role of the punitive state. The only laws that can exist after that are those of kinship and fraternal com-mitment. As a result, it is an affective oedipal conflict between Avinash and Baba that continues to override the propositional dialectic between law and crime. Avinash does his best to step out of the shadow of a notori-ous elder brother who has brought him up and whose rights to the uterine fold he cannot cancel. When he accuses Baba of being a Ravana instead of a Rama, as all elder brothers are supposed to be, the gangster replies, "Jab apni akhon ke samne apni chote bhai ka sookhe hoot ho aur bhookh se tarapta hua pet ho, to phir Ramayan yaad nehi rehti" ("When you are faced with a younger brother's parched lips and empty stomach, you don't remember the Ramayana"). Avinash keeps trying to bring Baba to book, but Baba relentlessly protects Avinash, whose police uniform is no longer potent enough to allow him to live in a violent world. Avinash is attacked several times by assassins sent by Sunny, the villainous crime boss who wants to take over the city by finishing off both brothers.

However, what is far more interesting than this oedipal conflict is the moment when it is abandoned along with the weak dialectic between law and crime to usher in a cosmic truce. This happens in the final stages of the film, when, in the midst of a bloody battle, Avinash and Baba come to know that it was Sunny himself who killed their mother. A cornered Sunny breaks into mocking laughter when police jeeps are seen at a distance. He gloats to a helpless and frustrated Baba that he will now surrender to the authorities and then use his considerable clout and money to escape justice yet again. It is at this instant that an epic pact is sealed between the brothers who had hitherto not seen eye to eye. Even as Sunny's evil laughter resonates with the approaching sound of the sirens, Avinash hands his gun to Baba, who takes it and shoots his mother's killer dead. The policeman does not arrive late here, as Madhava Prasad astutely observes in the vendetta films of the 1970s and 1980s;[15] instead, he witnesses a sovereign act.

When he hands over the gun, Avinash sets aside a modern reckoning of law, ethics, and duty, and ceases to consider the mother merely as a citizen who has been robbed of her right to live. By doing so, he not only allows her memory to assume its proper mythic dimensions, but also recognizes its sovereign scope. It is through him that the historical state (the same one whose machinery can be bribed and bought by the evil Sunny) announces its own abjectly formal status and withdraws to a witnessing stance. Once that is achieved, killing is possible without the taint of sin, or culpability for homicide. For under the auspices of this mythic horizon, identities have been already transposed: Avinash, the police officer is now Laxman, Baba the criminal is Lord Rama, while Sunny the criminal with rights and money is Ravana, the demon king who is the target of a legitimate killing beyond the law. Avinash corrects his prior reading of the Ramayana when he recognizes the mother as the one who has united with nature and created the very grounds on which there can once again be a proper passage from natural law to civic law. Hence, in stepping out of the formal norms of law, Avinash is not seen to have categorically betrayed his profession; rather, it can be said that he has been claimed by a greater covenant of justice which, in a deeper portal of time that has opened up, has overwritten his social contract with the state. Normal protocols can resume as soon as the deed is done. After shooting Sunny, Baba handcuffs himself and surrenders to his brother.

Aatish, in many ways, is a melodrama that privileges two principal themes in its dramatic outlay. The first is related to a primal act of surviving in the new, changing, and elementally violent city; the second concerns the idea of a life worth living in that city itself. The question of law and custodianship begins from the degree zero of political life, from the bare fact of living, and then fans out to a global expanse of desires, values, honors, riches, and entitlements that seem to determine a coveted form of existence that can transform the "refuge" in the city to a home. The urban mise-en-scène is a no man's land, marked by an incessant,

6.2: The outlaw gets the gun in *Aatish.*

differential flow of illegalities originating from many sources. With the
father already robbed of his right to live and reduced to a picture on the
wall, and the mother exposed to rape and murder, the question of custodianship becomes an open one. The formal state apparatus, debilitated
by corruption and formalism, is only one among many contending forces
of sovereignty. The cinematic city in *Aatish*, as an allegorical landscape
of ruins, is therefore seen to await what Benjamin has called mythic law
establishing violence.[16] It is this primal act that Baba conducts at the end
of the film, with his mother's son bearing witness.

Aatish falls within the genre of apocalyptic urban action thrillers which
gained widespread currency in popular Hindi cinema starting with the
Emergency and the comet-like arrival of Amitabh Bachchan as the definitive male star of the last quarter of the twentieth century. *Deewar* too falls
within this genre, as does *Shakti* (*Power*) (Ramesh Sippy, 1981), the other
notable *Mother India*-inspired film of the post-Emergency years. It is in
this context that the cinematic city becomes of cardinal importance in
films like *Aatish*. Within these spaces, the mother, as originary spirit of
the nation, is denied the naturalistic expressive landscapes of Mehboob
Khan's film; she is also bereft of a larger community of sons. In the urban
organizing of the population state, the mother is absorbed into its profane
demographics. The affective energies of the mother figure are thus distributed between the weakening aspect of the eternal on the one hand,

and the anthropological profiles of poverty, homelessness, and hunger on the other. It is not just her honor, but her biological existence itself that is imperiled in the crossfire of contesting legal and illegal powers. The mother can be killed in the city, which is what happens in *Aatish* and *Shakti*.

The mother has to come to the city because it is the domain that can historically determine a form of life worth living for her sons. And yet, the city itself is spectral because desire is democratized there and given an unbounded, planetary scope while the means to achieve it are not. In *Aatish*, this theme of a life worth living is no longer restricted to questions that could be referred back to the welfare state, as in *Deewar* (unemployment, social justice, stigmatized identity) or *Shakti* (unemployment, recognition from the police officer father). In Sanjay Gupta's 1994 film, the city is redrawn by the virtual architectonics of metropolitan information, and not confined to the resident realities. The cinematic milieu is a compact of historical Mumbai and touristic Mauritius, in which the commonplace problems of lived life (the hunger of little brothers) are in critical adjacency with the allures of transnational spaces, shopping malls, exotic restaurants, alien bodies, and a plethora of consumer goods. As in many films of the 1990s, the mise-en-scène in *Aatish* presents a sublime mass of global urban desire that is still prosthetic to the local commerce of money and ethics, and yet envelops it. This geo-televisual is "outside" the old ethical horizon of *Mother India* under which the rebel Birju merely gave expression to his libidinal tendencies by teasing village girls and pining for his mother's golden bangles which lay mortgaged in Sukhi Lala's iron chest. Apart from perhaps a bride and the restoration of the bangles symbolizing the mother's honor, there were no other things figurable in Mehboob's film that would make Birju's life truly worth living. In contrast, to be "common" in the milieu of *Aatish* poses a dual danger. First, the self and the refuge are unprotected from a normative circulation of violence. Secondly, one is rendered incapable of entering that realm of recognition and normativity defined by a new dispensation of capital. The status of political life is therefore not limited to mere biological sustenance, legal citizenship, or even that abstract thing called honor. It is marked by an anastomosis between the desire to live and freedom to consume that forms a new plane of language, affect, and common sense. In this realm, the mythic invocation of Ramayana can merge with a political desire for a new sovereign principle. The state, in relation to that, is formalized in an abject manner because its constitutional pieties cannot adequately address a new free market of isomorphic passions: a naturalized terror of fire power and a naturalized love of money power.

In *Mother India*, Radha derives her crucial sense of honor from an originary endurance of an organic milieu that has, since time immemorial, withstood the passages of history. It is because of this principle that she cannot finally condone Birju's libidinous refusal to await the gods. This assurance of an inevitable return of the Dharmic is severely tested in the capricious industrial city of *Deewar*; but in that film, Sumitra upholds the state's paramount custodianship of the Dharmic, now determined in terms of urban middle-class codes of production and property. This is precisely why she cannot permit her sons to become *chors*. The nameless mother of *Aatish*, on the other hand, issues a new Protestantism of globalized times. This new Dharmic calls for an infantile withdrawal from the formalized realities of citizenship in order to protect and enrich the uterine order. This task can be accomplished only within the scope of a hyper-nucleated existence because the community itself has been transformed into indistinguishable hordes of crime and commerce. In such a situation, Baba's exile from the family becomes an act of self-sacrifice and voluntarism; his imminent return is always licit since it is he who vouchsafes and sponsors the home. The mother refuses to call him a *chor* because in this new age religiosity which blends the ontology of the Dharmic with neo-liberal individualism, the formal third world state no longer has absolute name-giving powers. Similarly, one cannot live in the refuge offered by the city and be nostalgic about a pristine home (the organic spirit of the nation) that is outside the urban circulation of bodies and money. This is, indeed, an important lesson; unlike her predecessor, Sumitra, who thought that her home was only *formally* subsumed by capital, the mother in *Aatish* knows that hers is *really* subsumed by it.[17] The refuge/home, even in imaginative reckonings of time and space, is no longer outside the precinct of the market.

The idea of (anti-) heroic infantilism (incarnated best in the 1990s by the screen image of Shahrukh Khan) here approximates the word's Greek etymological root *in-fans*, which means beings without language. Infantile recession is thus an exercise of masculine energy that has withdrawn itself from the constitutive language of the state into a sphere of pure interiority. All questions of guilt, culpability, ethics, and interest are hereby addressed within a nucleated zone that has to be secured and nourished at any cost. When Baba says that one does not remember the Ramayana when faced with a hungry brother, what he denies is not the paramount authority of the epic *per se*, but the claims of the legal order on the domain of lived life and culture; in other words, what the formal state announces as Ramayana. This infantile oblivion pertains to a negation of a patrimony in twilight, the ineffectual law and readings of dead fathers. The latter would include powerful nationalist legacies like a Gandhian agrarian, anti-capitalist asceticism as a spiritual horizon, and also a Nehruvian-socialist form of development. This does not mean that the Ramayana can no longer be recalled. Quite the contrary, there already seems to be a new Ramayana in the market/city. In the new urban order, the figure of Rama can only be of local extraction, bound within a zone of middle-class, individual interests pertaining to security and a life worth living. The rebuke to the state is expressive of a desire for a new statism beyond the formal licenses and permits of the state as it is. The desire, as we noted in the Introduction, is for a new covenant with the father; mere contracts of the social can follow later.

Vaastav (Reality)

In *Aatish* there is once again a momentous handing over of the gun to an instrument of justice. The main difference is that in Sanjay Gupta's film it is the rebel who wields the weapon, instead of being killed by it. In *Aatish*, the rebel gets the gun because in the circumstances, he is the only one capable of exercising what Benjamin calls "law-making violence" as he is not formally bound by a statist charter of duties. These repetitions with difference from *Mother India* to Gupta's film, however, do not make a simple progressive series. That is, an ushering in and anointing of the Nehruvian paradigm in *Mother India*, its painful endorsement during the turbulent 1970s in *Deewar*, and its eclipse and abnegation in a violence-ridden, yet alluring globalized field of the 1990s in *Aatish*. Instead, each of these instances instantiates the complex nature of mythic recall. In Mahesh Manjrekar's 1999 retelling of the Mother India myth, the mother takes up the gun again, and unlike Baba, the rebel in this case does not survive and prosper. Through this film we shall also briefly explore the elemental genre of the crime thriller of the 1990s and after, one that is often set in a spectral underbelly of the city that is the war-torn other scene of the informatic–geo-televisual metropolis.

Unlike its cinematic predecessors, *Vaastav* begins with the nondescript. That is, the narrative is not launched by an abomination that destroys an idyllic, familial order, but begins from a "refuge" that is not yet a home. What I have been calling the refuge in the city is an inhabiting space for disposable populations,[18] populations that are either refugees or can become refugees in an instant, with subtle fluctuations in an overall commerce of money, violence, "development," communal riots, and politics. The refuge is a space to stay whose status, in terms of political economy, is not settled. In practical terms, this concept can be attached to the vast slums of Mumbai, largely built on landfills between what used to be a city of seven islands. It can be connected to the hundreds of thousands of living quarters protected by the Bombay Rent Control Act of 1947. Refuge can also mean the myriad, shifting habitations of a formidable population that lives on the streets: railway platforms, park benches, underneath flyovers, and many others. The refuge is thus the stark counterpoint to the spectral mansions in the marriage melodrama discussed in Chapter 2. These disposed yet recalcitrant figures and their subliminal economies of survival always vitalize the cinematic pictures of Mumbai in innumerable comic or monstrous forms: in Priyadarshan's 1993 film *Gardish* (*Sky*), Manishbhai Harishbhai is seen to run a highly sophisticated network of beggars in the city; in his other film, *Kabhi Na Kabhi* (*Sometime*) (1998), the arch-villain, Kachra Seth,[19] runs a massive garbage empire.

The narrative in *Vaastav* gradually exposes the inhabitants of a precarious uterine order to the diurnal violence of the city. In this film, the rebel is not created by the protagonist's obstinate questioning of the weak father's law. Instead, he is born of an urban irascibility, through a rootless floating of bodies and destinies in a whirlpool of *chance*. This admission of a pronounced and disheartening chance factor severely diminishes the mythic quotient in *Vaastav*. As we shall see, time is less of a curvature in this film; it is calendrical and devoid of a redeeming, messianic promise of a mythic recall. The hero in this case merely has to run his course till his luck runs out. This spirit of hardboiled urban disenchantment is what brings *Vaastav* closer to a new realism of the 1990s in the cinema of Mani Ratnam and Ram Gopal Verma, than with the instances of mythic repetition we have been discussing. The film is an abnegation of a national-spiritual monotheme of being, not an agonistic affirmation of it. It inhabits the tale of Mother India only to curtail its mythic impress and reduce it to a skeletal form in the light of present realities.

Raghunath Shivalkar is a young man who lives in a shanty town in Mumbai with his parents and his educated but unemployed elder brother, Vijay. Raghu's life acquires some direction when he starts a fast-food stall with a modest loan that his mill worker father procures for him. The business, run by Raghu himself and a few friends from the neighborhood, is a thumping success from day one. The sudden flush of money brings elation and comfort to the family's otherwise hand-to-mouth existence. Raghu's mother, Shanta, is proud of her son, his father feels vindicated, and arrangements are made to bribe officers to get Vijay a job. It is at this juncture that goons from the notorious "Fracture" gang begin to frequent Raghu's eating joint. The hoodlums never pay and bully the workers constantly; Raghu's patience is exhausted when they start beating up one of his friends. In the mêlée that ensues, he accidentally kills one of the gang members.

A frightened Raghu absconds and quickly understands that the malignant environment of the city allows no fair legal address of his circumstantial crime. The police officer investigating the incident happens to be on the "Fracture"'s payroll; he intends to hunt down Raghu and turn him over to his bloodthirsty enemies. The absence of viable citizenship rights in the real picture of the city evicts Raghu from his parents' refuge. Finally, he turns to Viththal Kaniya, a rival don and sworn enemy of the "Fracture" brothers, for shelter. Matters are made worse when arrangements are made to broker peace with the "Fracture" brothers. Kaniya agrees to pay them blood money in lieu of Raghu's life, but the treacherous brothers renege on the deal and attempt to kill Raghu when he meets them. The young man commits his second murder in order to save himself. This ends all possibilities of a return to normalcy. Raghu begins to take part in Kaniya's operations and soon emerges as one of the most feared mob assassins of Mumbai.

The cinematic metamorphosis of the innocent to the killer assumes the form of hallucination as a trope of melodrama: a drug–alcohol assemblage. A frightened Raghu takes his first shot of alcohol after his second accidental killing. From that point onwards, his filmic figuration is constructed by affects of insomnia, intoxication, fear, and other inner demons. Violence becomes endemic and disperses the integrated self, corroding all boundaries between the external and internal worlds. Raghu's aspect gradually loses its familial qualities and becomes a stage for the terror and multi-pronged aggression of the city itself. This becomes clear in the scene in which he visits his parents for the first time since embarking on his new career. Raghu, in a totally wasted state, lovingly demonstrates to his shocked mother the mechanical intricacies of his gun. His schizophrenic transformation reaches a stage of completion with this encounter because he has no memory of a lost uterine order. The abolishing of ethical consciousness through alcohol and drugs has extended to the forgetting of a primal and compelling love—precisely the love that was once capable of calling the prodigal back.

Ironically, it is only after the meek transmogrifies into a feared participant in the warring processes of the city that the paths of survival—the possibilities of turning the refuge into a home—open up for the family. Raghu threatens a headhunter to get a job for his elder brother, Vijay, and also clears the way for the latter's wedding by making his girlfriend's status-conscious father an offer he cannot refuse. Raghu himself falls in love with, impregnates, and then marries a prostitute called Sonya. Shanta welcomes her new daughter-in-law without any moral reservations. But subsequently, apart from Raghu's bad luck, the dreams of finding a home for the mother and preserving the unity of the uterine order are faced with a new problem. The educated white-collar employee Vijay fulfills his long-cherished ambitions by leaving the family set-up and lower-class neighborhood for a nucleated existence with his wife. Unlike his illustrious predecessors like the Nehruvian Ramu in *Mother India*, the firm and principled cop Ravi in *Deewar*, the educated model subject in this case abandons the mother.

Signatures of a sanitized, cowardly, and weak middle-income existence coalesce around Vijay. A relentless moral and emotional commentary invests him with a pathological despicability and selfishness as strong as Raghu's nihilistic death drive or drug abuse. Vijay leaves home even though his wife wants to stay with her in-laws. He is seen to be slavishly busy with office work even when his grievously injured father undergoes critical surgery in hospital. He refuses to acknowledge or welcome the presence of his brother even though it was the latter that got him his job and arranged his marriage. The abode of the new representatives of an atomized educated urban class is, however, an insecure one. Vijay's greed for the good life requires that his wife must work (she herself has no say in the matter); however, he is unable to protect her from sexual predators. He thus once again turns to his brother for help. Raghu is disgusted at his brother's inability to maintain his wife at home or ensure that her honor remains safeguarded in public. It is thus once again the felon brother that has to intervene to maintain private conjugal peace. Raghu protects his sister-in-law's chastity in the only manner he knows – the summary extermination of her stalkers.

The cinematic assemblage that constitutes the rebellious figure of Raghu has many expressive qualities. He is a combination of a street-savvy instinct for survival and an awry, drug-induced perception that increasingly detaches itself from the social. Raghu is a staging of the sensorium of the city itself, in which moral postulates like honor can no longer be connected to the realities of law and production. He is an ensemble of altruistic desire and pathological feelings that regularly explode into extreme violence. More than anything else, it is the absolute nihilism of his brutality that sets him apart from his predecessors. Unlike Birju, Vijay, or Baba, Raghu's outbursts often cannot be latched onto larger symbolic horizons pertaining to the quest for the mother as a seat of natality, or a counter-ethical recalcitrance against the state or cowardly fathers. Apart from being tormented by a world with a totally evacuated horizon of belief, Raghu, as he himself says repeatedly, is driven by a visceral hatred for the "white collar." This latter feeling, triggered initially by disgust for his gutless brother, drives him to schizophrenic fury several times. He kills a corrupt police officer and then a Parsee man who refuses to sell his property to an underworld-real estate nexus. These incidents disconnect Raghu from the calibrated economy of money, law, crime, and violence that runs the city. As a result, the very criminal-political order that had been sponsoring him now withdraws its support.

Raghu's spectacular rise to notoriety was due to the fact that he, as an unbridled reservoir of warlike energies, had been recruited by a special formation of power. This appears in the milieu of *Vaastav* in the form of Babbanrao Kadam, a thoroughly corrupt minister who wields tremendous clout brokered through a network of legal and extra-legal syndicalisms: parliamentary representation, real estate, street muscle, extortion, and hired killers. As an archetype, Kadam therefore belongs to the "Lalloo assemblage," discussed in Chapter 3. The type of formal/informal power he holds is habitually referred to in popular Indian cinema as *rajniti*. Despite being a Sanskritic equivalent of the signifier "politics," *rajniti* in this context acquires a terrifying aspect from the point of view of the modern: it pertains to the sum of all fears that realizes itself when there is an overall, perverse vernacularization of the metropolis, that is, not when a Sanskritized language of the state aspires to attain a globality of relevance (as we saw in the case of *Rudraksh*), but when signs of *dalitism* as non-being contaminates the entire body politic. The city then is no longer manageable into proper, equivalent metropolitan forms; it is seen to be ruled by competing hordes or tribes.

Encounters of the State and the Twilight of a Mythic Natality

When a power- and narcotics-pumped Raghu is recruited by the perfidious machinery of *rajniti* commanded by Kadam, he embarks on his journey to a tragic end. Despite the worldly-wise warnings of Kishore—his childhood friend and a cynical, bribe-taking police sub-inspector—Raghu organizes several assassinations and strong-arm maneuvers at Kadam's request. The most crucial among these is the murder of a pacifist Gandhian leader of the Muslim community which leads to communal riots in the city. This induction of the rebel into a grotesque war machine of *rajniti* is once again smothered by a melodrama of narcotic deterritorialization of the self. The heroic figure is no longer impelled by oedipal *angst* or a masochistic desire for reunion with the mother; it becomes a pure schizophrenic dissimulation of being across the city space.[20] As Raghu tells Inspector Kishore, alcohol, drugs, and the "high" of killing itself have become means for switching off the mind, to instrumentalize oneself for a cathartic expurgation of passions, and to foreclose thinking in a world devoid of any originary fountainhead of meaning.

The contract of violence, however, runs aground at a critical point, when Raghu's boundless *ressentiment* overrides the meticulously crafted economy of Kadam's operations. The latter decides to set Raghu up as scapegoat in order to save his political career. Kadam activates the legal war machine this time, which apprehends and kills the members of Raghu's gang in a series of encounters. "Encounter"[21] is a colloquialism used by the police in the Indian context to describe an extra-legal killing, by which the question of life and death is settled without recourse to law and juridical procedures. Encounter as such takes place in an intermediary zone between law-breaking/law-preserving violence and the sphere of juridical intelligence. The dead body as a result is produced in passing, in the temporal and spatial gap between the executive and the juridical. It produces a new corpus of the condemned lodged between the abstract form of the citizen and that of the prisoner with rights. The encounter is a newly manifest, "special branch" of sovereign execution not practiced by the cops that killed by answering fire with fire in the landmark films of the 1970s and early 1980s, like *Zanjeer* (*Chain*) (Prakash Mehra, 1973) and *Satyamev Jayate* (*Truth Always Triumphs*) (Raj N. Sippy, 1982). In the new dispensation of law and violence we see in *Vastaav*, Raghu therefore faces a predicament none of the rebels of the past did. Unlike Vijay in *Deewar*, he can no longer surrender to the police.

The clean-up is cynically publicized through the media by Kadam himself. At this juncture, Raghu tricks Kadam into a trap and finishes him off. Following that, however, the rebel exhausts his energies. The entire city by then has been sealed off, and a massive manhunt is already underway. Relentlessly on the run, Raghu somehow evades the police and reaches his farmhouse in the outskirts of the city where his entire family has been waiting. This tremendous journey across a war-ravaged landscape is, however, neither impelled by a hope for a mythic union with the mother who waits patiently, nor by a primordial survival instinct (for which the means have run out). It is a "mindless" flight to get away from an urban horizon overtaken by fear. This fear comes from neither the formal specter of legal death, nor from the possibility of facing the enemy on the warpath; it comes instead from Raghu's realization that in a battle for sovereignty between the state and other criminal forces, he has, for the first time, been absolutely rendered "bare."[22]

By the time Raghu reaches his family after a superhuman trek across

6.3: Raghu's final deliverance in *Vaastav*.

the countryside, he has already lost his wits. The mother escorts her hallu-
cinating and rambling son into the garden, where he gives her his money,
all his possessions, including the gun, and begs her to sell them and
procure some drugs to help him switch off his mind. The long-suffering
mother realizes that her son, who is already legally dead because of an
imminent encounter already announced, has crossed another threshold of
life. From henceforth, his body as well as soul can be resuscitated neither
by the nourishment of maternal love, nor by the pedagogy and punishment of God or the state. He can only be tormented by fear and insomnia, or mobilized as a killing machine only by the grotesque *jouissance* of
narcotics. The mother understands that the only form of life her son is
capable of does not permit a re-entry to the uterine order after performing
the rites of atonement; instead, it relates to a pure venomous pathology
of total forgetting. It is drugs that he wants, not union with her. A being-
eclipsing contact with *vaastav* (reality) has effaced the myth of the mother,
and created in its place an acute state of abjection in which the only way
to survive or find a home is to be in a perpetual state of hallucination. It
is then that the mother remembers the prophetic lesson Raghu had given
her about how to fire a gun. In an act of profound mercy which only

mothers are capable of, she shoots her son to deliver him from the fearful hunt of the city.

Notes

1. I am grateful to Kaushik Bhaumik for pointing this out to me.
2. See Carl Schmitt, *The Concept of the Political* (1976) and *Political Theology: Four Chapters on the Concept of Sovereignty* (1985).
3. See Sibaji Bandyopadhyay, *Atho Ma Faleshu Kadachon* (2003) and my recent and forthcoming essays "Hindutva and Informatic Modernization" and "The Indian Monotheism."
4. Ashish Rajadhyaksha and Paul Willemen, eds., *Encyclopedia of Indian Cinema* (1999): 350.
5. Radha had saved Birju's life from a fire that had broken out a little while earlier.
6. See Moinak Biswas, "*Mother India O' Roja*: *Jatir Dui Akhyan*" (1996). This reading of *Mother India* is heavily indebted to this analysis.
7. Gilles Deleuze, *Cinema 1* (1986): 87.
8. See Madhava Prasad's excellent reading of *Deewar* and the climate of the Indian Emergency in *Ideology of the Hindi Film* (1998): 138–59.
9. See Vinay Lal, "The Impossibility of the Outsider in the Modern Hindi Film" (1998). Here Lal talks about *Deewar* as a film concerned with the impossibility of being an outsider. Ravi, according to him, cannot have a true human relationship because he is caught between social institutions and the anthropological burden of kinship.
10. In between these scenes, the father, Anand, is seen from time to time, over the years, traveling endlessly by train. Unlike Shamu, the father in *Mother India* who is never seen again after he leaves the house for an unknown destination, Anand keeps reappearing, as a haunting reminder of a deracinated patriarchal presence that cannot exit to a pure outside. Anand's journey is thus driven by an unforgiving eschatology devoid of the messianic; it is an interminable drift through the historical that can end only in a death without ceremonial. This is precisely what happens many years later; his corpse is discovered in a train compartment.
11. See Rajadhyaksha's essays on early Indian cinematic forms and the notion of "frontality": "Neo-traditionalism" (1986), "Epic Melodrama" (1994), and "The Phalke Era" (1987).
12. Prasad, *Ideology of the Hindi Film*, 146–7.
13. The film is rife with events (especially in Vijay's criminal career and in his love affair with Anita) that the mother did not or could not have witnessed. Like many popular Hindi films, *Deewar* cites a psychological, individualistic perspective only to break away from and return to it without obligations.
14. Prasad points out in his reading that the ovation is claimed by the dead son as well.

15. Prasad, *Ideology of the Hindi Film*, 95.
16. See Walter Benjamin, "Critique of Violence" (1978).
17. Prasad uses the Marxist categories of formal subsumption and real subsumption to forge a descriptive of what he calls the "passive revolutionary" Indian political milieu after Independence. According to Prasad, this milieu is also characterized by the fact that the forces of production are only formally submitted to capital, and not subsumed by it. In the final chapter, entitled "Towards a Real Subsumption?", discussing the 1990s, Prasad speculates whether one can discern any indications of a process of "real subsumption." See *Ideology of the Hindi Film*, 6–14 and 217–37.
18. See Ronald A. T. Judy, "Provisional Note on Formations of Planetary Violence" (2006).
19. *Kachra* means garbage or waste in Hindi.
20. There is no quarrel with the father here; in one of the most memorable scenes, Namdev, Raghu's unfortunate father, embraces his son and cries out, "Why did this have to happen, son?"
21. Historically, the practice of the encounter is said to have become prevalent in Mumbai from the early 1980s onwards, after the closing of the city's famed textile mills created a fertile recruiting ground for Mafiosi. However, it was roughly from 1993, in the wake of the bomb blasts and a full-scale gang war between Dawood Ibrahim and his disgruntled former subordinate, Chota Shakeel, that encounters, in the extra-legal sense, were irresistibly systematized by the Mumbai police. On the trope of the encounter in Hindi cinema of the 1990s and after, see my "Encounters in the City: Cops, Criminals, and Human Rights in Hindi Film," forthcoming in *Journal of Human Rights*.
22. I am alluding to the idea of bare life in relation to modern sovereignty developed by Giorgio Agamben in *Homo Sacer* (1998).

Epilogue

It is perhaps pertinent that this book ends with a critical reading of *Vaastav*. The dark, stifling atmosphere of the film belongs precisely to that underbelly of the city that is denied the heady exhale of the geo-televisual as informatic. Yet it is a world that is irresistibly besieged by the overall diagram of desire and value of which geo-televisual informatics is an advertising component, that is, a diagram of financialization that universalizes desire, but segments life in the city into forms that are deemed worth living and those that are not. The elemental darkness of *Vaastav* comes from an acute rarefaction of light due to the withholding of metropolitan images from this picture. It is this withdrawal of forms of life that are "worth" living that makes the population a disposable one. This is poignantly underlined in the film. There are no non–obligatory geo-televisual excursions in *Vaastav*; however, it is the underworld's blood money that sponsors a fleeting vision of the other side. Raghu and his wife, Sonia, are sent by Babban Rao Kadam on honeymoon to Switzerland. *Vaastav* belongs to a sub-genre of urban crime films like *Satya* (*Truth*) (Ram Gopal Verma, 1998), *Gang* (Mazhar Khan, 1999), *Company* (Verma, 2002), and *Maqbool* (Vishal Bhardwaj, 2002) that demand a separate engagement. Such films are often set in an apocalyptic zone where state power, in its raw form, encounters powers of antagonism from the giant backwaters. The features of this penumbral city beneath the metropolis thus sadly remain outside this project, as do some other cinematic pictures of the other side: the jingoistic/communal war or terror-fighting films made around the Indo-Pakistan frontier war in Kargil (*Border*, J. P. Dutta, 1998; *Sarfarosh*, John Matthew Mathan, 1998, *Gadar*, Anil Sharma, 2001; *Indian*, N. Maharajan, 2001), or the filmic products of a new nostalgia/history industry that presented the "past" with new digital forms and geo-televisual textures (*Lagaan*, Ashutosh Gowarikar, 2001; *The Legend of Bhagat Singh*, Rajkumar Santoshi, 2002). I hope that the critical template of the geo-televisual presented in this book will help other scholars to examine them.

Let me, however, return to a usual suspect, the marriage/rich family melodrama, to ponder a curious final point. Despite the extravagance and plenitude we see in "Bollywood" products, such scenarios almost always come with a foreclosure of a defining power in the world: finance capital. Dharmesh Darsan's *Ek Rishta: The Bond of Love* (2001), for instance, is about a generational conflict between the aging patriarch of the family business and his code of paternalistic capitalism, and his American business school-educated son, an advocate of the new age principle of hiring and firing. This situation is further exacerbated when the patriarch's corrupt son-in-law attempts to take over the business by nefarious means. The latter and his cronies are punished in the end by the eldest son of the patriarch and the laborers as a community of sons. When the diagram of the *Khandaan* or feudal extended family inscribes that of the modern business establishment, the result is an assembled stage in which imprints of financialization cannot completely deterritorialize patriarchal authority into anonymous and dispersed shareholdings of money power. This is precisely why, in terms of proprietorship of women and custodianship of value, the patriarch Vijay Kapoor is never dispossessed of "richness" even when he is formally cheated of his property rights. The evil son-in-law cannot establish his "lawful" rights over the property when the workers barricade the gates; nor can he command conjugal rights over his wife who spurns him, or his paternal rights over his unborn child. In a utopian space where just authority is seen to take over all other contractual relations (of labor, money, property and woman), money *qua* money has no recognition apart from being part of a consummate richness of a singular upper-caste, upper-class, Hindu-Indian "tradition." The spectacular-ceremonial mode of the marriage films emerges precisely at that impossible interface between the ethical diagram of Indian womanhood and the new age diagram of "business" that is public, yet internal to the logic of the familial. The figuration of home in this milieu is thus that of absolute and total repose, a picture of custom removed from circulation. This feature too, along with the geo-televisual as informatic, deserves special investigation across genres and media. It too has morphed and assumed newer forms.

This book has been the story of the ideological and political underpinnings of the ways in which the Hindi film adjusted to a new dispensation of media, capital, and political Hinduism roughly between 1991 and 2004. I have thus examined the emergence of a "Bollywood" style in an environment of what I have called informatic or advertised modernization. While doing so, I have attempted to provide a lens for understanding not just the "Bollywood" phenomenon, but why exactly economic liberalization can actually bolster traditional, anti-modern authorities in third world situations instead of eroding them. To reiterate, such formations can rapidly gain technology without entering holistic domains of "science," embrace "cool" consumerism without bourgeois tastes or charters of rights, and work the formalities of a democratic polity without liberalism. They can therefore have information without "knowledge," a highly kinetic media universe without a civil society. India, the largest democracy in the world, can perhaps be situated at the moderate end, rather than the dismal extremes of this spectrum. And yet to this day, after a few more years of "development" and special alliances with Western powers, the Indian situation remains marked by a stark contrast between high-order metropolitan development at one end and the world's largest hungry population at the other.

That said, I think that the period between 1991 and 2004 I have earmarked for this project was one of special revels of the geo-televisual as absolutely informatic that have since abated, changed directions, or taken more complex forms. Rural India or the lower-middle-class, struggling India of the cities and middle-sized towns, for instance, made comebacks to A-list productions in *Swadesh: We the People* (Ashutosh Gowarikar, 2004), *Traffic Signal* (Madhur Bhandarkar, 2007), *Summer 2007* (Sohail Tatari, 2007), and even a Yashraj blockbuster like *Rab Ne Bana Di Jodi* (*A Couple Made by God*) (Aditya Chopra, 2008). Dominant generic templates like the marriage melodrama or the candy floss romance have been challenged and even displaced by a new order of speculative and partly experimental Multiplex cinema often in the English language. Indeed, an increasingly strong vein of modestly budgeted Multiplex films has subsequently explored formerly taboo territories of contemporary urban Indian atomization, *angst*, and desire: premarital sex, swinger lifestyles, polygamous temptations, and homosexuality. That is, unlike the middle-of-the-road art cinema of the 1970s, these themes have often been pursued within commercial idioms. That does not mean that the overall ecology of informatic modernization has disappeared, but it has become more striated and complicated.

It is always difficult to study the present. One needs the sobering distance of time in order to be able to do that. Perhaps the political consequences, traditions, and formations this altered (amongst other things, a post-BJP) scenario is engendering will be apparent to us in their true incarnations only a little later. The task of critical thinking in the meantime is not to negate the innovative powers of capital or neo-liberalization in the world, but to scrupulously track them and furnish new weapons of thought, ethics, and resistance. This is because it is not enough to understand the informatic ecology of Hindu normative nationalism in terms of representational politics and conscious ideological devoirs. The defeat of the right-wing BJP in 2004, while being an event strongly desired by all

Left-leaning people, does not alter a language environment that gradually defines the political spectrum itself in terms of a calibrated measure of hard, moderate, or soft Hinduness. The statism inherent in all of this does not propose the state as a clearly defined formal entity or a repository of decrees, but as a resonance chamber (as Deleuze would have called it) that is planetary in its ambitions; that is, a powerful impelling of signs towards a monotone of rhythm rather than a unity of theme. Here, more than what is clearly allowed and what is clearly forbidden in the world, it is more important to regularize the very terms of endearment and those of war. It is in such an order of information and assembling that it becomes, quite insidiously, a matter of absolute normalcy to become Hindu in the global metropolis.

Bibliography

Agamben, Giorgio. *Homo Sacer: Sovereign Power and Bare Life*. Trans. Daniel Heller-Roazen. Stanford, CA: Stanford University Press, 1998.
— *Means without End: Notes on Politics*. Trans. Vincenzo Binetti and Cesare Casarino. Minneapolis, MN: University of Minnesota Press, 2000.
— *Remnants of Auschwitz: The Witness and the Archive*. Trans. Daniel Heller-Roazen. New York: Zone Books, 2000.
— "Security and Terror." *Theory and Event* 5:4 (2002).
Allesandrini, Anthony C. "'My Heart is Indian for All That': Bollywood Film between Home and Diaspora." *Diaspora* 2:3 (2001): 315–40.
Amin, Shahid. "Gandhi as Mahatma: Gorakhpur District, Eastern UP, 1921–2," in Ranajit Guha, ed. *Subaltern Studies III*. New Delhi: Oxford University Press, 1984: 1–61.
Anand, Margot, ed. *The Kamasutra of Vatsayana*. New York: Modern Library, 2002.
Appadurai, Arjun. *Modernity at Large: Cultural Dimensions of Globalization*. Minneapolis, MN: University of Minnesota Press, 1996.
Arendt, Hannah. *The Human Condition*. Chicago: Chicago University Press, 1958.
— *The Origins of Totalitarianism*. New York: Harcourt-Harvest, 1973.
Auerbach, Erich. *Mimesis: The Representation of Reality in Western Literature*. Trans. Willard Trask. New York: Doubleday, 1957.
Avinavagupta. "On *Santirasa*: Aesthetic Equipoise," in *Indian Literary Criticism: Theory and Interpretation*. Ed. G. N. Devy. Hyderabad: Orient Longman, 2002: 61–73.
Bagchi, Jashodhara. "Representing Nationalism: Ideology of Motherhood in Colonial Bengal." *Economic and Political Weekly* 24:42–3 (1990): 65–71.
Balibar, Etienne and Immanuel Wallerstein. *Race, Nation, Class: Ambiguous Identities*. London: Verso, 1991.
Banaji, Shakuntala. *Reading "Bollywood": The Young Audience and Hindi Films*. New York: Palgrave Macmillan, 2006.
Bandyopadhyay, Samik. *Indian Cinema: Contemporary Perceptions from the Thirties*. Jamshedpur: Celluloid Chapter, 1993.
Bandyopadhyay, Sibaji. "Atho Ma Faleshu Kadachon." *Anustup Sharodiya* (2003): 2–232.
— "Punar Bishoye Punarbibechona," in Sibaji Bandyopadhyay, *Alibabar Guptabhandar*. Kolkata: Gangchil, 2009: 217–74.
— *Gopal-Rakhal Dwandhyosamash*. Kolkata: Papyrus, 1991.

Banerjee, Mita. "Bollywood Meets the Beatles: Towards an Asian German Studies of German Popular Culture." *South Asian Popular Culture* 4:1 (April 2004): 19–34.

Banerjee, Parthasarathi and Frank Jürgen Richter, eds. *Economic Institutions in India: Sustainability under Liberalization and Globalization.* New Delhi: Palgrave Macmillan, 2003.

Bardhan, Pranab. *The Political Economy of Development in India.* Oxford: Basil Blackwell, 1984.

Basu, Anustup. "The Human and His Spectacular Autumn, or, Informatics after Philosophy." *PostModern Culture* 14:3 (May 2004).

— "State of Security and Warfare of Demons." *Critical Quarterly* 45:1–2 (2003): 11–32.

— "Hindutva and Informatic Modernization." *Boundary 2* 35:3 (2008): 239–50.

— "The Indian Monotheism," forthcoming in *Boundary 2* (2010).

— "Encounters in the City: Cops, Criminals, and Human Rights in Hindi Film," forthcoming in *Journal of Human Rights* (2010).

Basu, Tapan, Sumit Sarkar, and Tanika Sarkar. *Khaki Shorts and Saffron Flags: A Critique of Hindu Nationalists.* New Delhi: Orient Longman, 1993.

Beeman, William O. "The Use of Music in Popular Film: East and West." *India International Center Quarterly Special Issue* 8:1 (1980).

Bell, Daniel. *The Coming of Post-industrial Society.* New York: Basic Books, 1999.

Benjamin, Walter. *The Origin of German Tragic Drama.* Trans. John Osbourne. London: Verso, 1985.

— "Outline for a Habitation Thesis." *Selected Writings. Volume 1, 1913–1926.* Ed. Marcus Bullock and Michael W. Jennings. Cambridge, MA: Harvard University Press, 1996: 269–71.

— "The Storyteller: Reflections on the Works of Nikolai Leskov." Trans. Harry Zohn. *Illuminations.* Ed. Hannah Arendt. London: Fontana, 1973: 83–107.

— "Theses on the Philosophy of History." Trans. Harry Zohn. *Illuminations.* Ed. Hannah Arendt. London: Fontana, 1973: 245–55.

— "The Work of Art in the Age of Mechanical Reproduction." Trans. Harry Zohn. *Illuminations.* Ed. Hannah Arendt. London: Fontana, 1973: 211–44.

— "Critique of Violence," in Peter Demetz, ed. *Reflections: Essays, Aphorisms, Autobiographical Writings.* New York: Schocken Books, 1978: 277–301.

Bennett, M. R. and P. M. S. Hacker. *Philosophical Foundations of Neuroscience.* Oxford: Blackwell, 2003.

— et al. *Neuroscience and Philosophy: Brain, Mind, and Language.* New York: Columbia University Press, 2007.

Bharatamuni. "On Natya and Rasa: Aesthetics of Dramatic Experience," In G. N. Devy, ed. *Indian Literary Criticism: Theory and Interpretation.* Hyderabad: Orient Longman, 2002: 3–14.

— *The Natyasastra: A Treatise on Hindu Dramaturgy and Histrionics.* Trans. Manomohan Ghosh. Vols. I and II. Calcutta: The Asiatic Society, 1961.

Bharucha, Rustom. "On the Border of Fascism: Manufacture of Consent in *Roja.*" *Economic and Political Weekly* 29:23 (1994): 1389–95.

— "Utopia in Bollywood: Hum Aapke Hain Kaun . . .!" *Economic and Political Weekly* 30:15 (1995): 801–4.

Bhaskar, Ira. "Allegory, Nationalism and Cultural Change in Indian Cinema: *Sant Tukaram*." *Literature & Theology* 12:1 (1998): 50–69.

Bhaumik, Kaushik. "The Emergence of the Bombay Film Industry, 1913–1936." Unpublished PhD dissertation, Oxford University, 2001.

Biswas, Moinak. "*Mother India O' Roja: Jatir Dui Akhyan*." *Baromas.Sharodiya* (1996): 58–71.

— "Historical Realism: Modes of Modernity in Indian Cinema." Unpublished PhD dissertation, Monash University, 2002.

Bordwell, David et al. *The Classical Hollywood Cinema: Film Style & Mode of Production to 1960*. New York: Columbia University Press, 1985.

Bové, Paul. *Poetry against Torture: Criticism, History, and the Human*. Hong Kong: Hong Kong University Press, 2008.

Brennan, Teresa. *The Transmission of Affect*. Ithaca, NY: Cornell University Press, 2004.

Brooks, Peter. *The Melodramatic Imagination*. New Haven, CT: Yale University Press, 1976.

Burman, J. J. Roy. "Shivaji's Myth and Maharashtra's Syncretic Traditions." *Economic and Political Weekly* (April 14–20, 2001).

Butcher, Melissa. *Transnational Television, Cultural Identity and Change: When Star Came to India*. New Delhi: Sage, 2003.

Byres, T. J. "Introduction: Development Planning and the Interventionist State versus Liberalization and the Neo-Liberal State: India, 1989–1996," in T. J. Byres, ed. *The State, Development Planning and Liberalization in India*. New Delhi: Oxford, 1997.

Castells, Manuel. *The Information Age: Economy, Society and Culture. Volume I: The Rise of the Network Society*. Oxford: Blackwell, 2000.

— *The Information Age: Economy, Society and Culture. Volume II: The Power of Identity*. Oxford: Blackwell, 2004.

— *The Information Age: Economy, Society and Culture. Volume III: End of Millennium*. Oxford: Blackwell, 2000.

Chakrabarty, Dipesh. *Provincializing Europe: Postcolonial Thought and Historical Difference*. Princeton, NJ: Princeton University Press, 2000.

Chakravarty, Sukhamoy. *Development Planning: The Indian Experience*. Oxford: Clarendon Press, 1987.

Chakravarty, Sumita. "The Erotics of History: Gender and Transgression in the New Asian Cinema," In R. Anthony Guneratne and Wimal Dissanayake, eds. *Rethinking Third Cinema*. New York: Routledge, 2003.

— *National Identity in Indian Popular Cinema (1947–1987)*. Austin, TX: University of Texas, 1993.

Chandravarkar, Bhaskar. "Growth of the Film Song." *Cinema in India* 1:3 (1981): 16–20.

Chatterjee, Gayatri. "Icons and Events: Reinventing Visual Construction in

Cinema in India," in Raminder Kaur and Ajay J. Sinha, eds. *Bollyworld: Indian Cinema through a Transnational Lens*. New Delhi: Sage, 2005: 90–117.

Chatterjee, Partha. *Nationalist Thought and the Colonial World: A Derivative Discourse*. Delhi: Oxford University Press, 1986.

— *The Nation and its Fragments*. Princeton, NJ: Princeton University Press, 1993.

— "Introduction," in Partha Chatterjee, ed. *Wages of Freedom: Fifty Years of the Indian Nation-State*. New Delhi: Oxford University Press, 1998.

— *The Politics of the Governed: Reflections on Popular Politics in Most of the World*. New Delhi: Permanent Black, 2004.

Chattopadhyay, Bankimchandra. *"Dharmatattva". Bankim Rachanabali*, Vol. II. Kolkata: Sahitya Sanshad, 1954: 512–615.

— *"Krishnacharitra." Bankim Rachnabali*. Vol. II. Calcutta: Sahitya Samsad, 1954: 407–583.

Chowdhury-Sengupta, Indira. "Mother India and Mother Victoria: Motherland and Nationalism in Nineteenth Century Bengal." *South Asia Research* 12:1 (1992): 25–6.

Corrigan, Timothy. *A Cinema without Walls: Movies and Culture after Vietnam*. New Brunswick, NJ: Rutgers University Press, 1991.

Crary, Jonathan. "Modernizing Vision," in Linda Williams, ed. *Viewing Positions: Ways of Seeing Film*. New Brunswick, NJ: Rutgers University Press, 1997: 23–35.

Damasio, Antonio. *Descartes' Error: Emotion, Reason, and the Human Brain*. New York: Penguin Books, 1995.

— *The Feeling of What Happens*. New York: Harcourt, 1999.

Damle, Shridhar D. and Walter K. Anderson. *The Brotherhood in Saffron*. New Delhi: Sage, 1987.

Dasgupta, Chidananda. *The Painted Face: Studies in Indian Popular Cinema*. New Delhi: Roli Books, 1991.

Dasgupta, Sudeep. *Hindu Nationalism, Television, and the Avataars of Capital*. Veenendaal: Universal Press, 2001.

Dawson, Ashley. "'Bollywood Flashback': Hindi Film Music and the Negotiation of Identity among British-Asian Youths." *South Asian Popular Culture* 3:2 (2005): 161–76.

Debord, Guy. *Society of the Spectacle*. Trans. Donald Nicholson-Smith. New York: Zone Books, 1995.

Deleuze, Gilles. *Cinema 1: The Movement Image*. Trans. Hugh Tomlinson and Barbara Habberjam. Minneapolis, MN: University of Minnesota Press, 1986.

— *Cinema 2: The Time Image*. Trans. Hugh Tomlinson and Robert Galeta. Minneapolis, MN: University of Minnesota, 1989.

— *Foucault*. Trans. Sean Hand. Minneapolis, MN: University of Minnesota Press, 1997.

— *Spinoza: Practical Philosophy*. Trans. Robert Hurley. New York: City Lights, 2001.

Deleuze, Gilles and Felix Guattari. *A Thousand Plateaus: Capitalism and*

Schizophrenia. Trans. Brian Massumi. Minneapolis, MN: University of Minnesota Press, 1987.

Derrida, Jacques and Bernard Stiegler. *Echographies of Television*. Cambridge, MA: Polity Press, 2002.

Desai, Radhika. *Slouching towards Ayodhya*. New Delhi: Three Essays, 2002.

Deshpande, Sudhanva. "The Consumable Hero of Globalized India," in Raminder Kaur and Ajay J. Sinha, eds. *Bollyworld: Indian Cinema through a Transnational Lens*. New Delhi: Sage, 2005: 186–203.

Deutsch, Eliot. "Reflections on Some Aspects of the Theory of Rasa," in Rachel Van M. Baumer and James R. Brandon, eds. *Sanskrit Drama in Performance*. Honolulu: University of Hawaii Press, 1981: 214–25.

Dhareshwar, Vivek and Tejaswini Niranjana. "*Kaadalan* and the Politics of Resignification: Fashion, Violence, and the Body," in Ravi S. Vasudevan, ed. *Making Meaning in Indian Cinema*. New Delhi: Oxford, 1999: 191–214.

Dienst, Richard. *Still Life in Real Time: Theory after Television*. Durham, NC: Duke University Press, 1995.

Dissanayake, Wimal. "Globalization and Cultural Narcissism: Note on Bollywood Cinema." *Asian Cinema* 15:1 (2004): 143–50.

Dudrah, Rajinder Singh. *Bollywood: Sociology Goes to the Movies*. New Delhi: Sage, 2006.

Dwyer, Rachel. *Filming the Gods: Religion and Indian Cinema*. London: Routledge, 2006.

— *Yash Chopra*. London: British Film Institute, 2008.

Eck, Diana L. *Darshan: Seeing the Divine Image in India*. New York: Columbia University Press, 1998.

Edelman, Gerald M. *Wider than the Sky: The Phenomenal Gift of Consciousness*. New Haven, CT: Yale University Press, 2004.

— and Giulio Tononi. *A Universe of Consciousness*. New York: Basic Books, 2000.

Foucault, Michel. "The Birth of Biopolitics," in Paul Rabinow, ed. *Ethics: Subjectivity and Truth*. Vol. I. *Essential Works of Michel Foucault*. New York: The New Press, 1997: 73–5.

— *Discipline and Punish: The Birth of the Prison*. Trans. Alan Sheridan. New York: Vintage, 1977.

— *The Order of Things: An Archeology of the Human Sciences*. New York: Vintage, 1994.

— "Security, Territory, and Population," in Paul Rabinow, ed. *Ethics: Subjectivity and Truth*. Vol. 1. *The Essential Works of Michel Foucault*. New York: The New Press, 1997: 67–71.

— *Society Must Be Defended: Lectures at the Collège de France 1975–76*. Trans. David Macey. New York: Picador, 2003.

Freitag, Sandra. *Collective Action and Community: Public Arenas and the Emergence of Communalism in North India*. New Delhi: Oxford University Press, 1990.

Friedberg, Anne. "Cinema and the Postmodern Condition," in Linda Williams, ed. *Viewing Positions: Ways of Seeing Film*. New Brunswick, NJ: Rutgers University Press, 1997: 59–83.

Fukuyama, Francis. *The End of History and the Last Man*. New York: Avon, 1992.

Gandhi, M. K. "World Federation, Democracy, and *Ram Rajya*," in Raghavan Iyer, ed. *The Essential Writings of Mahatma Gandhi*. New Delhi: Oxford University Press, 1990: 409–11.

Garwood, Ian. "The Songless Bollywood Film." *South Asian Popular Culture* 4:2 (2006): 169–83.

Gehlawat, Ajay. "The Bollywood Song and Dance, or Making Culinary Theater from Dung-cakes and Dust." *Quarterly Review of Film and Video*, 23 (2006): 331–40.

Gerow, Edwin. "Rasa as a Category of Literary Criticism," in Rachel Van M. Baumer and James R. Brandon, eds. *Sanskrit Drama in Performance*. Honolulu: University of Hawaii Press, 1981: 226–57.

Gledhill, Christine. "Introduction," in Christine Gledhill, ed. *Home is Where the Heart is: Studies in Melodrama and the Woman's Film*. London: British Film Institute, 1987.

Gopalan, Lalitha. *Cinema of Interruptions: Action Genres in Contemporary Indian Cinema*. London: British Film Institute, 2002.

Gopinath, Gayatri. "Nostalgia, Desire, Diaspora: South Asian Sexualities in Motion." *Positions* 5 (Fall 1997): 467–89.

— *Impossible Desires: Queer Diasporas and South Asian Public Cultures*. Durham, NC: Duke University Press, 2005.

Gramsci, Antonio. *An Antonio Gramsci Reader: Selected Writings, 1916–1935*, ed. David Forgacs. New York: Schocken Books, 1988.

Guha, Ranajit. "Dominance without Hegemony and its Historiography," in Ranajit Guha, ed. *Subaltern Studies*, Vol. VI. New Delhi: Oxford, 1989.

— "On Some Aspects of the Historiography of Colonial India," in Vinayak Chaturvedi, ed. *Mapping Subaltern Studies and the Postcolonial*. London: Verso, 2000: 1–7.

— "Discipline and Mobilize," in Partha Chatterjee and Gyanendra Pandey, eds. *Subaltern Studies VII*. New Delhi: Oxford University Press, 1992: 69–120.

Gunning, Tom. "Non-Continuity, Continuity, Discontinuity: A Theory of Genres in Early Films," in Thomas Elsaesser and Adam Barker, eds. *Early Cinema: Space, Frame, Narrative*. London: British Film Institute, 1990: 86–93.

— "'Primitive' Cinema: A Frame-Up? Or the Trick's on Us," in Thomas Elsaesser and Adam Barker, eds. *Early Cinema: Space, Frame, Narrative*. London: British Film Institute, 1990: 95–103.

— *D. W. Griffith and the Origins of American Narrative Film: The Early Years at Biograph*. Urbana, IL: University of Illinois Press, 1994.

— "The Horror of Opacity: The Melodrama of Sensation in the Plays of Andre de Lorde," in Christine Gledhill et al., eds. *Melodrama: Stage, Picture, Screen*. London: British Film Institute, 1994.

Gupta, Nilanjana. *Switching Channels: Ideologies of Television in India*. New Delhi: Oxford University Press, 1998.

Gutman, Judith M. *Through Indian Eyes*. New York: Oxford University Press, 1982.

Habermas, Jürgen. *The Structural Transformation of the Public Sphere: An Inquiry into a Category of Bourgeois Society*. Trans. Thomas Burger. Cambridge, MA: MIT Press, 1991.

— *The Philosophical Discourse of Modernity: Twelve Lectures*. Trans. Frederick Lawrence. Cambridge, MA: MIT Press, 1995.

Hansen, Miriam. "Early Cinema, Late Cinema: Transformations of the Public Sphere," in Linda Williams, ed. *Viewing Positions: Ways of Seeing Film*. New Brunswick, NJ: Rutgers University Press, 1997: 134–52.

— "The Mass Production of the Senses: Classical Cinema as Vernacular Modernism." *Modernism/Modernity* 6:2 (1999): 59–77.

Hansen, Thomas. *The Saffron Wave: Democracy and Hindu Nationalism in Modern India*. New Delhi: Oxford University Press, 2001.

Hardt, Michael. "The Global Society of Control." *Discourse*, 2:3 (1998): 139–52.

— and Antonio Negri. *Empire*. London: Harvard University Press, 2001.

Harvey, David. *The Condition of Postmodernity: An Enquiry into the Origins of Cultural Change*. Cambridge, MA: Blackwell, 1990.

Hassan, Robert. *The Information Society* Cambridge: Polity Press, 2008.

— and Ronald E. Purser eds. *24/7: Time and Temporality in the Network Society*. Stanford, CA: Stanford University Press, 2007.

Hayles, N. Katherine. *How We Became Posthuman: Virtual Bodies in Cybernetics, Literature and Informatics*. Chicago: University of Chicago Press, 1999.

— "The Seductions of Cyberspace," in David Trend, ed. *Reading Digital Culture*. Oxford: Blackwell, 2001: 305–22.

Hegel, G.W. F. *Phenomenology of Spirit*. Trans. A. V. Miller. London: Oxford University Press, 1977.

— *Philosophy of Right*. Trans. T. M. Knox. London: Oxford University Press, 1967.

— *Lectures on the Philosophy of World History: Introduction*. Trans. H. B. Nisbet. Cambridge: Cambridge University Press, 1975.

— *On the Episode of the Mahabharata known by the name Bhagwad-Gita by Wilhelm von Humbolt*, ed. Herbert Herring. New Delhi: Indian Council of Philosophical Research, 1995.

Heidegger, Martin. "The Age of the World Picture," in *The Question Concerning Technology and Other Essays*. Trans. William Lovitt. New York: Harper & Row, 1977): 115–54.

— "The Question Concerning Technology," in *The Question Concerning Technology and Other Essays*. New York: Harper & Row, 1977: 3–35.

— *Being and Time*. Trans. John Macquarie and Edward Robinson. Oxford: Blackwell, 1962.

Jaffrelot, Christophe. *The Hindu Nationalist Movement in India*. New Delhi: Viking, 1996.

Jagarnath, Vashna. "The Politics of Urban Segregation and Indian Cinema in Durban," in Preben Kaarsholm, ed. *City Flicks: Indian Cinema and the Urban Experience*. London: Seagull, 2007: 207–18.

Jaikumar, Priya. *Cinema at the End of Empire: A Politics of Transition in Britain and India*. London: Duke University Press, 2007.

Jain, Kajri. "Figures of Locality and Tradition: Commercial Cinema and the Networks of Visual Print Capitalism in Maharashtra," in Raminder Kaur and Ajay J. Sinha, eds. *Bollyworld: Indian Cinema through a Transnational Lens*. New Delhi: Sage, 2005: 70–89.

Jameson, Fredric. "Cognitive Mapping," in Cary Nelson and Lawrence Grossberg, eds. *Marxism and the Interpretation of Culture*. Chicago: University of Illinois Press, 1988: 347–57.

— *Postmodernism or, the Cultural Logic of Late Capitalism*. Durham, NC: Duke University Press, 1995.

— "Third World Literature in an Age of Multinational Capitalism." *Social Text* 15 (Fall 1986): 65–88.

— *A Singular Modernity*. London: Verso, 2002.

Jay, Martin. "Scopic Regimes of Modernity," in Hal Foster, ed. *Vision and Visuality*. Seattle, WA: Bay Press, 1988: 3–23.

Jha, Priya. "Lyrical Nationalism: Gender, Friendship and Excess in 1970s Hindi Cinema." *The Velvet Light Trap* 51 (Spring 2003): 43–53.

Johnson, Kirk. *Television and Social Change in Rural India*. New Delhi: Sage, 2002.

Joshi, Murli Manohar. "Role of Science and Spirituality for World Peace." Address of the Chief Guest at the Inaugural Session of the World Philosophers' Meeting, Geneva, August 8–21, 1998. www.here-now4u.de/ENG/role_of_science_and_spirituali.htm. Accessed May 24, 2007.

Judy, Ronald. "Provisional Note on Formations of Planetary Violence." *Boundary 2* 33:3 (2006): 141–50.

Kabir, Nasreen Munni. *Guru Dutt: A Life in Cinema*. New Delhi: Oxford University Press, 2006.

Kakar, Sudhir. *Inner World: A Psycho-Analytic Study of Childhood and Society in India*. New Delhi: Oxford University Press, 1978.

Kapur, Anuradha. "The Representation of Gods and Heroes: Parsi Mythological Drama of the Early Twentieth Century." *Journal of Arts & Ideas* 23–4 (1993): 85–107.

Kapur, Geeta. "Mythic Material in Indian Cinema." *Journal of Arts & Ideas* 14–15 (1987): 79–108.

— "Revelation and Doubt: Sant Tukaram and Devi," in *When Was Modernism? Essays on Contemporary Cultural Practice in India*. New Delhi: Tulika, 2000: 233–64.

Kapur, Ratna. "The Cultural Politics of *Fire*." *Inter-Asia Cultural Studies* 1:2 (2000): 379–81.

Kasbekar, Asha. "Hidden Pleasures: Negotiating the Myth of the Female Ideal in Popular Indian Cinema," in Rachel Dyer and C. Pinney, eds. *Pleasure and the Nation*. New Delhi: Oxford University Press, 2000.

Kaur, Raminder. "Viewing the West through Bollywood: A New Occident in the Making." *Contemporary South Asia* 11:2 (2002): 199–209.

Kaviraj, Sudipta. *The Unhappy Consciousness: Bankimchandra Chattopadhyay and the Formation of Nationalist Discourse in India*. Bombay: Oxford University Press, 1995.

— "Reading a Song of the City—Images of the City in Literature and Films," in Preben Kaarsholm, ed. *City Flicks: Indian Cinema and the Urban Experience*. London: Seagull, 2007: 60–81.

— "The Imaginary Institution of India," Partha Chatterjee and Gyanendra Pandey, eds. *Subaltern Studies VII*. Delhi: Oxford University Press, 1992: 1–39.

King, Richard. *Indian Philosophy: An Introduction to Hindu and Buddhist Thought*. Washington, DC: Georgetown University Press, 1999.

Kohli-Khandekar, Vanita. *The Indian Media Business*. New Delhi: Response Books, 2006.

Kothari, Rajni. "The Democratic Experiment," in Partha Chatterjee, ed. *Wages of Freedom: Fifty Years of the Indian Nation-State*. New Delhi: Oxford, 1998.

— *Politics in India*. New Delhi: Orient Longman, 1970.

Kumar, Shanti. *Gandhi Meets Primetime: Globalization and Nationalism in Indian Television*. Urbana, IL: University of Illinois Press, 2006.

— "Mapping Tollywood: The Cultural Geography of 'Ramoji Film City' in Hyderabad." *Quarterly Review of Film and Video* 23 (2006): 129–38.

Kurien, C. T. *Global Capitalism and the Indian Economy*. New Delhi: Orient Longman, 1994.

Lal, Vinay. "The Impossibility of the Outsider in the Modern Hindi Film," in Ashish Nandy, *The Secret Politics of Our Desires: Innocence, Culpability, and Indian Popular Cinema*. New Delhi: Oxford, 1998: 228–59.

Landy, Marcia. *Film, Politics, and Gramsci*. Minneapolis, MN: University of Minnesota Press, 1994.

— *Cinematic Uses of the Past*. Minneapolis, MN: University of Minnesota Press, 1996.

Larkin, Brian. "Colonialism and the Built Space of Cinema in Nigeria," in Preben Kaarsholm, ed. *City Flicks: Indian Cinema and the Urban Experience*. London: Seagull, 2007: 180–206.

— "Itineraries of Indian Cinema: African Videos, Bollywood, and Global Media," in Jonathan Xavier Inda and Renato Rosaldo, eds. *The Anthropology of Globalization: A Reader*, 2nd edition. London: Blackwell, 2008: 334–51.

Latour, Bruno. *We Have Never Been Modern*. Trans. Catherine Porter. Cambridge, MA: Harvard University Press, 1993.

— *Reassembling the Social: An Introduction to Actor-Network Theory*. New York: Oxford University Press, 2007.

The Laws of Manu. Trans. Wendy Doniger and Brian K. Smith. London: Penguin Books, 1991.

Lukács, Georg. "Reification and the Consciousness of the Proletariat." Trans. Rodney Livingstone. *History and Class Consciousness.* London: Merlin Press, 1971: 83–222.

— *The Theory of the Novel: A Historico-Philosophical Essay on the Forms of Great Epic Literature.* Trans. Anna Bostok. Cambridge, MA: MIT Press, 1971.

Lyotard, Jean-François. *The Postmodern Condition: A Report on Knowledge.* Trans. Geoff Bonnington and Brian Massumi. Minneapolis, MN: University of Minnesota Press, 1979.

McGuire, John. "Economic Liberalization and India: New Rhetoric, Old Theme." *South Asia* 21:1 (1998): 77–89.

Maira, Sunaina. "*Desis Reprazent*: Bhangra Remix and Hip Hop in New York City." *Postcolonial Studies,* 1:3 (1998): 357–70.

Mankekar, Purnima. "Brides Who Travel: Gender, Transnationalism, and Nationalism in Hindi Film." *Positions* 7:3 (1999): 731–61.

Manovich, Lev. *The Language of New Media.* Cambridge, MA: MIT Press, 2002.

Martin-Jones, David. "Kabhi India Kabhi Scotland: Recent Indian Films Shot on Location in Scotland." *South Asian Popular Culture* 4:1 (2006): 49–60.

Marx, Karl. *Eighteenth Brumaire of Louis Bonaparte.* New York: International, 1972.

— *Grundrisse.* Trans. Martin Nicholaus. London: Penguin Books, 1973.

Matilal, Bimal Krishna. *Ethics and Epics. The Collected Essays of Bimal Krishna Matilal.* Ed. Jonardhan Ganeri. New Delhi: Oxford University Press, 2002.

Mayne, Judith. *Cinema and Spectatorship.* London: Routledge, 1993.

Mazumdar, Ranjani. *Bombay Cinema: an Archive of the City.* Minneapolis, MN: University of Minnesota Press, 2007.

Mishra, Vijay. *Indian Cinema: Temples of Desire.* London: Routledge, 2002.

Mitra, Ananda. *Television and Popular Culture in India: A Study of the Mahabharat.* New Delhi: Sage, 1993.

Mufti, Aamir. "Toward a Lyric History of India." *Boundary 2* 31:2 (2004): 245–74.

Nahata, Komal. "The Future is the Multiplex." *Cinema in India* (January–March 2002): 33–4.

Nanda, Meera. *Breaking the Spell of Dharma and Other Essays.* New Delhi: Three Essays, 2007.

Nandy, Ashish. "The Intelligent Film Critic's Guide to the Popular Indian Cinema," in Ashish Nandy, ed. *The Savage Freud.* New Delhi: Oxford University Press, 1995.

— *The Secret Politics of Our Desires: Innocence, Culpability and Indian Popular Cinema.* New Delhi: Oxford University Press, 1998.

Nayar, Sheila J. "Dreams, Dharma, and Mrs. Doubtfire: Exploring Indian Popular Cinema via its 'Chutneyed' Western Scripts." *Journal of Popular Film & Television* 31:2 (2003): 73–82.

Negri, Antonio. *Marx beyond Marx: Lessons from the Grundrisse*. New York: Autonomedia, 1989.

Nicholas, Martin. "Foreword." *Grundrisse/Karl Marx*. Ed. Martin Nicholas. London: Penguin Books, 1973.

Niranjana, Tejaswini and Mary John. "Mirror Politics: 'Fire', Hindutva and Indian Culture." *Economic and Political Weekly*, 34:10–11 (1999): 581–4.

Olivelle, Patrick, ed. *Dharmasutras: The Law Codes of Apastamba, Gautama, Baudhayana, and Vasistha*. New Delhi: Oxford University Press, 1999.

Pandey, Gyanendra. "In Defense of the Fragment: Writing about Hindu-Muslim Riots in India Today." *Representations* 37 (1992): 27–55.

Patnaik, Priyadarshi. *Rasa in Aesthetics: An Application of Rasa Theory to Modern Western Literature*. New Delhi: D. K. Printworld, 1997.

Pendakur, Manjunath. *Indian Popular Cinema: Industry, Ideology, and Consciousness*. Cresskill, NJ: Hampton Press, 2003.

Pinney, Christopher. "A Secret of Their Own Country: Or, How Indian Nationalism Made Itself Irrefutable," in Sumitha Ramaswamy, ed. *Beyond Appearances? Visual Practices and Ideologies in Modern India*. New Delhi: Sage, 2003: 113–50.

Pinto, Jerry. *Helen: The Life and Times of an H-Bomb*. New Delhi: Penguin Books, 2006.

Poster, Mark. *Information Please: Culture and Politics in the Age of Digital Machines*. Durham, NC: Duke University Press, 2006.

Prasad, Madhava. *Ideology of the Hindi Film: A Historical Construction*. New Delhi: Oxford University Press, 1998.

— "On the Question of a Theory of (Third) World Literature," in Ann McClintock et al., eds. *Dangerous Liaisons: Gender, Nation, and Postcolonial Perspectives*. Minneapolis, MN: University of Minnesota Press, 1997: 141–62.

— "This Thing called Bollywood," *Seminar* 525 (May 2003) www.india-seminar. com/2003/525/525%20madhava%20prasad.htm. Accessed September 25, 2005.

Punathambekar, Aswin. "Bollywood in the Indian American Diaspora: Mediating a Transitive Logic of Cultural Citizenship." *International Journal of Cultural Studies* 8:2 (2005): 151–73.

Rajadhyaksha, Ashish. "Neo-Traditionalism: Film as Popular Art in India." *Framework* 32–3 (1986): 21–67.

— "The Phalke Era, Conflict of Traditional Form and Modern Technology." *Journal of Arts and Ideas* 14–15 (1987): 46–82.

— "The Epic Melodrama: Themes of Nationality in Indian Cinema." *Journal of Arts and Ideas* 25–6 (1994): 55–70.

— and Paul Willemen, eds. *Encyclopaedia of Indian Cinema*. New revised edition. New Delhi: Oxford University Press, 1999.

— "Rethinking the State after Bollywood." *Journal of the Moving Image* 3 (2004): 47–90.

— "The 'Bollywoodization' of the Indian cinema: Cultural Nationalism in a Global Arena," in Preben Kaarsholm ed. *City Flicks: Indian Cinema and the Urban Experience*. London: Seagull, 2007: 111–37.

Rajagopal, Arvind. *Politics after Television: Hindu Nationalism and the Reshaping of the Public in India*. New York: Cambridge University Press, 2001.

Ramaswamy, Sumathi. "Visualizing India's Geo-body: Globes, Maps, Bodyscapes," in Sumitha Ramaswamy, ed. *Beyond Appearances? Visual Practices and Ideologies in Modern India*. New Delhi: Sage, 2003: 151–90.

Ranade, Ashoke. "The Extraordinary Importance of the Indian Film Song." *Cinema in India* 1:4 (1981): 4–11.

Rancière, Jacques. *The Future of the Image*. Trans. Gregory Eliot. New York: Verso, 2009.

Rangoonwala, Feroze. *Indian Cinema Past and Present*. New Delhi: Clarion, 1983.

Rao, Shakuntala. "The Globalization of Bollywood: An Ethnography of Non-elite Audiences in India." *Communication Review* 10 (2007): 57–76.

Ray, Manas. "*Chalo Jahaji*: Bollywood in the Tracks of Indenture to Globalization," in Preben Kaarsholm, ed. *City Flicks: Indian Cinema and the Urban Experience*. London: Seagull, 2007: 138–79.

Sabjani, Nina. "The Challenges of a Sleeping Giant." *Design Issues* 21:4 (Autumn 2005): 94–105.

Sangari Kumkum and Sudesh Vaid, eds. *Recasting Women: Essays in Colonial History*. New Delhi: Kali for Women, 1989.

Sarkar, Bhaskar. *Mourning the Nation: Indian Cinema in the Wake of Partition*. Durham, NC: Duke University Press, 2009.

Sarkar, Tanika. *Hindu Wife, Hindu Nation: Community, Religion, and Cultural Nationalism*. New Delhi: Permanent Black, 2001.

Savarkar, V. D. *Hindutva: Who Is a Hindu?* Bombay: Veer Savarkar Prakashan, 1969.

Schmitt, Carl. *The Concept of the Political*. Trans. Charles Schwab. New Brunswick, NJ: Rutgers University Press, 1976.

— *The Crisis of Parliamentary Democracy*. Trans. Ellen Kennedy. Cambridge, MA: MIT Press, 1988.

— *Political Theology: Four Chapters on the Concept of Sovereignty*. Trans. George Scwab. Cambridge, MA: MIT Press, 1985.

Schwarz, Susan L. *Rasa: Performing the Divine in India*. New York: Columbia University Press, 2004.

Sharma, Arvind. *The Hindu Gita: Ancient and Classical Interpretations of the Bhagwadgita*. La Salle, IL: Open Court, 1986.

— "On Hindu, Hindustan, Hinduism and Hindutva." *Numen* 49:1 (2002): 1–36.

Shresthova, Sangita. "Swaying to an Indian Beat . . . *Dola* Goes My Diasporic Heart: Exploring Hindi Film Dance." *Dance Research Journal* 36:2 (Winter 2004): 91–101.

Simmel, Georg. "The Metropolis and Mental Life," in Donald N. Levine, ed. *On Individuality and Social Forms*. Chicago: University of Chicago Press, 1971: 324–39.

Sirkar, Ajanta. "Romancing the Rural Belle: Bombay's Love Story." *Deep Focus* VIII: 3 & 4 (1998): 135–44.

Sobchack, Vivian. "New Age Mutant Ninja Hackers: Reading *Mondo 2000*," in David Trend, ed. *Reading Digital Culture*. Oxford: Blackwell, 2001: 322–33.

Spivak, Gayatri-Chakravarty. "Can the Subaltern Speak?" in Cary Nelson and Lawrence Grossberg, eds. *Marxism and the Interpretation of Culture*. Chicago: University of Illinois Press, 1988: 271–313.

Staiger, Janet. "Hollywood Mode of Production to 1930," in David Bordwell et al., eds. *The Classical Hollywood Cinema: Film Style and Mode of Production to 1960*. New York: Columbia University Press, 1985: 85–153.

— "The Hollywood Mode of Production, 1930–1960," in David Bordwell et al., eds. *The Classical Hollywood Cinema: Film Style and Mode of Production to 1960*. New York: Columbia University Press, 1985: 309–38.

Stam, Robert. "Beyond Third Cinema: the Aesthetics of Hybridity," in Anthony Guneratne and Wimal Dissanayake, eds. *Rethinking Third Cinema*. London: Routledge, 2003: 31–48.

Stiegler, Bernard. *Technics and Time, 2: Disorientation*. Trans. Stephen Barker. Stanford, CA: Stanford University Press, 2009.

Sunder Rajan, Rajeswari and Anuradha Dingwaney Needham, eds. *The Crisis of Secularism in India*. Durham, NC: Duke University Press, 2007.

Thapar, Romila. *Interpreting Early India*. Delhi: Oxford University Press, 1992.

— "The Ramayana Syndrome." *Seminar* 353 (January 1989).

— *Time as a Metaphor of History: Early India*. Delhi: Oxford, 1996.

Thomas, Rosie. "Indian Cinema: Pleasures and Popularity." *Screen* 26:3–4 (1985): 116–32.

— "Sanctity and Scandal: The Mytholization of Mother India." *Quarterly Review of Film and Video* 11 (1989): 11–30.

— "Not Quite (Pearl) White: Fearless Nadia, Queen of the Stunts," in Raminder Kaur and Ajay J. Sinha, eds. *Bollyworld: Indian Cinema through a Transnational Lens*. New Delhi: Sage, 2005: 35–69.

— and Adina Bradeanu. "Indian Summer, Romanian Winter: A 'Procession of Memories' in post-Communist Romania." *South Asian Popular Culture* 4:2 (2006): 141–6.

Thoraval, Yves. *The Cinemas of India*. New Delhi: Macmillan, 2000.

Thussu, Daya Kishan. "Hollywood's Poorer Cousin—Indian Cinema in an Era of Globalization." *Asian Cinema* (Spring/Summer 2002): 17–26.

Uberoi, Patricia. "Dharma and Desire, Freedom and Destiny: Rescripting the Man-Woman Relationship in Popular Hindi Cinema," in Meenakshi Thapan, ed. *Embodiment: Essays on Gender and Identity*. New Delhi: Oxford, 1997: 145–71.

— "The Diaspora Comes Home: Disciplining Desire in *DDLJ*." *Contributions to Indian Sociology* 32:2 (1998): 305–36.

— *Freedom and Destiny: Gender, Family, and Popular Culture in India*. New Delhi: Oxford University Press, 2006.

Upadhya, Carol. "Counter-Fire." *Economic and Political Weekly* 34:21 (1999): 1299–300.

Upadhyay, Deen Dayal. *Integral Humanism*. New Delhi: Jagriti Prakashan, [1962] 1992.

The Upanishads. Trans. Juan Mascaró. New York: Penguin Books, 1965.

Vanita, Ruth, ed. *Queering India: Same-Sex Love and Eroticism in Indian Culture and Society*. London: Routledge, 2001.

Vartak, Malavika. "Shivaji Maharaj: Growth of a Symbol." *Economic and Political Weekly* (May 8–14, 1999).

Vasudev, Aruna. *Liberty and Licence in the Indian Cinema*. New Delhi: Vikas Publishing House, 1978.

Vasudevan, Ravi S. "The Politics of Cultural Address in a 'Transitional' Cinema: A Case Study of Popular Indian Cinema," in Christine Gledhill and Linda Williams, eds. *Reinventing Film Studies*. London: Hodder Arnold, 2000: 130–64.

— "Shifting Codes, Dissolving Identities: The Hindi Social Film of the 1950s as Popular Culture," in Ravi S. Vasudevan, ed. *Making Meaning in Indian Cinema*. New Delhi: Oxford University Press, 1999: 99–121.

— "The Exhilaration of Dread: Genre, Narrative Form and Film Style in Contemporary Urban Action Forms," in Preben Kaarsholm, ed. *City Flicks: Indian Cinema and the Urban Experience*. London: Seagull, 2007: 21–32.

— "The Melodramatic Mode and the Commercial Hindi Cinema: Notes on Film History, Narrative, and Performance in the 1950s." *Screen* 30:3 (1989): 29–50.

— "The Cultural Space of a Film Narrative: Interpreting *Kismet* (Bombay Talkies, 1943)." *The Indian Economic and Social History Review* 28:2 (1991): 171–85.

Virdi, Jyotika. *The Cinematic Imagination: Indian Popular Films as Social History*. New Brunswick, NJ: Rutgers University Press, 2003.

Virilio, Paul. *The Art of the Motor*. Trans. Julie Rose. Minneapolis, MN: University of Minnesota Press, 1995.

— "Speed and Information: Cyberspace Alarm!" *Reading Digital Culture*. Ed. David Trend. Oxford: Blackwell, 2001: 23–7.

Vitali, Valentina. *Hindi Action Cinema: Industries, Narratives, Bodies*. New Delhi: Oxford University Press, 2008.

Wilkinson-Weber, Clare M. "The Dressman's Line: Transforming the Role of Costumers in Popular Hindi Film." *Anthropological Quarterly* 76:4 (2006): 581–608.

Willemen, Paul. "For a Comparative Film Studies." *Inter-Asia Cultural Studies* 6:1 (2005): 98–112.

Zielinski, Siegfried. *Deep Time of the Media: Towards an Archeology of Hearing and Seeing by Technical Means*. Cambridge, MA: MIT Press, 2006.

Index